Words about this book:

"The title says it all. *Happy Actor* is ̲ ̲ ̲ ̲ ̲ ̲ ̲ ̲ ̲ ̲ ̲ ̲ ̲ ̲ ̲ inspired ways for actors to be happy in a business that can be tough. This book is really needed in our industry!

Eric Dawson, Emmy-winning casting director – *American Horror Story, The Mentalist, Glee.*

"Justina explores the psychological, scientific, and even the spiritual aspects of truly being happy and comes up with some of the best advice I've ever heard on the topic. *Happy Actor* is a must-read for every actor at any stage in their career."

Mark Atteberry, award-winning actor, photographer and co-author of *The Working Actor's Guide to LA.*

"(Justina Vail is) a fabulous teacher. She reminds us to take a journey— to 'keep growing and learning in the midst of impermanence and unknowing'—a lesson we often forget!"

Margie Haber, acting coach and author of *How To Get The Part Without Falling Apart.*

"With razor sharp wit and a sensitive hand, Justina's genius approach to the business lies in a formula that is easily applied to most aspects of life. As actors, the challenges we are conditioned to view as mountainous magically diminish with each passing chapter, until we are on a pleasant journey through friendly, manageable terrain. If 'could've', 'would've', 'should've's mean anything, this book tells you that you still can. Read this book and fire your therapist!"

Alex Manette, actor *We Need To Talk About Kevin, Shame, 2 Days In New York, Law & Order and The West Wing.*

"Be happy with yourself. Then be a happy actor. Justina shows us how. (This book is) a breath of fresh air that's all about enjoying the journey. Because having a successful career is all about the journey. It never ends. Book a job. Finish a job. Need a job. Repeat. Why not make it a happy journey?"

Anthony Meindl, artistic director of Anthony Meindl's Actor Workshop.

"Justina Vail has articulated some of the best kept secrets of longevity and joy behind all great acting. There are valuable assists that get to the heart of inspiring all important art. Her insights are hard won and spot on. I wish this book was available when I was starting out as an actor so that I could have spent more time and energy on craft, and less on choosing an appropriate anti-depressant. I am so happy that it is now in print for others to learn lessons from a true master."

Jeffrey Marcus, actor and acting coach.

"Justina's book is not only a valuable asset to actors, but to all filmmakers. It confirms that being happy and fulfilled is what we deserve, and is essential to being successful in the business. Increasing the good in our lives is up to us, and is contagious—like this inspiring book."

Evette Vargas, writer/director/producer.

How to be a
HAPPY ACTOR
in a Challenging Business

A Guide to Thriving Through it All

JUSTINA VAIL

How to be a Happy Actor in a Challenging Business

A Guide to Thriving Through it All

Copyright © 2012 by Justina Vail

Disclaimer: Because of the author's confidentiality agreements with her real clients, all "clients" and their situations described in this work are fictitious and are created solely to illustrate a process. Any resemblance to real persons, living or dead, is purely coincidental.

Edited by Rebecca Howard
Front cover design by Justina Vail

ISBN: 1477522212
ISBN-13: 978-1477522219

Library of Congress Control Number: 2012911921
CreateSpace, North Charleston, SC

www.HappyActor.com
www.JustinaVail.com

Acknowledgments

Without the following people this book would not be written. I owe many thanks.

First of all I would like to thank my given family, the Vails. They put up with my sometimes dysfunctional beginnings, and had the compassion to believe in what I've worked to become. Most especially I would like to thank my mother who taught me the value of curiosity, laughter, and caring for others, and who has made it her job, through thick and thin, to care for me in her unique and extraordinarily generous way.

I am grateful to all my teachers. I've been blessed to have many. Thank you especially to Laurence Frauman, Ivana Chubbuck, Margie Haber, Holly Holmes Meredith, Russell Friedman, Tim Hallbom, and Suzanne Samson. I am also grateful to all of the world's many teachers of art, philosophy, spirituality, and psychology whose books I have learned so much from.

Thanks to my wonderful clients who inspire me every day and who have given me the profound opportunity to follow my passion and be on my right path. I am honored that they have asked me to be a part of their journeys and commend each one of them for their courage to grow and evolve through such challenging times as these.

I also want to deeply thank David Nutter, Christine Lahti, Mark Teschner, and Risa Bramon Garcia, whose contributions to this book are immeasurably valued and valuable. Their insights and their art will no doubt continue to influence and uplift others for many years to come.

Lastly, I want to thank the love of my life, my husband Dr. Jeff Evans. He is a great mind, a generous spirit, an inspiring teacher and a deeply connected human being. I am eternally grateful for the lessons I have learned through the ever-expanding relationship we have. This wonderful man has shown me what unconditional love is, and, through that, he has given me the opportunity to be happier than I ever imagined possible.

Contents

How to be a

HAPPY ACTOR

in a Challenging Business

A Guide to Thriving Through it All

CHAPTER 1

Bottom Line

Happiness is the meaning and the purpose of life, the whole aim and end of human existence.

~ *ARISTOTLE*

Setting The Stage

You chose this book for a reason. You are an actor. The business you are in can be tough and you have probably struggled with it. The competition, rejection, and uncertainty may have had you wondering what you are doing wasting your time. Let's face it; you've probably been unhappy enough that, more than once, you've thought about quitting.

I get it. I was an actor for over twenty years and I know, in my bones, what it's like to be part of that struggle. I wanted so much to be happy and fulfilled on the path I had chosen. *Is that too much to ask for?* I thought. It was a path I had believed would be exciting, creative, and rewarding, and instead it felt like being in a bad relationship. It seemed that being an actor, by itself, was not going to be a source of happiness for me.

It wasn't just the business of acting that I felt was making me unhappy. Happiness had been elusive for much of my early life—partly due to genetics, partly due to a string of traumatic events, and partly because I simply didn't know how to be a happy person. Just like many people, and without knowing it, I was actually very good at being unhappy. I had some habitual thinking, beliefs, and behaviors that had kept me firmly stuck in a cycle of suffering, and once I chose to pursue an acting career my search for relief just became all the more challenging.

Like many actors the element that initially drew me in was the craft itself. The artistic side to acting made me feel alive and inspired. Then, as I realized it was going to be my *business*, the struggle began. The rejection

1

and uncertainty kept bringing me down. I was on a roller coaster, going from the occasional high of an acting gig back to the misery of unemployment. I started to find that even when I did book a role, I sometimes felt worse knowing that it would end and that I would be on the hunt for the next gig once the week was over.

One day in 1996, standing on the set of the sitcom *Seinfeld* shooting a guest-starring role with some of the most talented comedians in the business, I realized that despite the extraordinary life I was living, I wasn't enjoying myself at all. In fact, I was overwhelmed, frightened, and profoundly sad. I understood something that day. No matter what was going to happen for me as an actor, this cycle of misery couldn't continue. Something needed to change and it would have to be something *inside me*.

For years I had been a student of psychology, spirituality, and philosophy, and I decided to renew my focus, not so much on the theories anymore, but on the practical lessons. I began to change some very specific things in my life, adopting new ways of thinking, beliefs, and actions. I committed to myself and my shift, just as I had previously committed to my career. Fairly soon my whole world began to change, including my acting career which shot forward overnight. It was a massive shift.

I also realized that those things, those practical lessons, were not going to work just for me. They are universal to all human beings. There are intentional activities that can make each one of us happier *no matter what life brings*, and what's really encouraging is that there is research to prove it.

Life doesn't come with a book of instructions. This thing called *living* is a challenging mystery to us human beings and because of this, and because our world is going through such profound shifts, there has been an explosion of interest in the subject of human happiness in recent years. As a species we have looked for answers about how to best navigate the terrain of human existence, and we have done that through our spiritual, psychological, and now, more than ever, our scientific realms. Over recent years many of our top universities have pinpointed specific activities and intentions that prove to increase our sustainable levels of happiness. You, an actor in a challenging business, have every reason to gain from this information.

The changes I made in my own life happened because I searched for answers and acted on them. As I changed myself and the ways I functioned in the world, my life began to respond in kind and I got different results.

I went from being a struggling actress in Hollywood— occasionally working, nearly broke, two months behind on my rent, and getting ready to move into my car—to feeling confident, happy, relaxed, and profoundly connected, which instantly began to change my relationships and my experience of life. My new focus and activities shifted the way I engaged the world and the world then engaged me differently. And how differently that turned out to be! Within fourteen months of making these conscious changes I landed a lead role on a network television series, was earning over half a million dollars a year, had a new car and a new apartment in Hollywood, and had a far more satisfying social life. More than anything I was happy, and I realized that in order to sustain that I needed to continue the activities and nurture my new, resourceful ways of thinking and being. Those things—not what showed up in my life—were the source of it all.

Your Happiness

Ultimately we all want to be happy—actors, accountants, and farmers alike. We live in a world that challenges, disappoints, hurts, surprises, pleases, excites, bores, and continues to present us with the ups and downs of human existence. Many of us go through life believing that outside events or material things are the source of our happiness or unhappiness, and we subsequently work hard to attempt to control them.

As an actor, you face a unique set of challenges and advantages. It's said that the stress an average actor experiences during opening night is higher in intensity than a jet fighter pilot's is while in combat. Whether that's true or not, many actors will agree that acting (on set, on stage, or in auditions) can be acutely terrifying, at times to the point of amnesia or a feeling of "what just happened?" Along with the actual acting process, the repeated rejection and career uncertainty of being an actor is also uniquely challenging, and no matter what level of success you reach, if you do have a career the knowledge that it may be over at any moment is ever there.

Of course, there are some profound advantages to being an actor. If there were not, no one would be doing it! The variety, creativity, wealth, personal exploration, human connection, and the ability to be of service are real possibilities. It can be an extraordinary profession to be in.

So, being an actor has experiences on each end of the spectrum. The waves you ride can be incredibly high one moment and very low the next, and though roller coasters may seem thrilling for a while, to live on one full-time will begin to wear on you no matter how resilient or strong you are!

Along with that, we humans are extremely adaptable. When positive things happen to you (when you book that wonderful role, you get that powerful new agent, or you have a beautiful new car) you probably go into a high, and when something unwanted happens (a "negative" event or circumstance occurs) you drop into a low. Yet neither response will likely last. That's because you've *adapted* to your new situation. You've simply become used to your change in circumstances and will inevitably, and quite quickly, return to what's called your *baseline state*.

The baseline state is what psychologists also call a *set point*. It's the combined emotional, mental, physical, and spiritual way in which each of us tends to experience being alive on this planet. It's the unique organization of *what life is like for you* most of the time—and whether wanted or unwanted events show up in your life, that baseline state is where you will eventually return, usually within nine months at the most. If that baseline state is *not very happy* then it doesn't matter what positive events come your way, you will return to being *not very happy*. If you land that huge movie deal, for example, and your usual state of being is just *fair*, then the feelings of happiness about your new circumstances will eventually wear off and you will go back to feeling *fair* again in a short period of time. The patterns you may have had—like being negative, thinking pessimistic or obsessive thoughts, involving yourself in activities and relationships that sap you, or holding onto resentment or regret—would be some of the factors that return you to that state. It doesn't matter if you win the lottery or book a television series, it won't make a very long-term positive impact on you unless you change those old misery-making patterns.

If, however, that baseline state or set point is *happy, fulfilled, and congruent*, then no matter what happens out there in the world you will keep returning to an overall happy disposition. You can be at any level of your acting career and still be enjoying the journey. Because of this, fulfillment is not contingent on whether you book that role, and you tend to enter the meeting or audition for it in a far more trusting, creative, and confident state. Your happiness, therefore, creates more success in your life and your career!

What Is Happiness Anyway?

The ancient Greeks used the term *eudaimonia*, which means "human flourishing." Buddhism describes happiness as "the cessation of suffering."

With its ups and downs, life as we know it is like that roller coaster, and the entertainment industry is no exception. Yet we somehow hope or expect that all unfolding events will be smooth sailing and easy for us. We humans tend to get upset when they're not. However, it's that *response, not the events themselves*, that creates our unhappiness.

Suffering and pain are not the same. Pain is inevitable. When we fall down and break a leg we will feel pain. When someone dies we will feel pain. Pain is a natural part of the human experience. The anger, frustration, and sadness that may be felt because of that pain are like our own weather system, and while we are still in human form they will move through us whether we are fully enlightened or not. We will probably feel disappointment when we don't get the jobs we have our hearts set on.

Suffering, on the other hand, is dissatisfaction with the reality of the human condition. It's what occurs when we expect and demand that life be without pain and then let the fact that it's there drag us down. The constant attempt to escape pain and get comfortable is the cause of suffering. Happiness, or "the cessation of suffering," is what we grow into when we accept and become present with the truth of life's pain and pleasure, ups and downs, hot and cold, dark and light. There is both a detachment from the drama and a connection to the authenticity and fullness of life when we accept the variety of human experience. And when we move into that acceptance, time slows down just when we need it to.

You may understand this acceptance in your creativity. It's similar to when you're in the midst of an acting scene and you suddenly become very present. You find an awareness of the spaces in between the moments, and you fill those spaces with those creative, instinctive, essential parts of you. That presence then connects to whoever is in the room with you or watching you from their theater seats. You inspire them, they feel what you feel, they want to be part of it, and your life expands in a multitude of ways because of it.

Accepting life's pain creates space. The roller coaster continues to move up and down as it does; yet you traverse it all from a far more expansive state. You become the evenness of your life—not neutral or dull, just deeply fulfilled.

Happiness is a *state*, not an emotion. Many people confuse happiness with emotions like excitement, anticipation, nervousness, obsession, and gratification. *Elation*, for example, is that short burst of excitement and pleasure you feel when you get great news or something turns up that you had been hoping for. It's a feeling that soon dies away once the novelty of whatever triggered it goes away. Elation is a great feeling that might *feel* like happiness, but again, it's not a sustainable experience. You can't hang onto that pleasure for long no matter how hard you might try! Elation and depression are on opposite ends of the spectrum of the human experience, and attempting to stay in the "high" end tends to create a habit of swinging back and forth between the two. If you allow yourself to ride on the roller coaster of life's events, whizzing up and down on the tracks, rising into elation when you book a role and down into depression when you don't book that role, there is little chance for long-term, sustainable happiness. You become a passenger of life, not the driver.

Once we have the basic needs of shelter, food, and safety met, even circumstances like winning the lottery or becoming a millionaire overnight can't be counted on to bring any of us long-term happiness. It's well-known that lottery winners, once they have adjusted to the change in circumstances, can sometimes even fall further once the novelty wears off. They just have more money to fund their misery. Money can certainly make things easier for a while and bring choices to life, but our life *style* has to change as well in order for our inner workings to benefit long-term.

In his book *A New Earth*, spiritual teacher Eckhart Tolle writes about the three modes of *awakened doing*: acceptance, enjoyment, and enthusiasm. "Each one represents a certain vibrational frequency of consciousness. You need to be vigilant to make sure that one of them operates whenever you're engaged in doing anything at all, from the simplest task to the most complex. If you're not in the state of either acceptance, enjoyment, or enthusiasm, look closely and you will find that you're creating suffering for yourself and others."

When we are simply in the moment with something and we can't enjoy it, we can at least accept it. If we can enjoy it then we are tapping into the source of life. If we have a goal or a plan that our present moment is connected to, then we can turn that enjoyment into enthusiasm. The word *enthusiasm* comes from *en* which is "in" and *theos* which is "God." The intensity we experience in enthusiasm is the intensity of being connected to a divine creative force. It is not to be confused with excitement, which has a stressful intensity. Many of the people we most respect and admire don't run around in a state of excitement, but rather in a state of deep enthusiasm.

So, for you as an actor and as a *person*, if your life takes a turn and you book that great gig, you meet that delicious person, you get those gorgeous things, or earn that extra money, why not make the baseline state you return to—once you've adapted to the novelty—one that has you accepting, enjoying, fulfilled, empowered, enthusiastic, and happy?

Happiness and Your Craft

Remembering that pain is an inevitable part of life, it's important to be aware that a sustained foundation of happiness is not going to be mutually exclusive of grief, anger, and sadness. Genius is often born in our darkest realms, and artists of all kinds have created some of the world's greatest works of art, poetry, film, and music through the source of human pain. Long-term happiness has to include sadness and anger. They are healthy and important emotions that are a fundamental part of being human, and, as an actor, having a full range of them is part of what a well-rounded craft comes from. You will need to be able to access a full spectrum of feelings and emotional experiences in order to be a multifaceted vehicle for your work. The question, as a human being, is more about *where you tend to reside most of the time.*

If you habitually live in anger, sadness, or fear there is not much room for you to flourish. Artists often think they need to suffer for their art, yet there is no reason to do that in order to be great. You're entirely capable of creating great art through just the fact that you're human and have experienced the tragedies of life as well as the thrills. In fact the very nature of the business you're in will keep you on your toes.

Award-winning casting director Risa Bramon Garcia works with actors in many different capacities. Not only is she one of Hollywood's top casting directors, she also runs acting workshops, directs, and produces. She has been involved in the business for over thirty years and has a passionate interest in the nature of human unfolding. Risa described her thoughts with me about actors and emotional health.

"I've seen amazing performances by actors who are deeply messed up, but that doesn't last forever. There is the actor who comes out of the Mickey Rourke journey of years of insanity—the actor who does that one definitive part because he can access all of the pain and wounds. But ultimately, people can't keep creating if they're in a bad place. You can't honor yourself as an artist if you don't know what that is for yourself. You don't know who you are."

So, I ask you, when you're old or in your last days on Earth and you look back at your life, is it all going to be about those anguished moments that you've had—those few moments as an actor? Or is it going to be your life as a whole and who you've *been* that you will look back on?

By nurturing your happiness in the middle of all the "stuff" life brings you, your craft can remain filled full of all of your humanity *and* you can also live a life that's deeply fulfilling. It is entirely possible to be a great actor *and* a happy actor, and you owe it to yourself to be both.

Becoming Good at It

If you think of your happiness level in terms of an overall baseline state and rate it on a scale from zero to ten (zero being "not happy at all" and ten being "the most happy you can imagine"), what number would you come up with? If you then asked yourself what number you would rather be at, what would you then arrive at? Would you choose a seven, eight, or dare you go for ten? I am here to tell you, in the business you're in, being generally happy and fulfilled is not only something you deserve, it's absolutely essential to your success as an actor. Happy people tend to be healthier, wealthier, more creative, and more successful in their careers, and those things, in turn, are some of the elements that can increase happiness. In other words, consciously raising your baseline state of happiness is going to give you a better chance at creating what you want in your life, your career, and your relationships. You get to live in a positive cycle of increasing happiness and fulfillment in life.

Not only that, the fact is happiness is contagious and the people in charge of hiring actors for film, theater, and television want to feel good just like anyone else. They want to be around people who inspire them, move them, and make them laugh, and no matter what character you're playing in what type of story, if you're essentially a happy person you will inspire others because you will be able to bring your best self to the table personally and professionally.

Being happy means you will also be able to handle the success that then comes along with maturity and emotional intelligence, and that's what makes many actors real stars. Though it's the dysfunctional, unhappy celebrities who tend to get the most press, there are a significant number of successful actors who are grounded, stable, and fulfilled. Take Tom Hanks, for example. He comes across to me as someone who is a fairly happy person. Anne Hathaway and Hugh Jackman come to mind. Will and Jada Pinkett Smith also seem to be consciously creating healthy, happy lives for themselves and their children. And that beautiful, radiant being Goldie Hawn has dedicated much of her life to the study, practice, and teaching of happiness. Through The Hawn Foundation Goldie has taken much of the research and, with her team of experts, improved the lives of others by put it all into practice.

All of the actors mentioned appear to be not only highly skilled and professional, but also generally healthy and happy in their lives. Certainly, life has its ups and downs for everybody (remember, no one is always in a state of bliss, and there are actors who have career success despite the fact that they are not happy), *and* having generally healthy relationships, a stable home life, and a good, strong emotional life makes the whole journey that much more fulfilling.

So, what can you do about all this? It turns out *happiness is something you can actually become good at.* Scientists at the University of California, Berkeley, believe that 50 percent of our happiness is genetic, 10 percent is circumstantial, and a huge *40 percent* is in our hands to cultivate at will. That's really happy news. It says we are, in fact, capable of controlling the quality of our lives far more than we may have been led to believe in the past.

The Keys to Happiness

What are the intentional activities that raise our baseline state of happiness and increase the good in our lives? For a start, research in both traditional and new psychology says that positive thinking and optimism have been proven to change people's lives for the better in profound ways, as do healthy relationships, strong spiritual beliefs, good role models, forgiveness, and meditation, among others. The element that stands out in all research on happiness is the importance of successful relationships—ones that are mutually respectful of the other person's needs, desires, and feelings in speech, action, and intention. Learning to be a more loving person and learning to have better clarity around your own needs and boundaries with others is a big key, as is gathering a tribe around you who fits who you want to be and how you would like your vision to unfold. The relationship that determines how all your other relationships will be is, first and foremost, the one you have with yourself. Developing a friendly, healthy relationship with yourself is a big step toward creating a healthy life. In order to have good self-esteem you have to move toward greater self-awareness; to know who you are, you also have to make peace with your self and know how to resolve the inner conflict you have.

Another very important factor in building a happy foundation for your self is a trust in something bigger than you. From the beginning of time humans have grappled with the idea of faith and whether to believe there is something infinitely powerful in the universe. Scientists recently described this "something" as a single quantum energy field that functions in intelligent, predictable ways to make up the universe. They call it the *Unified Field*. Religious and spiritual words for it are *God*, *Providence*, *Allah*, *Spirit*, *Nirvana*, and *Great Soul*, as well as many others. It is held as the all-knowing, infinite, all-loving, wise existence that creates and sustains everything. It is a universal, superconscious mind, and it's believed that we are all part of this "one mind." It has been found by researchers in both science and spirituality that having strong faith in the benevolence of this infinite energy field is a very significant element in how happy we will be in life.

We connect with this Unified Field through many channels. Prayer, meditation, art, dance, song, and relationships are just some of these possible channels. Research shows that meditation, for example, is a multi-faceted source of happiness. It trains our minds to become more present with the truth of life as it is now, putting it into a relaxed and positive perspective. The idea is that the present moment is the only thing that's ultimately real. The past is gone and the future is yet to materialize. The present moment is where we can find a deep peace and trust, and teaching our minds to live in that state more often through daily practice is known to increase our happy factor in dramatic ways.

Our habitual beliefs, thoughts, and language will also determine what life is like for us, no matter what our circumstances. Training our brains to be more resourceful—to focus on the things that serve us and our joy—contributes greatly to our success in life. In addition to that, it appears to be vitally important to have a clear, strong sense of purpose and mission. That comes out of an awareness of what's deeply important to us, our core values.

Another key piece is about the past and how we hold it in our systems. That will also either be a drain on our happiness level or a resource to draw from. Furthermore, how we see, feel, and hear the future has a great effect on how it turns out.

What we focus on daily and what perspectives and interpretations we choose make up how we experience life. Thinking in terms of collaboration or competition, gratitude or lack, forgiveness or resentment, instincts or "shoulds," optimism or pessimism, will determine how life is painted and therefore how happy we are. Whether we go into situations intent on serving something good and honoring the needs of others, or on getting what we want, we will have very contrary experiences. When we work toward meaningful goals that are consistent with cherished values, we will find that life turns up differently than if we head toward a general idea that we thought up years ago and that we haven't reviewed. The environments we spend our time in make a difference. When we take care of our bodies in certain ways we find our psychology changes. When we take care of our minds in certain ways we find that our physicality changes. When we take care of our emotions and our spirit in certain ways, we find that our lives change. What we believe about our world and our place in it determines our experience of life.

These and many other specific keys to your happiness will be revealed as our story unfolds. You will soon become privy, not only to the formal research about all this, but also to the personal discoveries and experiences of other actors as they too adopted these keys and moved toward a happier life. I will also share words of wisdom with you from some of our top industry professionals as they reveal their years of knowledge and perspective.

Your level of happiness may have been low based on genetics and circumstances, yet it doesn't have to remain that way when you include these tried and tested intentional activities in your life. What we explore in this book can potentially be a great source of your joy of living. In the process of raising your happiness level, you will bring into your life the activities that nurture and sustain it, and let go of the ones that don't. It's really that simple. Trying to change life and its varied terrain is futile. You can't escape pain by trying to change the nature of life "out there" through the attempt to control it. You can only become happier and make life's inevitable ups and downs more manageable by changing what's inside you, and you do that by changing what you focus on.

Mark Teschner, legendary multi-Emmy and Artios-winning casting director, is most well-known for his extraordinary work casting the daytime series *General Hospital*. Mark has shared many of his thoughts with me regarding his experience with actors, and one in particular emerged right after he had come out of a casting session.

"I met an actor an hour ago who's been in a wheelchair since he was twenty-three. There's passion, fire, and great joy in him, yet for a lot of people that's something they wouldn't be able to find. He's carved out some acting gigs, he's done a lot more than a lot of actors without disabilities, and he wants to do more. There was a spirit, a joy, and a happiness in him that wasn't dictated by being in a wheelchair, but by finding what he loves and finding ways to create, like writing scripts. When he entered my room I didn't feel like I was in front of an actor looking for a job. I felt I was in front of a creative, happy guy whose life took a detour that no one would want their lives to take, but he was making it all it was worth."

"And that's what we want to be around," I replied.

"That's correct," Mark said.

So, no matter what life may have delivered to your door, for the sake of your career and of your life in general, are you willing and ready to commit to your happiness? Ultimately to grow your happiness as an actor, as a human being, *you* are the answer—and that's where I invite you to start.

Dear one, we are all on the adventure of our own unfolding whether we know it or not. Be open to the possibility that you are about to emerge into someone you have never met before—a person whom you admire, trust, and know as being part of a great plan to uplift our world.

CHAPTER 2

Start with You

Be yourself; everyone else is already taken.

~ OSCAR WILDE

It's an Inside Job

Have you ever waited to hear back about that wonderful role you auditioned for and noticed your inner voice going down a deep, dark hole? Your mind went back over every line you spoke and every gesture you made, and because you hadn't heard back from your agent by the end of the day you wondered, *What happened? Did I blow it? Why have I not heard back?*

Then when you found just the right excuse to call your agent in case he had heard anything, he says casually, "Yeah, they went in another direction."

That inner voice launches in again, *What do they mean "another direction"? What direction is that? I did it again, didn't I? I really shouldn't be in this business—I can't even remember how to act. I was probably terrible and the casting director, or even worse, my agent isn't telling me. What's wrong with me?*

This may or may not seem extreme to you, and I can only imagine given the nature of the industry, the way it's organized, and what it attracts that every actor experiences hearing a voice like this coming from inside at some time in their career. I certainly did, and I can imagine if you've ever put yourself through this it didn't make you feel any happier, nor did it make you *do* any better with the next audition. In fact it probably made you feel shaky and less confident the next time because you would have anchored all those feelings of fear and self-doubt right smack dab into the middle of the whole idea of auditioning at all.

Dear creative spirit, you do not have to live your life as an actor like that. It's an archaic and ridiculous concept that artists have to suffer for their art or feel powerless in their chosen careers. As you know, the *craft* of acting is

13

incredibly important to being successful in film, television, and theater. What is sometimes overlooked by actors is the work of building confidence and self-esteem, which is ultimately what will hold in place any skill you've acquired through the workings of the craft. For you, if those elements are not intact, the skills and talents you have may not be available to be seen by anyone. After all, if you walk onto a set feeling bad about yourself you will likely find that any work you've done on your role will be compromised. You're also in a relationship business, and when it comes to interacting with casting directors, agents, producers, directors, cast, and crew, your inner life affects how you come across as a person. That, then, is absolutely going to color your career. Any industry professional will tell you that.

There are people in the industry who believe you have to be crazy to work in a crazy business. I believe it serves a greater purpose to be as healthy, grounded, and sane as you can be so you can flourish in a business that might *seem* crazy at times. If you're not, you take the risk of being swallowed whole by the uncertainty, rejection, and fear within it. As it is, being an artist takes tremendous courageous, and to give yourself as many resources and advantages as possible seems only fair to you, and to those who love you, as you travel the road of creativity and service.

It's estimated that 85 percent of people feel they have low self-esteem and lack of confidence. This means that the huge majority of people walking around our planet don't feel good about themselves. That's something to consider. It's not surprising, therefore, that so many people are unhappy. We tend to feel happier when we feel good about who we are. Human happiness is determined in great part by the quality of our relationships, and the relationship you have with yourself determines the relationships you have with others. If you have a fulfilling and peaceful relationship within your own being, you will have fulfilling and peaceful relationships with others. The happier you are within yourself, the happier your relationships will be, and the happier you will be in turn.

Confidence is part of this whole equation. If you think about your own sense of self-confidence, you will probably be able to identify your own special brand of it. You will be able to think of at least one time, if not a few, when you've felt particularly confident—whether it was when you were acting or doing something entirely different—and you will be able to remember in your body what that confidence feels like.

Confidence is not arrogance. It's never cocky or boastful. It's an attitude of quiet *knowing* concerning your value and the value of others. It's also an honest knowing of what you're good at. When you learn to focus on what you have real talent for—whether it's cooking, adding numbers, or listening compassionately to people—you deepen your ability in that area. Confidence means you don't need to convince others or have others tell you that you have a talent; you just enjoy what it is that you can do. So much so that being good at it is not the important part, *serving* good is. When that happens, and you trust your abilities and your worth, you find you walk into any room giving others the opportunity to have confidence in you too. That then attracts the relationships and consequently the career you want.

And what about *self-esteem?* Esteem means "regard." When we hold someone in high esteem we respect, admire, and like them. *Self*-esteem shows up as the ongoing friendship with the one person you're guaranteed to be with for the rest of your life: you. Again, it's not arrogance or egoism and it's not about being self-obsessed or feeling better than others. Self-esteem takes nothing away from the importance of others. It's simply the practice of being kind, compassionate, and forgiving with yourself. There is an acceptance and gratitude for the person that you are right now, today.

Many actors confuse self-esteem with self-obsession, and that can get in the way of their happiness in profound ways. Any time you worry about how you're going to come across or whether people are going to like you or not creates the very thing that you may be trying to avoid, which is not being loved or accepted. Fear attracts and creates what it is we fear. On the other hand, when you feel good about who you are, you relax. The world can then relax around you, and people tend to like people who are relaxed!

Beginning to like yourself more involves turning old, limiting beliefs into kinder, more resourceful ones. Having self-esteem means that the voices coming from inside your head are those of a wise, loving friend—even when you make mistakes, even when you mess up that meeting, forget your lines, or don't book that role. When that happens you get to learn from your mistakes and grow as an artist and as a human being.

Self-esteem also makes it possible to respect and love others more. How we behave with ourselves is very likely how we will behave with others. If we are being hateful, judgmental, or impatient with ourselves, at best we might *believe* we are being loving to someone else, but that harsh inner life will show up in ways that don't feel loving to *them,* guaranteed. *We will always somehow act out the relationship that we have with ourselves.* Therefore the kinder we know how to be with ourselves, the kinder we will know how to be in our relationships. The happier we are with ourselves, the happier others will be in our presence. When you do something that hurts another person, for example, and you have good self-esteem, rather than swimming in guilt or shame, you grow up. You create room to feel remorse and make amends. You get to decide *who you want to be* and how you want to live from there on out, and you honor everyone in that.

As an actor it's absolutely essential to be friends with yourself in a healthy, balanced way. The business of acting can be unpredictable and challenging, and your interactions with your fellow actors, casting directors, producers, directors, and crew are going to be colored in a multitude of ways by how you feel inside. Everything you experience in the world is an out-picturing of what's in your interior, and the relationship you have with yourself is the foundation of that. Your success depends on it. Both within the craft of acting as well as the strategic business side of it, when people are drawn to you (as they will be when you're confident and happy) you will attract the life, the openings, and the opportunities you want. When you're kind and loving with yourself, you're naturally more confident and relaxed. That gives the people casting the roles a feeling of peace and confidence that you can do the job. It's far more important to most casting directors, producers, and directors that an actor is in his or her "own skin" and has a sense of something positive inside themselves, above and beyond any clever acting skill they might display. In fact, very often what stands out as "talent" is when someone walks in and has some sort of connection to something deeper and in-the-moment, which may be seen as confidence or power.

Casting director Mark Teschner told me, "One of the things that's very appealing about an actor when they walk in the room, before they even read, is confidence. Not arrogance, confidence. It's very attractive. Even before they read, there's something present about them that I respond to. I can tell when an actor walks in scared or vulnerable or not owning their uniqueness."

It doesn't matter so much to casting directors, producers, and directors if you know all your lines, or have done hours of character study and worked the piece to death if you walk into the room disconnected and feeling fearful and judgmental of yourself. That just makes everyone else in the room feel fearful and judgmental, and they don't want to feel that way—so they probably won't be inspired to invite you back. They want to feel connected and present and powerful. The people who hire actors want you to have a type of confidence that they may not even be able to describe, something intangible, whether it's a connection to a truth you feel, or an ability to play in that moment, or a courage you have to free-fall into the unknown.

The people in our industry have a lot on their own heads and they want to be able to bank on someone who will deliver the goods. They want you to come in with the attitude that you're providing a reliable, high quality service. They want to know that you're professional, skilled, polite, stable, punctual, prepared, and consistent. Your *clients* (because that's what they are) want and deserve a good, solid product when they spend their time and money on you. A lot is at stake for them and they are putting a lot of trust in the people they hire to do a good job. Most of these people are under tremendous pressure and have limited time. They are often tired, stressed, and afraid, and (again like anyone) they want to feel good. What makes that possible is being able to trust that you will deliver. Then they can relax, enjoy, and focus on doing their own jobs.

To get to a place where these people will feel that way about you, you must not only treat your job responsibly and professionally, you owe it to yourself (as well as to your clients) to take care of the product you provide with the greatest of care. That product is you. And you're not just the human being walking around waiting to hear back from your agent or working on your lines or dreaming of the next step in your fabulous adventure. You're a magnificent and eternal spirit who happens to be taking a human journey toward remembering about *love*.

"Love?" I hear you say. Yes. Deep, sustainable happiness is an inside job, and, to get to the bones of it, the source of that happiness is love. Love of the self, love of others, and love of life. Love is not just a feeling of fondness; it's a multifaceted creative force that expresses itself through connection, intention, and action. Fortifying the connection and understanding you have of your own eternal essence and learning to love and take care of your human self are the foundations of this journey.

The world we live in today, more than ever, needs and wants leaders, artists, and teachers who are connected to their deepest essence, strong in who they are, and focused on creating good. The relationship you have with *you* is not only what determines the nature of the relationships you have with others, it also affects every single one of your experiences. Your reality is *infused* with how you feel about yourself and what you believe about your worth, and this in turn shapes the experiences you have with your finances, your career, your body, your health, your creative energy, your life.

Self-Love and Celebrity

Have you ever noticed how newborn babies allow themselves to express exactly what they feel, apparently without judging, berating, or editing themselves? They appear to have no shame and no regret. Their consciousness is plopped into a tiny, brand new body that they seem to relish. There is no concept that it's somehow flawed. They appear to have no inner conflict around their emotions or the ways that they think. Still in their natural state, they love themselves entirely because they haven't learned anything else yet. Babies are living manifestations of love and trust—as are we. That hasn't changed. Only our *concepts* of ourselves changed as we grew up. The fact of the matter is, it's your natural state to feel great about yourself and to trust who you are. Embracing your own humanity, and accepting and loving your body, your mind, and your emotions is a huge part of creating a peaceful inner life, one that will nurture your happiness.

You've probably heard people talk about self-love in negative terms, making statements like *Boy, they really **love** themselves!* Incredibly the word *love* has been used in some judgmental and damning ways. Many people don't have a good frame of reference for what self-love really is and are therefore resistant to the idea of it simply because they don't want to be associated with vanity or conceit. That's understandable. We have plenty of collective training that it's egotistical to love ourselves, and that's because of a cultural confusion between self-love and narcissism.

I certainly didn't understand the difference until I was already in my early thirties and was introduced to the idea of self-love by my therapist. I had been raised with the mistaken belief that it was egoism, which meant I lived in a very unhappy internal relationship for most of my life until that point. I was, at first, uncomfortable and resistant to the idea, yet I eventually realized there was no way out of self-judgment or criticism with the kinds of beliefs I'd had. Coupled with past circumstances that had led me to believe I had little value, I was certainly in need of a different world view by the time my therapist posed the idea. The doors he opened for me probably saved my life.

Understanding and embracing self-love has also significantly improved the lives of many of the people I have coached. It's a foundation that can't be ignored. In fact, without it, the things we work so hard to build don't stand very long. Lack of self-love will show up and show up again as issues in our lives until we stop, turn within, and begin to heal.

I have an office in Los Angeles a few miles west of the heart of Hollywood. It's near the beautiful sandy beaches of Malibu and just a few minutes from the major film studios and neighborhoods where many of the industry's top working actors live. Unless they prefer I coach them on set, on location, or in their home, this is where I see my private clients. One of these actors, a beautiful, successful television actress whom I will name "Bridget," came to me initially because she had taken some time away from her career to have a family and wanted me to help her create a plan for her comeback. As we explored what her thoughts and feelings were about the industry, she began to realize how nervous she was to return to it. It had been a while and she felt rusty, *and* she also realized as she talked to me that she was very concerned that people may no longer like her. She said the career she'd had before just sort of "happened." A talent scout discovered Bridget when she was quite young and her career had been fast-tracked by the high-powered agency that then groomed and guided her. There had not been a lot of the rejection that most actors pounding the pavement experience, and her charm and great looks meant that she was well-liked and appreciated by most people in the industry, by the media, and by the public. Yet, she realized she had always had an underlying fear that she was just faking it, that she really didn't deserve to have the career she had, and now she was facing the reality of her own doubts.

Bridget had been raised by a father who was highly critical of her. He was an army man who had high standards when it came to most things and as a child Bridget had felt she never quite reached any of them in his eyes. She had worked very hard to please him, getting good grades, winning at sports, being the most polite and pretty girl she could be, and a great part of her success came out of the standards of excellence and professionalism that came out of that history. There had been some positives that had come out of it all, yet the image she had of herself was someone who wasn't of value unless she was *perfecting* something. Feedback was therefore really important to her. In our conversations she began to realize that she didn't have a sense of what "perfect" was unless it came from someone else, nor did she have a stand-alone sense of her own worth. She was realizing very quickly that in order to enter the world of acting again in a healthy way and create any sort of long-term happiness in that arena (or *any* arena for that matter) she was going to need to start building a foundation within herself of love, trust, and compassion.

Many people become actors in part because of a desire to understand themselves and to be heard, seen, and loved, and yet they are taught, just by the nature of the business, to look for those things outside of themselves rather than within. As you navigate your life in the entertainment world, you're required to focus on your *self* as the product. As you do that, the surest way to be happy in the process is to make sure you have a solid connection to the deepest part of who you are, rather than an attachment to how you're seen or what others think of you. It's easy to get caught up in what others think of you, and yes, it can be very valuable to take feedback as a learning tool and a way to grow. However, it's essential that there is a healthy balance. You can't base your value on whether they think you're the "next best thing" or if they say you're not worth a second look.

In the sea of actors struggling with the rejection that comes with being in this industry, I've met many who have an obsession with the need to be famous. And what does that mean, ultimately? Is fame a way to feel loved?

I had the opportunity to experience a mild version of what it's like to be a celebrity during the three years I was a lead actor on a network television show. This first started to happen for me when the pilot got picked up and we were required to do a number of press junkets and therefore the "red carpet" thing. The very first time I walked down a red carpet I was surprised by photographers shouting, "Justina, over here, over here!" as they begged me, almost desperately, to look their way so they could snap my picture. A smile crept over my face, not so much for the cameras' sakes, nor because I was particularly enjoying the attention, but because I was amused by the human game of life occurring in front of me. I was acutely aware that just a day or two prior to this they had probably never heard my name and had no idea that I existed at all. Yet at this moment they were acting as if I were a celebrity and that their day's work relied on me looking at their camera lens! It was a surreal moment. As I moved through the scene, posing for photographers and talking to journalists, I found myself detached from it, yet at the same time very, very present, relaxed, and connected to something solid. Time seemed to slow down. The bustle and drama around me continued, yet inside me was a kind of silence, peace, and observance.

I had spent previous years growing and healing the relationship I had with myself, creating a foundation that was specifically meant to be unconditional to life around me. I had plenty of room to grow in that area still, *and* I had come far in comparison to where I had started out. This meant that in that first red–carpet moment I was grateful for the work I had done thus far. If it had occurred a few years earlier than it did I may have been more caught up in it, perhaps letting it launch me into a high of excitement. I might have bought into the sudden "success" and the drama of all that attention. I might have identified with the role of "celebrity" that was being projected onto me. As it turned out, the work I had done meant that I was able to watch the show unfold around me knowing it was just that: a show. None of what was being said or acted out was going to define me. I had been as valuable yesterday, before any of these people knew I existed, as I was in that moment, and I would be just as valuable, still, if they instantly forgot me again.

The way the business is, if an actor makes it to the red carpet and experiences celebrity being put on them, the odds are they will very likely be forgotten again when they are no longer the flavor of the month. This means it's truly essential—even if you become or already are a celebrity— that you value yourself no matter what's happening in the world around you. Even the rare phenomenon of permanent fame and celebrity is not always going to be a positive experience. When people, the public, and the media put anyone on a pedestal they very often end up pulling them down off it again at some point.

So, the "love" you might feel when you become the center of attention is not necessarily real, and it is certainly not to be relied on for a gauge of how valuable you are. What happens when the fanfare is over and the attention turns to someone they think is younger, hotter, and more interesting in the moment? Then life is over, right? Not if the attention and love you desire come from *within*. If you're filled full with a deep knowledge and a connection to something far bigger that you're a part of, an eternal source of universal love, then you won't find yourself desperately trying to be the one they pick to be the "next best thing." This foundation greatly fortifies the human journey you're on and is where your happiness will grow.

My client Bridget was actually in a really healthy place because, with coaching, she was quickly able to recognize the fears that would have blocked the plans she initially wanted to create. She was willing to get to the core of the matter and had the courage to make some deeper shifts. She wanted to get back to work after having had a family and was eager to do it differently, more authentically, through whom she felt she genuinely was as a person. Bridget committed to improve her relationship with herself. She did that through being more conscious about her inner voice, and by replacing the unkind, unsupportive things that voice was saying with positive, supportive thoughts. She found herself being far more relaxed and trusting about her return to acting, and even her relationships with her husband and friends improved. She soon began working as an actor again, this time, without the belief that she had to be perfect.

Real, healthy self-love is a source of happiness for you and those around you. It could not be further from narcissism. In fact, you are doing everyone else a favor by loving yourself. If you're busy beating yourself up, there is little room for the love, care, and compassion of others. If you're engaged in judging, criticizing, blaming, or doubting yourself your energy gets tied up and you become self-absorbed. Self-love is about service toward a greater good for *all*. It's inclusive, collaborative, and generous, and it brings creativity and joy. It looks *within* for the source of happiness, and it shares that happiness with the world. It sets you up to be fulfilled and filled full. Self-love means you deeply trust that you have value and that you are part of an equally valuable human family. You don't have the need to brag or advertise that, and have no need to pull yourself down. You are free to focus on creativity and serving the world and others.

Narcissism

To be an actor with a healthy, happy platform to operate from, in an industry that can test not only the ego but also the emotions and psyche, you really will only benefit from having that good friendly relationship with yourself. At the same time, many research psychologists believe there to be an epidemic of what is called *narcissism* (or egoism) in the entertainment industry. That's not really a big surprise. Just read the news or watch many of the reality shows out there. There are plenty of people in the entertainment industry that prove the researchers are hitting the mark. It has probably been that way since the first humans entertained other humans with storytelling. If you think about it, many people who end up in the spotlight are there simply because they crave the spotlight. Certainly there are many people who are just very creative, expressive, and have full imaginations—all of which need to be channeled through a craft of some kind—and they end up on stage singing, dancing, acting, or speaking. Some find being in the spotlight rather uncomfortable or just a necessary part of the overall job, *and* there are many who go into the entertainment field in great part because they have narcissistic tendencies that have driven them there.

We all have the capacity for everything human and each one of us has *some* tendencies toward narcissism. Those of us not labeled a "narcissist" by psychologists may still have some level of narcissistic tendencies or traits, meaning we go to similar behaviors in our weakest times. The most undeveloped parts of us display the traits. It's basically the ego showing up and taking over.

All this means that, as an actor especially, it's important to know the difference between narcissistic traits and the healthy and necessary development of self-love.

Narcissism is what most people are referring to when they talk about the ego or conceit. It's considered a very real and painful personality disorder that comes out of deep fear—the fear of being invisible and unloved and the need to compensate for that. It's an obsession with the self, driven by a desperation to be seen and adored. Narcissism looks *outside* of itself for the source of happiness, which means it will never, ultimately, be satisfied.

The narcissistic personality is considered to come out of a tremendously dysfunctional childhood and the belief, held deeply in a person's subconscious, that they are fundamentally flawed and unlovable. Yes, the irony is, despite all appearances, someone who acts as though they are the center of the universe may actually have a deep fear of not being enough. They may look happy but they are inevitably desperately *un*happy, just like an addict is miserable unless they are getting their fix, which for the narcissist is attention and adoration. Those are things that can't be relied on, and so life is a terrifying gamble.

Narcissism, in many instances, can come out of a person being raised and taught by direct communication or by example that they are above everyone else and that they don't have to pay any consequences for their actions. They believe they are entitled to do or say whatever they choose and their entire identity becomes based on this belief. They then take this out into the world, which will most likely not accept or reflect that back. The world around them begins to corrode the picture and a deep and unconscious fear of being discovered as fundamentally flawed begins to develop. People who suffer like this don't recognize their fear, often expressing that they feel good about themselves, yet in reality there is an underlying terror of not being enough. They then compensate by trying to restore the picture for themselves that they are better than others. They act entitled to special treatment, take advantage of others to achieve their own ends, and show a pattern of grandiosity, a need for admiration, a self-involvement, and a lack of empathy. Some narcissists will do just about anything to get attention, as in the case with some celebrities who habitually act out to trigger a frenzy of paparazzi and the media. A narcissist will also do whatever it takes to maintain the learned picture that they are not only better than others, but that they are above everything, including the law.

Interestingly enough, narcissistic traits can *also* develop when a child is taught, to whatever degree, that they are stupid, ugly, flawed, or worthless. Imprinted deeply into their being, they will grow up holding those beliefs as true, no matter what the outside world reflects back to them. That is, unless they discover and nurture something else.

It's a fundamental human need to feel seen, heard, and loved. Without attention and touch, human babies are prone to have health issues, not grow as well or as fast as other babies, and have significant emotional disorders later in life. Love and attention are vital to healthy, normal development. We all need to feel seen and heard, let alone believe that our existence is of some value. When a person doesn't deeply believe that, they will desperately try to make the world around them prove otherwise, and they will cry out for the attention they never got as a child by bragging, being demanding, and creating drama.

All this doesn't mean people with these tendencies are bad. They are scared, disconnected from reality, have been taught some very distorted perceptions, and have found ways to cope through their attitude and behaviors. Again, just about every human being on the planet will display a measure of *narcissistic traits* at some point in their lives even if they are not diagnosed as being narcissistic. We have all had moments of acting arrogantly, being self-involved, and craving fame, accolades, attention, and superiority. We all have egos. Some of us have lived through periods of being obsessed (negatively or positively) with our looks or intelligence. That happens most understandably and especially in a business where the product that's being assessed at all times is *us*. The real gauge of health and balance is about *where we live* most of the time. These types of narcissistic behaviors, if occasional and a passing phase, don't necessarily indicate the personality disorder narcissism. It's just a part of being human and is something that can be grown out of. We each have the opportunity at any point to heal the parts of us that are afraid, and we can do that with love.

If we truly understand that narcissistic tendencies operate out of fear, and that confidence and self-esteem come out of love, we also understand that self-love and narcissism are worlds apart. Love is the highest and most powerful creative force there is and all the good in the world arises from it. *Self*-love is the natural state you belong in because it aligns with that good.

When you're in your ego you're afraid of not being enough. In fact, whenever you feel superior *or inferior* to another, that is the ego in you. It's the most frightened part of your human self and it's in constant fear of annihilation. It speaks through a filter of doubt and blame. It says you're a victim. It says that you're guilty, bad, wrong, flawed, or it decides that others are. Because of this you may find you're trying to control others or your environment so that you can feel better. The ego has us humans strutting around and getting attention in different ways because we don't feel like we are enough just being who we are. It's a lonely, frightening place to be.

So, what would you notice if you were to stand in each place for yourself? Perhaps, if narcissism is the ego, it says it wants you to be "the best." Love, on the other side, says it desires you to explore your own highest potential and wants the same for others. The ego says it wants you to seek fame and attention. Love says it desires you to be creative and of service. The ego says it wants you to put others down to feel more valuable by comparison; it has a sense of "better than." Love knows your value and encourages others to know their own value. The ego is disconnected from the feelings of others. Love is empathetic and compassionate. The ego is controlling and forces the self into things. Love has self-control, is kind, and is efficient. The ego feels entitled and will only accept *yes* from others. Love feels worthy and can accept *no*. The ego is attached to appearance. Love is grateful for both inner and outer beauty. The ego is afraid of criticism and tries to control how others perceive it. Love trusts its own worth no matter what happens in the world. The ego seeks power over others. Love cultivates power *with* others. The ego wants attention from others. Love desires connection with others. The ego says, *What can I get here?* Love says, *How will I contribute here?*

In the path toward loving yourself more you can practice recognizing when the ego (your fear) comes up and be compassionate. Having an ego is part of being human, and however much you might like to get rid of it, you can't destroy it.

There is a film I rather like called *The Fifth Element* in which evil shows up as a massive sphere hurtling toward Earth. The Earthlings decide to fire atomic missiles at it in hopes that it will be destroyed before it destroys Earth, yet each time the missiles hit the sphere of evil it grows, expands, and becomes stronger and fiercer. The humans' missiles are sent out into space with violence and the intent to destroy, and the only effect they have is to increase the size of the sphere. This is because their missiles and the intention with which they are used are made out of *the very same substance* as the mass of evil: fear.

We can't fight for peace nor hate evil in hopes that we will win over it, or that it will go away. When we berate ourselves for being afraid or we criticize ourselves for being critical, we are doing just what the Earthlings did in the film. We are trying to destroy a fire with a firebomb. If we get angry with ourselves for being afraid, defensive, or egotistical, we simply compound the fear. When we send hatred to the dark places in us, we only increase them. Fear is simply the absence of love, as darkness is the absence of light. The only way to transform darkness and fear is to return to love.

In the film the humans eventually save Earth by using a combination of the Fifth Element (perfect human form) and the power of love. The marriage of our higher humanity with that of love creates the essential self, which in turn creates a glorious light sent out into the sky where it floods the sphere of darkness, dissolving it in a blaze of good.

Actor, Know Thyself

As long as there is relative health and fitness, as we get older we tend to get happier. One of the reasons for this is that we know ourselves better as we mature. Self-awareness is an ongoing journey that, if traveled consciously and with intention, can be a strong ingredient toward raising our happiness levels. Being self-aware means we can trust ourselves more with the directions we choose to take in life, our relationships are better, and we are more confident and aligned with our purpose. Happiness will come in proportion to the courage we have to take the journey of self-awareness. It takes doing some exploration, which sometimes requires working with a therapist or coach. If they are skilled and a good fit for you, a professional guide can be a very powerful catalyst to finding out about who you are, how you tick, what your fears are, what your tactics are, what your strengths are, and what you really want underneath it all. Becoming conscious of these things will serve you well for your own personal growth as well as in your relationships.

Because you're an actor and a student of the human spirit I would imagine you've already done some amount of self-exploration and soul searching. Whether you are beginning your journey as an actor or have been in the industry for many years, at some point you will have asked yourself the question, *Who am I?* Exploring yourself through your craft can give you an awareness that non-actors might not have. It's important to know who you are so that you can use those aspects within the roles you play. The work of slipping into the life of a character requires it. Playing a part is, in its ultimate form, you accessing parts of yourself, which you then use to portray the life of the character. You begin to live their life through your own life.

With that in mind, what is the *self* anyway? We are made up of many, many dimensions and "parts" as individual *beings*, and the *self* is a perceived aspect of that being. The mistake many of us make is to assume that this is who we are in our entirety. When we do that our identity becomes enmeshed only in our humanness, our bodies, our appearance, our thinking, our doing, our emotions, our fears, our memories, and our beliefs. We are, in fact, so much more than that. We are everything. *You* are everything. You are part of the entire universe. So, rather than seeing yourself as just a general *you,* busy running around trying to make things happen, it can be enlightening and empowering to explore more deeply what your other dimensions and parts are.

It can be said that, ultimately, we are *consciousness* and that this consciousness is expanding through its current expression, which is human form. This consciousness is thought to be an eternal part of the whole universe.

When we are babies we come into the world *at one* with everything. We are not interested in being separate from others, the world around us, the air, the ground, or the love we feel. Separation grows on us as we grow into our humanity. The great challenge of the human experience is the separation we feel. It can create incredible suffering. When we return to our oneness with the whole universe we have entered into what's considered the divine experience. We "tap in." This is the ultimate goal of most spiritual practices. Oneness is what we all seek whether we know it or not, and whether we are doing things to run away from it or not. Many actors report a sense of that connection and oneness while working, sometimes right in the middle of a scene or performance. You may have experienced a sense of this yourself as an actor, or even outside of the acting process, when thinking ceased and you became acutely present. This is your consciousness and it's the truth of all of us. It is the *essential self*.

Your essential self is without fear or doubt. It doesn't have patterns, habits, belief systems, and judgment, nor does it live in the past or future. It is fully present, in a state of love, and nonending. The essential self is considered in spiritual terms to be *God individualized*. It is also sometimes called the *higher self*, the *true self*, the *individual superconscious*, the *spirit*, or the *soul*. Whatever your religious, spiritual, or nonspiritual beliefs, I simply invite you to tap into the part of you that's powerfully alive, peaceful, and intuitive. Our greatest and most inspiring spiritual teachers live through their essential selves more than most of us. They have awareness that— rather than the ego or human self—it's the *essential self* that is the truth of who they are. It's their connection with the divine in this way that makes them such extraordinary teachers.

Your essential self and the relationship you have with it are fundamental to your happiness. Being conscious that you are a part of the divine allows you to live *as* the divine with its loving, wise, and eternal compassion. Every person has the potential to be an inspiration to others and we do that through the highest parts of ourselves. That's what comes through you when you're being creative. The word *inspiration* comes from *spirare*, which is related to the words *spirit*, *courage*, *vigor*, and *breath*. So *inspiration* is "in spirit" or "breathing life into." Whatever your passion and human purpose is, your work as an actor is part of that divine expression. You breathe the life of your spirit into what you do when you are inspired.

In exploring your essential self, in becoming more aware of it you might ask, "Where has that inspirational, wise, loving 'me' been when I've been out there in the world dealing with relationships, work, money, auditioning, and going to meetings?" We all learn things that limit the connection we have with our essential selves. As children and in adult society we are often directed to outside forces and taught that the ultimate power of good is something separate from us. A "man up in the sky" even. This tends to send us away from ourselves when we need answers, support, and strength. The truth is there is also a source of wisdom right inside each one of us, a source that's a part of the ultimate and infinite wisdom of the universe itself. Our higher purpose is to awaken to this.

Becoming aware of your own deep wisdom takes consciously connecting with it. That can be accomplished through meditation, quiet moments of contemplation, or even simple reminders during the day to become aware of the present moment. As you do that, as you think less and become more conscious. You expand, living as the core essence of *you*. That in turn creates a foundation of deep and sustainable happiness.

Your Humanity

Let's now examine the *human self* that you're inhabiting while you are on the human journey.

The human self is made up of your body, your thoughts, and your emotions, as well as your beliefs and values. The ego is also part of the human self. One of your major roles in life is to take care of and evolve your own "human being" while you're traveling around on the planet. Caring for yourself and all your parts as a parent and friend is essential to your happiness and health, and ultimately to your success. Personal development is essential for every one of us, no matter what we do for a living. For you as an actor, taking care of your own personal development is going to be as important as any acting skill you acquire. After all, you are the vehicle for your art. Successful, happy, and fulfilled people take care of themselves emotionally, physically, mentally, and spiritually—not because they can afford the time, money, or effort it takes to do so. They take care of themselves because they know *they cannot afford not to.*

One of your many human parts is, of course, your body. This physical body you're in can be thought of like a space suit, an outfit you wear as you travel around on this planet, just like an astronaut might use while exploring unknown territory out in the cosmos. When you're finished with the journey you leave your space suit behind on Earth.

Whatever opinions you have about your body, the truth is, it's an extraordinary miracle. Your skin, your organs, your skeletal system, and your muscles are a spectacular, magnificent creation. You are utterly unique. Your body expresses you through those eyes, those lines and folds, the ways you stand, walk, and talk, and the ways you interact. It speaks to others about who you are and what's happening inside. It works diligently to heal itself. Whenever you get sick, it immediately begins to get rid of the offending poison, virus, or bug. It digests food, works to eliminate the waste, and adjusts to your every need and action. It has billions of different cells with different jobs, all working around the clock to make sure everything is running smoothly. We have barely begun to understand how this magnificent creation works.

As an actor, your body is one of your most important tools. It's the physical vehicle through which you express the human spirit. One of the great adventures of being an actor is that you will use your body in many more ways than the average person. You will get to step into and live through your characters' physical traits, abilities, and limitations. You will be able to explore many, many physical experiences through the roles you play! As a human being with the desire to be happy it's vital that you take great care of this extraordinary body of yours. If you let it down, it will let you down, and without your health you will have real limits to accomplishing what you want to accomplish. This means you must be conscious about how you treat your body. This is done in a number of ways, not only by being discerning with how and what you consume, how you exercise, and what your lifestyle is like, but also in how you *regard* your body. As you criticize less, and accept, appreciate, and have more gratitude for the space suit you live in, you will find yourself being far healthier and happier.

One of the things that might have prevented you from appreciating your body is what you were taught about it. Most of us living in the "developed world" are bombarded with images of models and actors that we are encouraged to measure ourselves against. The thing is, those images are not realistic and they have us believing we are not enough the way we are. A very small handful of exceptions to nature actually look like the people we see in magazines and on television. Much of the time the models of beauty we measure ourselves against have been created (or at least enhanced) by surgery, specific eating habits, personalized physical training, designer clothing, chemical and laser treatments, dermal fillers, and makeup and hair products. The photos and footage of these people are also enhanced and manipulated with special lighting, photo retouching, and computer graphic imaging. Too many of us have bought into the idea that the resulting standards of appearance are what we should aspire to *without* the advantage of the right genetics or the many tools that create the illusion of those genetics. The catch-22 is that there is judgment when those tools *are* used, so the pressure is enormous.

Is there anything wrong with using tools to improve your looks? Your body is a large piece of the product you're selling on a day-to-day basis as you audition and perform. It has to be in top condition in health and appearance, *and* if you're going to improve on nature it's important to consider how that is approached. Everything you do in life is going to be permeated by the initial intention and energy behind it. If you take part in any action through fear of not being enough (or any fear for that matter) the end result is very often going to reflect that. If you move into an action through celebration and care you will likely have a happier experience. If you're going to use any tool (whether it's cosmetics, lighting, surgery, clothing, supplements, exercise, or food) celebrating your space suit, decorating it, and making improvements must be done with long-term loving care, taking into account any risks and making sure you take the most appropriate path. If you abuse your body physically or with your thoughts, you will only create misery down the line. Your happiness will increase as you care for your body, fueling it with the nutrition and supplementation it requires, taking part in nurturing and health-giving activities, and respecting its long-term needs. Your body is here for you to enjoy and care for as it carries you faithfully on your journey. How thankful you must be, whatever your space suit is like. It's really a miracle for each of us that we are even alive.

Another part of your human being is your mind. It's believed that the root of suffering and the root of happiness are both in the mind. You can tell when you're in your human self because you're thinking. Being *conscious* is not about thought; it's about being present.

Your mind is a complex and brilliant machine containing a huge database. We have barely begun to tap into the vastness of our minds' capabilities. Some researchers believe that the mind is made up of four levels. Firstly, there is the *conscious* mind, where you have daily thoughts and where reason and logic are processed. This is the part that keeps you occupied most of the time. It tends to think about the past or the future and jumps around from thought to thought. It is also the part of your mind that can decide to become focused on the present moment.

You also have a *subconscious* mind, which is where some of the beliefs and patterns from your past experiences lie hidden, affecting how you respond to your life and what you create. It is the part of you that you have little or no awareness of in your conscious day-to-day life, yet most of what drives your life and the outcomes you experience come from what's in your subconscious. It's where memories, deeper thoughts and feelings, and self-understanding are stored. Metaphor, symbolism, and imagery are the types of thinking that can access the subconscious. Recent studies have shown that our subconscious minds are actually thirty thousand times more powerful than our conscious minds! Your subconscious contains all the things you learned about yourself and the world through what you heard, what you saw, and what you felt in your body. Your mind made interpretations about all of it and created beliefs. Your beliefs, whether they are resourceful or not, are a powerful creator of your experiences.

Then there is the *superconscious* mind, which is sometimes called the *soul*. We are moving away from the human aspects of you as we enter the realm of the soul. This superconscious mind is moving into the essential self as described earlier. It's the part of you that can sense and influence the energy fields in yourself, others, places, and things. Bypassing logic and using intuition are thought to be the channels into your superconscious mind. Using and developing your intuition are also big parts of how you learn to trust yourself and know who you are.

Then there is the *collective* mind, or the *universal* mind. Science understands this as a single quantum energy field that functions in intelligent, predictable ways to make up the universe. This is what scientists call the *Unified Field* and what religion or spirituality calls *God, Allah, Spirit, Nirvana, The Universe, Great Soul,* or *the Source,* as well as many other names; and they hold it as the all-knowing, infinite, all-loving, wise existence that creates and sustains everything. We are all part of this One Mind through our essence. Meditation and focused, peaceful concentration allow us to access this universal superconscious mind. When we connect with the universal mind through meditation, we simply become love.

That's the mind. If we look at the physical brain, which is where a good part of the mind is thought to reside, its neuropathways can be equated to the body's muscles. They develop in certain areas and not in others depending on what we use more—or in the brain's case, according to what we focus on. The more we use certain parts of our minds with what we think about, the stronger and more influential those parts of the brain become.

What you have the opportunity to do now, as you get to know these parts of yourself, is to decide if the *thoughts* you're well practiced at are really serving you and your happiness. What is in the contents of your mind from day to day? What are the images, metaphors, and words that habitually pop up? In order to create positive experiences in your life and to be a happy person, you have to transform the thoughts that haven't been serving you and discover new thoughts that are more productive and positive, teaching your mind to become stronger in those areas.

A significant part of your path to becoming happier is through exploring what lies beneath conscious thought. Your subconscious beliefs and patterns can be the source of your success or your failure in life. This is where you're called to bypass your intellect and move into the next levels of your mental body: your subconscious and superconscious minds.

The potential for success and happiness already exists within your mind. It's an amazing tool for analysis, discernment, processing, connection, and magnificent creation. Only through exploring your mind in all its levels can you learn to harness the amazing power you have to make your dreams become your reality.

Recent scientific research is now showing that consciousness doesn't just originate in the mind, but also from a communication between the mind and body, and the heart plays a significant role in this process. Not just a pumping organ, the heart is now understood to have its own "brain" that receives and processes information. It learns, remembers, and makes functional decisions independent of the brain. Not only that, but if you know anything about electromagnetic fields, the heart's field has been found to have a magnetic component five thousand times stronger than that of the brain! This field can be detected several feet away from the body by magnetometers and is believed to be directly involved in intuition, which it perceives before the brain does. The heart is a powerful force. When we are "in" our hearts, as opposed to "in" our conscious minds, we may well be tapping into a far more powerful and intelligent part of ourselves than we previously thought possible.

Our emotions are believed to come from the heart-center, which is in the middle of the chest just to the right of the physical heart. It is said that the emotional self actually has a "body" of its own, though it's not a dense body like the physical form. Rather it's what we might think of as an energy field, expanding out to about an inch outside of the solid body. The emotional self is a powerful built-in tool for us to tell what feels right and not right. The ability to trust in that part of you can create a great source of happiness in life. Confidence is the result of understanding your emotions and knowing how to navigate through them. By doing that you're empowered to heal what needs healing, grow what wishes to grow, and shift what has not been working for you into what does. You also get to consciously infuse your acting roles with your emotions if you want to. Your palette becomes further reaching and more authentic. Exploring your emotions, not just as a set of tools for your craft as an actor but as a resource for your own personal power, is yet another way to expand your happiness.

Your human self has many, many aspects to it, and to be curious about how you function and what your processes are will only serve to create confidence. Along with that, taking care of all the needs you have through health and healing will only mean your life is enhanced and your happiness levels raised. We are understanding more and more what a profound effect our activities and internal dynamics have on our evolution as individuals. As you get to know your needs, boundaries, and growth areas, you will find yourself making new choices about how you behave, how to think, and what to believe about you. This, then, shifts what shows up in your life. Remember, successful, happy people take care of themselves because they have learned that they cannot afford not to.

Baby Elephants

Actors are, more than most people, connected to their humanity and their feelings. Actors are storytellers, artists, and shape-shifters who courageously explore their hearts, fears, and personalities like no other community of humans—and they do it publicly. It's also very likely that many of those drawn to the craft of acting had some trauma as children. Many of us were taught some things that really limited us. We learned from authority sources that we were not important or valuable and that we didn't deserve to be happy. We learned that our bodies, our opinions, and our emotional needs were not worthy. We became drawn to artistic things, expressing ourselves and making people laugh, inspiring and moving them. And perhaps later in life, some of us went out into the world and found ourselves trying to make up for our imagined limits in ways that were desperate, fearful, or regrettable. In times like those we forgot who we really are.

Have you heard about baby elephants? These wonderful, enthusiastic creatures are quite the lot for their handlers, so they keep them in place by shackling one of their ankles to a small stake driven into the ground. It's an easy and effective way to keep the little guys from running away. A baby elephant may attempt to escape at first, tugging frantically at the chain, yet after time he will give up knowing that he can't break free. He gets on with life within those bounds.

The interesting thing is that as the elephant matures and becomes a huge and powerful adult, he doesn't test the stake again, even though he could easily pull it out and be on his way. He gave up trying to break free a long time ago. He learned as a baby that the stake would keep him in place no matter what. The elephant doesn't *get* that he has grown. He doesn't recognize the truth about his own size and strength. In fact, very often, all that's required to keep an elephant in place is a small metal bracelet around one of its ankles even when it's not attached to anything at all! Having once learned that the bracelet is chained to a stake, the elephant will stay. There are hundreds of grown-up two-ton elephants all over this planet that think they are still little and can't move forward.

This same thing has happened to many of us. We forgot that we have grown up and that the things that used to feel so huge, so controlling, and so able to hold us back are now tiny and small compared to who we have become.

Part of creating happiness inside yourself is the recognition that the things from the past have no hold over you anymore unless you decide to believe so. It's the little one, the baby elephant inside, that has had you believe you're still at the mercy of others. As an adult it's up to you to bring reality to the forefront, remembering that you have, indeed, got choice.

Children are like sponges. They are open vessels; never having built up walls or learned what to filter out, they are highly sensitive and will take in everything around them on a profoundly deep level. They feel and hear everything. When you have a child who is especially aware and sensitized to the world around them, negative experiences will have even more profound consequences. Many artists and actors are very sensitive people. There is an opportunity, then, to use your creativity for personal growth. One of the ways you can make your shifts and heal your past is through self-parenting. Rather than spending your life looking at the past and wondering what caused what and why, you can bring the past into the present and heal the beliefs and emotions of the child in you now. You can do this by becoming the ideal parent to your child self.

How do you do this?

As time is now believed to be nonlinear there are those who also believe that we carry with us, in our systems, all the ages we have been, our past selves traveling with us on the road as we go. There are also some who believe that we carry all of the ages we *shall* be as well, our future selves existing within us ready to be lived out. Each of us has had the experience of feeling and acting like the child we once were, and at times like the wiser and more experienced version of ourselves. There are times when we are afraid, unsure, or in need of reassurance. When things come up that, for example, your three-year-old self is afraid of, even though you're an adult you're going to get really scared. You might intellectually be able to talk yourself through it for a while, yet that fear will keep coming up in different circumstances and in different relationships or jobs until the three-year-old is loved and cared for consistently over time.

Most of us have the desire in some way to be heard. The fact that you're an actor means that's probably even more likely to be the case for you. Actors choose their profession for many reasons, and one of them has to do with being heard. For a child, as well as for adults, *not* being heard is the most fundamental and intense type of invalidation. The need to be heard can drive some people through every decision they make in their lives. It can create movie stars and it can create serial killers. When children are not listened to and their feelings are invalidated they will have a hard time understanding their worth and any sense of healthy boundaries, so it's fundamentally important that you get to feel heard to a healthy degree in your life now as an adult. That's not something you can control when it comes to being heard by others, though you can raise the odds by being around respectful, interested, and loving people.

It *is*, however, something you can commit to for *yourself*. You have the chance now to play that very important role: your own parent. A parent that listens, nurtures, teaches, forgives, and protects, and who will always be there.

The children in this world who have been abused rarely ever have anyone around who will let them know that they don't deserve it and that it's not okay. They are not given a sense of boundaries, self-worth, or any reference points for loving themselves. Abuse for a child is devastating and sometimes even life threatening. It can take years of hard work and courage to survive, let alone thrive after a childhood that contains abuse to the physical, sexual, emotional, or intellectual being. I can tell you that it is not only possible to survive this kind of a history, because I did, but it's potentially a ticket to creating a very powerful and rich life. A past containing an unusually large amount of adversity is one of the most common factors among our world's most inspirational leaders. Some of the most successful people in our world have risen from great pain and hardship to become the inspiring, powerful people that they are today.

In your journey now, you get to unlearn the myths about yourself and return to your natural state. That state is to love yourself again in a healthy, uncomplicated way. There is the opportunity to step in as the powerful adult that you are today, recognizing that you're no longer tethered or shackled to anything. Frankly, you will need to do that in order to continue putting yourself out publicly without feeling annihilated. You've chosen to make your body, your emotions, your psyche, in fact your very essence the materials for your creative expression, while at the same time marketing those materials in a business that can be brutal. The happy news is that you're in one of the most likely groups on the planet to be able to nurture and strengthen the internal relationship. You and your fellow actors have special access to those inner places like few other humans and what you do with that now, knowing that it's possible, is you learn to trust yourself more, find out what's really important to you, and have a friendship inside that you can truly count on.

It's all good and well to understand the importance of having a good relationship with yourself, but to actually *develop* it there has to be change. Practical steps, new habits and thinking, and reminders or "anchors" to the new relationship are essential. If, as you grow your happiness levels, you start with *you*, there is a foundation being built. Just like when you build a house, the foundation has to have strong rebar and good concrete, and the hole has to be nice and deep. Otherwise, the building itself won't last the earthquakes and the rains of life. Whenever you grow anything, you start with what's in the soil; so go down into the roots of your life and make peace with yourself somehow.

Many of the areas we will explore in this book will fortify the relationship you have with yourself. To love yourself may take some unlearning of old, limiting beliefs and a relearning of more resourceful ones. We will look at what sort of self-talk you have and how you communicate with yourself and begin to find kinder ways. We will explore your values and what's really important to you, and as the understanding you have of yourself becomes stronger, that in turn builds trust. You will be invited to complete unfinished business from the past, and to build new resources into your life, both daily and in stages.

Until you really understand what self-love is, and that it's not only acceptable but also crucial to a happy, healthy life, you will be stuck in a cycle of unhappy relationships and circumstances. In learning more about what self-love is and understand that it has nothing to do with conceit or narcissism, you will find that a foundation, fortified by your knowledge, will begin to grow inside you and show up as a faithful friend in your life and your career. Again, the level of self-love you have determines how you interpret everything. Your interpretations will then affect how you behave and how you come across, and that will affect how others respond to you, which then affects much of what shows up for you as experiences and events. It's a domino effect. All of this is true, not only for you, but for every human being on the planet, whether you're an actor or an accountant, and committing yourself to improving just this *one* thing may well be the greatest investment you will ever make. So, arm yourself with love, shield yourself with light, and wrap yourself in compassion.

Ultimately the choices we make in our lives are between darkness and light, between fear and love. You can only accept light into your life when you have accepted it inside yourself. You can only accept unconditional love when you have learned to love yourself.

You have to build a strong foundation to build a strong life, and that foundation, dear, wonderful, creative spirit that you are, is the relationship you have with you.

CHAPTER 3

Living in Alignment

But what is happiness except the simple harmony between a man and the life he leads?

~ *A L B E R T   C A M U S*

Got Peace?

Do you love the craft of acting but find the logistical, business side of it frustrating and challenging? Do you enjoy being fit or want to lose weight yet do everything you can to avoid going to the gym? Is there a part of you that dreams about being rich and famous and another part that feels uncomfortable and out of place walking into high-end department stores? Do you love the idea of being in a relationship yet find yourself shutting down when things start to get serious? A *yes* answer to any of these means you know what it's like to be in conflict with yourself. You also know that leads to unhappiness and blocks on your path.

The world we live in would obviously benefit from more peace. We are inundated with wars breaking out all over the world, political battles in our own countries, gang fights in our neighborhoods, bickering between our friends, and bad blood between family members, and we wish for peace. Yet do we really think about where it begins? Does peace begin "out there" where the bombs are blasting and the missiles are being fired? Does it begin with our politicians and our leaders? Does it begin with our neighbors and family members? Or does it begin *within us*? Is it really any use to want global, social, and relational peace and to want the violence to stop if we are living in our own internal war zone? What if the condition of the world around us is simply an out-picturing of our own individual worlds within? What if the times we have been critical and judgmental of ourselves and those around us, the times we have been ashamed or felt unworthy, or the times we have simply had a limiting belief—*what if those moments are the roots of war?*

As we have established, your human self is made up of many parts and many of them have wanted different things. Imagine for a moment that each of your parts is an actor playing a role in the movie of your life. Each actor (or part), with his or her own purpose and character, is here to benefit you somehow. These interesting and diverse actors make up the cast that's the whole you. However, as with any group there has to be a leader, a producer/director. If that producer/director is not focusing on the job there is most likely going to be some confusion, disagreement, disparity, and conflict on set, which can make the ultimate goal of the group (creating the desired movie of your life) hard to achieve. The truth of it is you're a multifaceted being and some of your parts may not agree with others. Conflict and lack of communication between your parts is one reason you may have had trouble creating what you envision and one significant reason for a lack of happiness. Getting your cast of "actors" to communicate effectively and in harmony so that the overall goal (your dream) can be met is the job of the producer/director of this system, and ideally that's the one who observes all of this happening. That part would be your essential self.

Peaceful relationships create a higher overall level of happiness, and that includes the relationships within yourself. In order for inner harmony to occur you first need to be able to *imagine* it. You can't create what you can't envision.

Many years ago a young actor I will call "Taylor" came to me because he was having trouble finishing projects and felt a life coach might be a way to motivate him to shift that habit. I first explained that a large part of my job was to help him discover his own inner workings. This way he would be able to expand on what was working and reorganize what wasn't. Through our exploration he realized that his trouble finishing projects had a lot to do with inner conflict. Taylor had been so busy questioning himself, wondering whether he was going in the "right" direction, or what the "right" stopping point would be, that he had ended up feeling deflated and stuck on just about everything. There had been so many debates in his head about what he "should" or "should not" do that he had not been able to get to a point of completion on most things he had started.

"It's like I have a war going on inside me!" Taylor said in amazement as he observed his own thinking process for the first time. As I waited for

Taylor to have a few moments with this I noticed his eyes darting about as though there were a number of people in the room chatting at once. It looked to me like he was attempting to hear what each of them was saying. I let Taylor know what I observed and he affirmed my suspicions.

"Yes, it's like there are a dozen different opinions and they are all shouting to be heard and I really can't hear any of them because of it. It's overwhelming! I can't make heads or tails of any of it."

"What would you like to do with this?" I asked.

"I'd like to shut them up for a minute," he laughed.

"And how would you like to do that?" I continued.

"Ummm, maybe by putting my hands over my ears." Taylor placed his hands firmly over his ears and scrunched up his eyes.

"Okay, so as you do that now, notice what difference it makes."

"It doesn't make any difference because they're inside my head!" Taylor lamented.

"Yes," I said.

"So what shall I do?" Taylor asked me with a frustrated smile.

I smiled back and said, "You will know what to do. If you like we can brainstorm some ideas."

"Okay, great," he agreed.

After a while we came up with a few ideas on the best ways to deal with his many insistent voices. What was most important for Taylor, as we explored the possibilities, was that all the voices in his head had relevant and valuable opinions and needed to be honored. Instead of fighting them and trying to shut them up, he realized he needed to stop and listen to each one of them individually. Right then and there we decided to play with that. On a particular project he had not finished (a film script), Taylor wrote down what each voice inside him had been saying about it. Once he had listened to them all, he stopped, took some deep breaths, and centered himself.

I guided Taylor to relax even further and become aware of the present moment. As he connected with his own consciousness deep beneath the chatter of his mind, his physical and energetic demeanor changed. He became lighter, calmer, and more open.

"So, from this new perspective as you observe those different voices and begin to listen to the overall truth, you now get to consider—not so much in thought, more in your *being*—the script you have on the go. What comes up for you?" I asked.

Taylor opened his eyes with a powerful smile and said, "I know exactly what I want to add to the script, and it's *this*." He then told me what direction he felt truly "right" about going in with his project. He added, "I'm meant to finish all the projects I have like this, feeling that I can trust myself!"

Taylor realized that as he listened to his own deeper voice in the stillness he was able to make stronger choices. He also realized that many of the voices in his head had ultimately wanted the same things but had not been heard properly over the noise of the others. Now that each voice was being listened to and validated, Taylor noticed that they had become either completely silent or much softer. He went home and got many of his projects completed within a few days. He was astounded at how little time it took and realized it had not been the projects that were the issue but his inner conflict. Once he created a peaceful environment in his own mind, completing projects became easier and his life began to flow.

A foundation of long-term happiness requires a commitment to inner peace and congruence. The places inside each of us where we relate to ourselves are the places conflicts first have to be resolved. War is about opposing forces. When you have opposing forces within you—whether from your feelings about eating a food that has an adverse effect on your body, or the beliefs you have that stop you from reaching your goals, or a vision you have for the future that opposes your core values, or even your feelings about someone that don't match up with what you think you ought to feel— resolving conflict and creating peace is paramount. You can't be happy when there is a war inside you. Your job as the center of your own being is to sort through what has not yet been resolved and to create a system of harmony. You've got to align with your innermost self. Only then can you begin to align with your own life.

You may say, *I'm an actor! I walk in the shoes of characters dealing with conflict, high stakes, and big changes. How will all this potential harmony and happiness affect my ability to play the challenges in my roles?* This is such a great question, and here is what I've found to be the case. As you begin to really trust the process of life, as you become more aligned and confident, you will find your work as an actor becoming stronger. Your ability to be compassionate and empathetic increases. You draw from an understanding of your own humanity and the humanity of others and you're able to use that knowledge in your work. Rather than living in the middle of a human drama, you're more at liberty to stand on solid ground as your characters fall apart and come together into their new shapes. Just as a sturdy ship courses though a massive storm at sea, your solid base of peace will allow your work as an actor to become fuller, broader, and more present and interesting as a result. Trust that. Trust that peace has what it takes to be creative.

The question now is, can you commit to being here, with yourself in this moment? Can you commit to finding congruence and understanding inside? Can you commit to having compassion with what you find? Can you commit to communication and patience? Can you commit to unconditional kindness? Can you commit to raising yourself like a loving parent? Can you commit to being loyal to yourself like a true friend? The journey you're taking toward greater happiness requires that you commit to inner peace step by step, moment by moment, and day by day. Only then can you begin to have peace in your relationships. Only then can you begin to tend to others with a compassion and understanding that comes from a deeper and more central experience of yourself and love the people in your life in ways that feel like love to *them*. Only then can you align with yourself, with your life, with others, with your vision and your goals, and with the experience you have of life around you; and when that happens the world opens up. What is possible, then, is deep, sustainable happiness.

Why Acting?

Why are you an actor? What is it about acting that gets you up every morning and fills your dreams at night?

I've had a number of up-and-coming actors turn up at my office feeling dejected, exhausted, and flattened by the process of auditioning, working for short spurts and then going back to auditioning again. They often think there is something wrong with them because, out of that, they have lost their energy for the whole business of acting. Do you relate to that? Have you felt tired of the whole journey? The first thing I suggest to actors wanting guidance with this is that, rather than there being anything *wrong* with them, perhaps on the contrary those feelings show that there is something very healthy and sane occurring!

Imagine walking through a small town knocking on doors every day, hoping to be welcomed with a *Come in! Come to our party; we would love to have you be part of our team!* and instead finding that the majority of the time the blinds get pulled down, the doors are not answered, or the locks get bolted. And if a door *is* answered, more often than not the inhabitant says, *No thanks, not today.* This describes the sort of life a door-to-door salesperson would have today, and I would bet not many people would come home from a job like that saying, *Wow, I am so energized by my month! What fun! I had fifty no's and one yes.* That attitude might even be considered a bit crazy. It's one thing to be peaceful and neutral about events, and quite another to celebrate rejection. Certainly it's very important to be optimistic, *and* it's also important to honor what you're being faced with each day and how that might affect a human being. The sane human response might be to feel a bit deflated. Nonreciprocity does have a tendency to do that in all systems. It's what you *do* with that deflation that matters. For an actor, because uncertainty can be such a big part of life (no matter what level your career is at) and because there's the added experience that the product you are presenting at those doors is yourself, it becomes really important to reconnect with a deeper meaning behind *why* you're even in the business you're in. What is the *meaning* behind it all?

Meaning taps into the core parts of who you are. It's what you place value on and it's what inspires and ignites you. It's what refills the deflated spirit. This important area is known as your "values", and they are essential if you're going to have purpose and a vision for your future.

There is a tendency, when we think of our values, to mistake the ones we were raised with for those of our own. We are not talking about "perceived values" (the values of your family, religious community, or social groups). We are talking here about the principles that are truly *yours*, the ones you find uniquely, deeply important and inspiring to you. We are talking about your core values. These are some of the most fundamental ingredients for building peace and trust in yourself. Your values are the fingerprints of your soul.

There are three main ways we find out what our values are. One is when they are violated. Our physical and emotional bodies have a wonderful built-in mechanism that can signal what's truly a part of us in the deepest sense by how something *feels* to us. When we feel uncomfortable or upset, we can usually bet that a value has been violated. The second way we understand our values is when they are fulfilled somehow. We get a sense that something important has occurred and it feels good. Now, that being said, being upset is also often a result of the ego being bruised, and feeling fulfilled is sometimes because the ego has been satisfied, so it's important as we explore our values to separate out the ego's wants from what's deeply and intrinsically important to us. The third way to know our values is through self-examination and a conscious effort to discover them. This is the surest way to separate our own values from those of others.

You can feel values in yourself when you love an object or person. There is an opportunity when that happens to look at what it is *about* them that connects for you. What is it that feels good and stirs the deeper parts of you to life? Is it the sense of play and lightness you get there, or the intimacy, or trust. Or is it the warmth, the freedom? It's very important to know that it's not the car, the mountain, the dog, the person, or the earrings that are ultimately going to make you happy, even though the ego may convince you that it is. The truth is it's the values that you find *in* those objects, animals, or people and the feelings you get when you're around them that will create long-term happiness. Your values are there even when the object is not. Of course there are profound connections we can have with other people and animals, and that is included in and goes well beyond this idea. The thought is that a car might stir feelings of comfort, beauty, and efficiency, all of which are values. Values can also be described with words like *creativity, communication, freedom, independence, learning, self-control, fairness, humor, punctuality, justice, love, connection, challenge,* and so on. Your happiness doesn't come from a car or a relationship, but from the core values it fulfills in you. Values are what we find deeply "value-able" (or valuable).

One of my clients (I shall call him "Ryan") had come to me partly because he had lost his passion for acting. He was a talented actor who had had some real success in television and film. Understandably, the wind had left his sails after the fanfare of a hit movie had died down and he found himself in the auditioning circuit again, even though now it was for major films opposite A-list stars. He was uninspired by the return to the high level of investment required to deliver great readings, and the low return on how many roles he might book per audition. No matter that he was on a higher rung on the ladder of success as an actor, he was still dealing with rejection and competition in his mind and he was simply tired of it. He felt flat and defeated. Ryan was no longer juiced up by the idea of acting. The thing to do, it seemed, was to get back to the fundamental reason this boy was even in the business at all. Why be here if it wasn't fun anymore? Most importantly, what was it about acting that he loved? So I asked him, "If you take a moment to think about acting and when you're most enjoying it, the times you can really say to yourself, *Aaah, this is why I do this!* what comes up for you?"

He shifted on the couch and just slightly visibly lightened. I encouraged him, "Imagine being in that experience now with whatever feelings you have in your body, immersing yourself in how it affects you, and what it brings up in you, and then ask yourself, *What does this feeling allow me to have, be, or do?* Then notice what comes up."

Ryan's body became more open and his eyes widened as he remembered. "Well, when I'm really in the moment and things are rolling, in the zone, I'm hooked into something with the other person, I feel plugged in."

"Plugged in," I repeated.

"Yes, plugged in, and I feel like I'm in the flow, like there's this freedom. I can feel myself just being free to create."

"So, you're in the flow, and you have freedom, and creativity."

"Yes, it's like something else takes over and it becomes effortless and all my troubles are gone. Even when the character is in trouble, I am channeling some kind of power through that. I also get to laugh a lot when I'm acting. I love that."

"Those sound like some really important things to you."

"Yes."

"When you get the feeling of those important things, those values for you in acting—in the moment, rolling, in the zone, hooked in, plugged in, in the flow, freedom, creativity, effortlessness, channeling, power, laughter—which one really stands out right now for you?"

"I think creativity."

"What has creativity allowed you to have, be, or do that's even more important?" I asked.

"Umm, creativity has allowed me to connect to other people I guess," Ryan said quietly. "I'm not sure how easy that has been to do in life, to be intimate, and acting is an arena I've been able to really do that. Like there's permission."

"Connecting. Intimacy," I said.

"Yes. I think it's really the connecting."

"Yes. And what has that *connecting* allowed you to be or have that's even *more* important to you?" I pressed. Ryan smiled sideways at me. I smiled back and stayed silent.

After a few moments, Ryan emerged and said, "To be inspired. It's *inspiration.*"

"Ah."

"Yeah." His whole being was glowing.

"I am noticing your shift. How is it to be in that *inspiration?*"

"Oh, it's everything. It's just the most incredible . . . I feel strong and powerful and I feel like I have so much energy to go out there and make things happen and at the same time like I can just sit here and just know it's all happening. Does that make sense?"

"Absolutely." I watched for a while and then offered, "Ryan, this may be what you're here to remember, this feeling, this inspiration again. How does that sound?"

"Yes, that sounds right."

"This feeling is the truth of who you are. You didn't make it up, you didn't steal it from anyone else, it came from within you and this is who you really are. All the other 'stuff' that you had been feeling was coming from your mind and how you were framing things. *This* is why you're here doing what you're doing, and now you get to remember it, align with it again, and anchor it back into your consciousness and your experience of living in your body. If that's something you would like to do."

"Oh, heck yeah I would!"

"Okay," I laughed.

Ryan chose a body posture and a word that summed up the feelings he had of *inspiration.* He used them to anchor that feeling back into his body, and that value became something he could align with again. When I asked him how he felt about auditioning now that he had reconnected with his passion, he felt very differently, far more inspired to go out there and enjoy the process rather than try to book the roles. Very quickly Ryan began attracting different things into his life because of how he felt about it and what he was focusing on. He had tapped into his own sense of meaning and he got his juice back. Within a couple of months he booked a television series. He was very pleased with the turn of events because to him his life was flowing. He felt he was plugged into something important, most specifically because the project was creatively fulfilling, the people on his new show were respectful and kind, and he felt he could really connect with them. He told me later that driving home from the first day of shooting he found himself saying out loud, "I'm living my dream!" A month prior Ryan may not have thought that being on a television series was his idea of the "dream" per se, yet *creativity* and *connection* had been two very important values for him, and they were being deeply fulfilled by his new situation. That was creating a new level of happiness for him. The show would eventually have to end at some point, *and* staying conscious of his core values would keep that happiness level up and keep the cycle of good in his life flowing no matter what the outside circumstances held for him.

Exploring what is so valuable for you about being an actor is fundamental for you, not only as an actor, but also as a human being. You will find that those values have meaning and importance in your life in general and that you will make far more fulfilling choices based on them than you will on what you think you "should" do. This is not about intellectually understanding the reason you want to be an actor. Asking the right questions gets you in touch with the *experiences* that your system seeks in making the goals you make. When you experience your values as you move toward the core, you get your system aligned with the higher purpose behind it all. You then trigger a creative movement in your life. In order to manifest anything, you need to feel it in your physical, emotional, and intuitive bodies.

When you return to your original purpose for being an actor you align your beliefs, values, interests, desires, actions, and the sense of who you are. You get your whole being involved. Those great feelings, along with effective action, are what will create the outcomes you want. Values will take you beyond your human purpose (like being on a show or acting in movies) into your higher purpose (which, ultimately, for all of us, is to become fully conscious). With values, you understand more what your mission in life is. Your mission is the infusion of your human purpose with your higher purpose. To attempt to fulfill your human purpose without attempting to fulfill your higher purpose, no matter how hard you work on it, is not going to bring happiness.

Finding your mission aligns you with your life. When you then make goals based on your mission, your actions get into alignment as well. Mission-based goals are exciting, inspired, and fun, and they are a profound source of happiness. It's where you really get to live out your passion.

One of the most wonderful things about connecting with what your values are is that you no longer have to battle within yourself over whether it's legitimate that something feels right or not. It's just clear and personal, and you can honor yourself by honoring your values. That's the stuff that the essential self is made of.

Align with Your Dream

Dreams are the beginning of creation. You have no doubt had some sort of dream for yourself as an actor and have moved toward it as best you can, making choices that you believed would take you closer to making it come true. Some of what has probably prevented your dream from already happening is that the appropriate steps haven't yet been taken. Some of it is because the opportunities haven't yet become available. Some of it is because you haven't been aligned with your dream. As we have established, when you're out of alignment with something, you're in conflict with it.

If you want to be peaceful, happy, and successful, and yet have found yourself sabotaging it, it's likely there are parts of you that hope to protect you from harm. Being out there in the world with its challenges can seem threatening at times and you may have developed parts designed *specifically* to stop you from moving forward because of that, even if it means forfeiting your success. Many actors are both driven toward *and* afraid of their own success because of what comes with being in the spotlight. Not being successful is a way to avoid things like being judged or scrutinized, living with higher stakes, having to be perfect, being responsible for others, being tied to contracts, and many other possible outcomes of being a successful actor. The human system is always trying to protect you from whatever might be a threat. The tricky piece to this is that those "protecting" parts are usually in the subconscious, so you may not be entirely aware of them. Even if you are, what do you *do* about them?

One thing to consider is that, rather than trying to get *rid* of a part of you, it's important to honor every aspect of your being. This doesn't mean you just live with things the way they have been, but rather you bring those parts to your conscious awareness and then communicate with them, understand what they are *trying to do for you*, and then give them more resourceful ways to take care of you.

Let me give you a specific example and one that comes up over and over again with the performers I work with. Artists have free spirits, some more than others, and they often feel that having structure to life is like being put in a cage. Structure can be anything from having to work a specific number of hours to having plans and setting them out on a calendar. For some artists the thought of actually getting a job can be quite frightening, even one as a series regular on a network television show, because that would entail "losing" their freedom. It would require their commitment, energy, time, and being tied to someone else's agenda. The resistance to achieving a dream of success is often because of this fear of losing that freedom, and it's usually subconscious. The free spirit wants so much to be free to create and express and to be loved doing it, yet it is so confused as to why it has not been happening. All the while an underlying, subconscious protector has been saving that free spirit from being trapped and smothered by structure, agendas, contracts, appointments, responsibilities, business meetings, and call times. The inner conflict is extraordinary and the artist is not even aware of it being there, just that things feel stuck and frustrating.

The key, when this becomes known in consciousness, is not to try to get rid of that natural need for freedom, but rather to look at the dream and to make sure that freedom is somehow built into the goals that come out of it. That might mean changing the goal to one where the hours are more flexible, or making sure there are breaks planned in, or that there are clear boundaries around time away or contract lengths.

Later in this book you will discover ways to create powerful goals—goals that align with your values, your vision, and your needs. When you create your path, you will want to create that path's edges. Those edges are the boundaries you set around what you want and what you don't want to be included in the journey. They are the parameters by which you live your values. Those boundaries are what will ultimately create the freedom that the artist in you so desires.

Trust the Process

In the early '90s I met the actor David Duchovny when I guest starred on his television show *The X-Files*. We had some interesting conversations during the shoot, as well as for a few months beyond that on the phone. We shared a bit about ourselves and our backgrounds as well as our philosophies and beliefs about life. One of the thoughts David shared with me was about the craft of acting itself. He told me that his acting coach had encouraged him to *do nothing* except hit his marks and say his lines, which at the time wasn't such a well-considered acting technique as it is today. David stood out among many of the other actors on television at the time because of taking this advice. Acting was far more *pushed* then than it is these days, emotions more expressed, intentions more indicated, thoughts more transparent, and the story more *told*. Actors were doing a whole lot more *acting*. Today television is high-definition, big-screen, close-up—every detail, every twitch of the mouth and flash of the eye magnified—and partly because of this acting has become far more subtle craft than it was. In fact, you could say that today's actors do a lot less acting than some reality television stars do!

So, I consider David Duchovny to be a pioneer of sorts. He proved to us that an intelligent, funny, curious, complex human being would show up on screen without having to telegraph any of it. Of course, you know there is no such thing as *doing nothing*. We humans are always doing *something* even when we intend to practice just *being*. Yet within that realm we can at least have the intention of relaxing and trusting a little bit more than we may have previously done. As an actor the direction to do nothing might be interpreted as the intention to relax and trust the material, the dialogue, and the story, and perhaps even the production team, the director, the editors, and the studio. It may be to trust that there is a larger force at work with a collective direction that you can simply be a part of. More than anything *doing nothing* might mean relaxing and trusting that you are enough, and that you're infused with enough natural humanity and spirit to fill those lines without having to work so hard. To take it even further, perhaps this is what you can apply to your life in the business as a whole.

You may have noticed (in the most inconvenient of times) parts of you that get triggered by the industry and its dynamics. The industry presents you with *stuff*. Emotional, physical, and mental stuff. I call it *stuff* because, after all, though we give it all kinds of clever names, that's what it is, right? That *stuff* is your challenge, not just in the industry but also within all other areas of your life, and it shows you what needs to be dealt with inside you. It highlights things that are unhealed, unfinished, or limiting. For example, if you have boundary issues in your own system, you will find that the experiences you have in the industry will let you know that. If you have control issues, self-worth issues, grief, or stuckness, the industry will let you know that by showing up in a way that highlights them. These trigger moments can be painful and are often a blow to the ego or to self-esteem, yet they can also be a profound gift.

We become aware of things only when we are ready to heal them, complete them, or let them go. The choices you have, then, are to go off and work on this unfinished business or to put it away for another day hoping it will disappear. You could sit silently with it, lean into it, analyze it, write about it, or ignore it. The options are endless. Before all that, though, think about what you have had a tendency to do in the past. Have you spent your life working diligently to heal endless stuff? Have you become really good at avoiding it all and ignoring your own unhealed items, maybe focusing on the healing work of others? Or have you focused on how hard it has been and felt a need to talk about that a lot with your friends and family? There are so many variations on how each of us deals with our growth areas, negative experiences, or beliefs. I'll give you three examples of extremes, using myself as one of them.

I spent most of my early adult life looking to find answers, wanting to heal myself from a very traumatic past and wanting to be the best person I could be by understanding myself, the world, and the human spirit. The film industry dynamics touched on many of the unhealed parts of me and let me know where I still had room to grow. I went through approximately five hundred hours of psychotherapy in a fifteen-year period starting in my mid-twenties. I was blessed to have had a wonderful therapist and teacher who actually helped me out. I am aware that this is not always the case. Just as in any other profession there are skilled therapists, as well as some who can do more harm than good. However, toward the end of that fifteen-year period I found (despite all the growth achieved) that I was still somewhat in the mode of "got to blast through that one" when something incomplete presented itself. Now, I have to give myself some credit for having the kind of courage and willingness that is needed to work through things that are painful or limiting. Still, there does need to be balance. The pattern of wanting to blast through a dysfunction or limit had become unloving to myself. It had turned into a default "enforced healing" pattern. Thankfully, I learned over time to relax and be still with where I found myself, and I eventually found a more compassionate balance.

At the other end of the spectrum is one of those people who has many friends coming to her for help and comfort. For decades she has been a tremendous support to those in crisis. She is not a helping professional, yet she advises other people to go to therapy and gives them many great resources for their troubles. There is great value in loving and caring for others, and again, there has to be balance. This person will rarely talk about herself when it comes to the past or her own emotions. She has done almost no personal growth work of her own. She shuns therapy, coaching, or any formal support, and in times of conflict with others usually refuses to take responsibility for her own part. She does not seem to want to explore her own growth areas and has taken the avoidance and deflection route, putting on a face that everything is rosy. Eventually this sort of façade wears down and starts to crack, and the darkness underneath seeps out in compulsive and sometimes destructive ways. It takes a tremendous amount of energy to shove down negative feelings about ourselves and others, and this person is (not surprisingly) sick much of the time. She has had illness after illness. After all, living like that is exhausting and can't be kept up for long without the body, mind, and emotional selves expressing *dis*-ease.

Our third example is an actor who feels very badly treated by the entertainment industry. He believes he is being constantly passed up and rejected by casting directors, and when he goes to auditions he sees the other actors in the waiting room as either his competition or "losers" who should not even be there. He feels angry about it and very sorry for his lot, spending many an afternoon with one or more of his actor friends in his local coffee shop bonding over how hard the business is. This group enjoys pulling apart, line by line, the job that so-and-so did on that whatsit show the night before. They agree passionately that they could have done the job far better and that they should have been cast instead.

People like this unhappy actor deal with negative feelings, experiences, or beliefs by blaming circumstances and other people, and then continue to live right in the middle of the problems they have. They then create a persona for themselves that fits that picture. They talk about their misfortunes a lot, identifying with the negative experiences or beliefs as though it's part of who they are and how the world is. They might even begin to give themselves the title to match as they introduce themselves: *Hi, I am an abuse victim,* or *Hi, I am an out-of-work actor,* or *Hello, I am a single parent whose husband left me.* These people take on that idea as though it's something they *are,* rather than it being something factual that has happened or even (often more accurately) something that has been *interpreted.* They tend to filter everything through the belief that because of who they believe they are, they will, yet again, be the victims of their lives or of other people. It perpetuates itself and grows. What we focus on gets bigger and becomes our experience over and over. People do experience some very real, factual tragedies and a key to healing them is to remember that we are responsible for our *responses* to them. We can learn to detach from the old interpretation of what facts might mean.

Of course there are many other variations on how each of us deals with our pain or growth areas, and when it comes to dealing with a business like the one you're in, with its diverse dynamics, none of the three examples above are ultimately useful to such an extreme. So, what is?

There is other ground that might be more solid to stand on. The invitation here is to put aside judgment and notice what *your* unique pattern has been when it comes to processing stuff. Have your patterns been useful? Are they now? How balanced have your choices been? Have they been in alignment with your values and beliefs? Can you decide to take forcing out of the equation for yourself? Again, as a society we have become very good at *doing*. We make things happen. It's tremendously important to have a vision for the future and take action on it. Doing is part of the equation of progress. When it comes to personal development and creating happiness in life, a lot can be accomplished by courageously pushing through our fears or resistances, *and* in stepping back, how much is relying on that one choice going to be of benefit? To what degree do we keep pushing ourselves before it becomes abuse? Forcing something, either to heal or to go away, may not ultimately serve.

Many years ago when I first started to meditate I would get upset with myself if I didn't get it in every day. Understandably, I began to get quite tense about the new regime I had committed to. This meant that my stress levels became worse than if I hadn't decided to meditate at all! Thankfully I saw the irony over time and asked, *How can I force myself to relax and then be the relaxed person I am hoping to be?* Human beings respond in the very best way to love, and forcing anything down, out, in, up, or any which way is usually not love. It's fear.

We are all here to become enlightened, to become more conscious, and to gain knowledge. When we become enlightened about anything we have simply become aware of it, and that's often enough. It's the gift itself. When we put our awareness onto something that has previously been in the darkness, it's then bathed in the light of our consciousness. Our physical, mental, and emotional systems are naturally moving toward health and very often all we need do is pay attention and be present. There are many healing techniques that work on this principle. Just *noticing* can be the catalyst that allows for our health and wholeness to become manifested. Simple awareness is the greatest agent for change.

As you invite yourself to trust the universe around you without the need to try so hard to control it or to make things happen the way you think they "should" happen—without having to indicate, impress, try, force, fix, suppress, deny, or deflect—perhaps you can begin to trust that there is something greater at work. Something you can simply and knowingly be a part of and align with. And perhaps as an actor you can trust yourself to be a conduit for something creative and good in the world without having to push it in any way, knowing that you're perfectly cast for the role of "you" and divinely infused with all that's needed to fill it.

Be Here Now

One of the primary ways to become more trusting of the process of life is to practice being present with it. Having established that raising your baseline happiness levels requires taking part in certain intentional activities, we know that meditation is a major activity on that list.

Navigating the world of being an actor means you're living in a world of variety. You face a lot of unknowns. Will you be working next week? What will your hours be? What town will you be in? Who will you be meeting or spending your time with? Will your life change dramatically today? This kind of life requires being pretty grounded and having ways to stay in your own presence and power.

There are several life practices widely regarded as central and essential for effective transpersonal development: having an ethical lifestyle, redirecting motivation, transforming emotions, training attention, refining awareness, fostering wisdom, and practicing service to others. It's known in many cultures that meditation is a vehicle for many of these practices. If we look solely at the practice of training attention, we know that a focus on being in the present moment is a very powerful way to move toward being happy and fulfilled. Human beings tend to spend a lot of time thinking about the past or the future, and it's very often not resourceful thinking at that. In fact, the tendency is to think neurotically, the mind chattering wildly, jumping from thought to thought like a monkey jumping from tree to tree. This kind of thinking is sometimes called *monkey mind*. In monkey mind we are usually busy in thought either regretting the past or worrying about the future. This is not a resourceful way to be. In reality, the past is gone and the future has yet to materialize. Yes, we need to learn from the past and plan for the future and we can only do that effectively if we are *present* to begin with. The present moment is where we can connect to the process of being alive with a peaceful trust. Being present very often relaxes us and put things into a perspective that suddenly makes things far more manageable, perhaps easy, often funny, and sometimes even blissful. If you think about the times, as an actor, you've been most connected and "in the zone," you've probably also been the most present. Time slows down and things become clearer and more connected. You get to really experience a truth about the moment you're in, and that affects you and others in profound ways. This can happen at times by accident, but if you're someone who practices training your mind to be present, you're far more likely to reach those places in your craft.

Multi-award-winning actress Christine Lahti has traveled the acting road for most of her life and has managed, through all the ups and downs of her tremendous, sustained success, to find a balance. One of the many ways she has done that has been through a consciousness of her own ability to be present. "All those mosquitos that buzz around," she shared, "you just want to quiet them. All the worry and the *I'll never work again*, and *What's wrong with me?* and all that . . . it's just to quiet that, live in the moment, which is the most cliché thing, but in your work you have to be able to live in the moment. In your life I think that would be a great goal. That's one of my goals as well."

Meditation, or any type of focused, peaceful concentration is what allows us to access the universal superconscious mind, Unified Field, or God. It is a multifaceted superhighway to peace, growth, creativity, clarity, wisdom, groundedness, and, of course, happiness. Teaching your mind to be more present through daily practice (focusing the mind on one thing regularly, as though training a muscle) is known to increase the happy factor in dramatic ways.

Meditation has been practiced in many forms in numerous cultures over many centuries. We have at least three thousand years of known history of meditation practice as a species, and goodness knows how many years unknown prior to that. Meditation is a central discipline at the contemplative core of each of the world's great religions.

Since the 1960s, meditation has been the focus of increasing scientific research. Several hundred studies have shown meditation to have significant positive effects on the physical, psychological, and emotional well-being of humans, and the practice of meditation is increasing, at least in the Western world. In the United States a 2007 study by the US government found that nearly 9.4 percent of US adults (over twenty million) had practiced meditation within the previous twelve months, up from 7.6 percent (more than fifteen million people) in 2002, and so it continues to rise.

Matthieu Ricard, a French academic turned Buddhist monk and an interpreter for His Holiness the Dalai Lama is considered by scientists to be the world's happiest man. The "happiness" levels shown in his brain through MRI research were off the scale. M. Ricard also took part in trials that show that brain training in the form of meditation can cause an overwhelming change in levels of happiness, proving again that happiness is something we can create in our lives and that it's a "skill" to be learned. In these trials MRI scans showed that he and other long-term meditators (who had completed more than ten thousand hours each) experienced a huge level of "positive emotions" in the left prefrontal cortex of the brain, which is associated with happiness. The right-hand side, which handles negative thoughts, was suppressed. Further studies have shown that even novices, by taking part in only a little meditation, have significantly increased levels of happiness, and that it can actually affect the structure of the brain.

In January 2011 a team led by Massachusetts General Hospital researchers reported the results of a study, the first to document meditation-produced changes over time in the brain's actual grey matter. They tracked sixteen people over eight weeks participating in the Mindfulness-Based Stress Reduction (MBSR) program. New-to-meditation participants practiced exercises meant to build the skills of *mindfulness*, which is a moment-by-moment awareness of one's thoughts, feelings, bodily sensations, and surrounding environment. For many years those who had completed the MBSR training had reported feeling less stress, more positive emotions, and a sense of well-being both emotionally and physically. In this particular study, however, researchers went further and scanned participants' brains both before and after the program and found that their grey matter had become significantly thicker in several regions.

One of these regions was the hippocampus, which is involved in learning, memory, and the regulation of emotions. The grey matter of the hippocampus is often reduced in people with depression and post-traumatic stress disorder, so a thickening of this area would seem to be good news. The researchers also found denser gray matter in the temporo-perietal junction and the posterior cingulated cortex of the participants' brains (regions involved in empathy and taking the perspective of someone else) and in the cerebellum (which has been linked to emotion regulation). All this suggests that meditation can physically improve our brain's ability to regulate our emotions, control our stress levels, and feel empathy for others. I have personally found that the times in my life when I've increased my meditation practice are also when I've had the most breakthroughs and been the most on track. I have also felt the most powerful, compassionate, connected, and healthy, had the most successful relationships, and of course, been the happiest.

Years ago, a friend of mine, a lovely and inspiring yogi, told me a story about himself, his wife, and their young daughter (who must have been three or four at the time). The yogi and his wife had decided to practice being more present and to set a chime to go off every half hour to remind them to stop what they were doing and just notice the "now" moment. It was a wonderful exercise for the three of them until *adaptation* set in. The two adults slowly became so used to this new routine that eventually their minds began to ignore the chime and they carried on with their day, passing over the moments they had planned to notice. The interesting thing was that their little daughter *didn't* adapt to the chimes. Her consciousness was in a different place and her mind still heard them, so she would tap her parents on the shoulder and say "now" when they went off. Sometimes it takes a child to remind us to be awake!

Simply stopping occasionally throughout the day, surrendering to the moment, and relaxing your body with a deep breath—just like my yogi friend, his wife, and their little girl did—can be a very powerful addition to your lifestyle. You can breathe out as far as you can go, and then breathe deeply into the lower belly. Doing this three times or more any time you can remember will affect your health, your mental and emotional clarity and serenity, and your immune system profoundly. The answers are always in the quiet spaces. As an actor, you have the power to let those emerge in the most unlikely of times.

This kind of consciousness requires that you allow stillness into your life. It's not always an easy thing to be still! In fact many of us spend our lives doing all we can to avoid it. We surround ourselves with things to do, people to chatter with, drugs or food to numb out feelings, drama to contend with. We are then human *doings,* not human *beings.* If we stop and get still we meet the void, and that void can feel terrifying. Yet in free-falling through space we open ourselves to the most powerful parts of living.

I sometimes incorporate an exercise into my teachings or workshops where the group is asked to stand in two lines facing each other and, just breathing, look into each other's eyes without trying to *do* anything or trying to *affect* the other person in any way; just being with that person and with themselves, being still and silent. It's often very challenging for participants simply because we are not used to being still, for a start! On top of that, to be still with another person, looking directly at them without trying to make something happen is almost never how we engage each other. Yet the power in it can be profound. It can open us to otherwise unknown parts of ourselves. It can show us how afraid we are to be seen, and yet how much we desperately want to be. It can show us how we really don't take the time to see others as they *are* but instead we see them through the lens of our own stuff. It can be painful, beautiful, it can shut us down, and it can reach in and pull us out of ourselves simultaneously. It teaches us that when we really let ourselves become present with whatever and whoever is there and we allow intimacy (into-me-you-see) we begin to learn a very different way of being with others and with ourselves.

The discovery can be to know that within the void everything lives. Yet, if we continue to rush around as though possessed, we drown out the sound of our deeper selves and of the wisdom inside. We forget to respond and move toward what allows our happiness because all we can hear are "should's" and "ought to's" and the chatter of our monkey mind. Every one of us, whether we have kids or huge jobs or are dealing with illness of some kind, can afford ourselves a few moments each day to stop and breathe and just *be.*

So, how do you meditate? If you're not already familiar with a meditation practice, there are some simple beginnings. There is no "right" way to meditate. It's an exploration. The most common type of meditation is to sit in peaceful repose and cultivate a state of being, like compassion or peace, or to focus on the breath, a point in the room, or a chant or prayer. For some, activities like yoga, surfing, skiing, writing, or flying airplanes bring the mind to an acutely focused and quiet place. When you practice meditation in whatever form, you train your mind to become more present with now, connecting with both the minute details and the larger perspective, becoming conscious of what is internal as well as external. As you learn to surrender to the moment you also learn to empower yourself by detaching from outcomes.

Here is my suggestion to you as you navigate whatever your life is like, both as an actor as well as in all other aspects. Take some time each morning before you start your day to simply sit with yourself, having the intention to connect in a loving way. If you don't already meditate daily, just one minute to start with in the mornings will make a big difference. Open-eyed meditation can be a great way to practice being wholly open to being in the world and conscious of the inner realms simultaneously. You may want to check in with your body. Notice how it feels and what it's telling you. Become aware of your emotional body and breathe quietly without having to do anything, just being wherever you are. Notice your thoughts and let them pass through you like clouds, without judgment or the need to do anything with them. Just remain in observation, allowing a friendship with the present moment, and then return to your breath.

As well as a formal practice at certain times of the day, you can adopt a habit of reminding yourself throughout the day to be present, bringing awareness to the now, surrendering to the moment, making sure that you're kind with yourself when you notice you're off wandering around in the past or the future. Even something as simple as putting your hand on your heart and taking a moment to breathe deeply, saying *hi* with an inward smile, can be quite powerful.

Taking the time to be still, quiet, and present, with an intention to be peaceful, will lay down a powerful foundation for your happiness. Meditation is your greatest spiritual teacher. With meditation as a life practice, you become more confident and empowered, and happiness emerges as an essential and eternal source.

Power and Belonging

I went through much of my early career as an actor feeling scared, lost, and intimidated. Back in the '90s actors didn't have the Internet to inform us (for goodness sakes, most of us didn't have cell phones yet) and many of us felt like outsiders. It was a bit like groping around in the dark, relying solely on word of mouth, industry papers, and the occasional tidbit we might get from our managers. There were very few seminars available about the business side of the business and even less concerning an actor's personal power. It was all about the craft of acting. Thankfully there are many more resources for actors now and many more ways to feel like a part of the business. Yet, of all the people in the world, actors need to know how to retain their own power and to feel that they belong. Far too many actors give their power away to casting directors, agents, managers, producers, studio executives, acting coaches, to roles and jobs, to the idea of "success," and by relying on others' opinions or on external feedback for a sense of self or value. Because of the way the film and television industry is structured it feels to many actors as though there is an "inside" and an "outside" to the business. The "inside" is where all those "successful" people get to play and make movies and shows, and the "outside" is where you sit waiting for the phone to ring hoping that you will be let in some day. There are even actors who work regularly and are considered successful who feel this way. And there are some people in the industry who seem to enjoy perpetuating that myth, yet it's just that: a myth. There are no actual moats, electric fences, or armed guards (except, of course, at the studios) and certainly those things are not there *literally* keeping you out of being part of something that's creative and rewarding in the industry. In truth, if you believe that you're on the outside you will be, and if you give your power away to someone they will have it.

First of all, only *you* can bring your power back to where it belongs: with you. Also it's important that you know *no one has ever been able to take your power from you.* Think about that. Have you ever been able to go up to someone, take his or her power away, and walk home with it? No, and nobody can do that to you either. You can certainly *give* your power away if you choose to, but no one has the power to take it!

Second of all, for you to feel that you belong in the industry you've chosen, you have to find out what it is that you connect with and make it intrinsically part of your life. It's up to you to live the life you want to be a part of, however you can do that. If that means you buy a used camera and make movies of your own or you turn up at certain events that put you in the world you want to belong to, you have the power to do that. There is that word again. *Power.*

The nature of the industry requires that you step into the truth of who you are and claim your space in the world. This means knowing what your own personal power is and developing it. Your personal power is an intrinsic part of who you are, and it's essential to restore, nourish, and fortify it so that you can thrive happily in the business of being an actor.

How do you do that? The opportunity you have as a human being, let alone as an actor, is to find the part of yourself that's on a *higher plane*. This higher plane is the part of you that trusts your unique worth and the things that are deeply important to you. It "gets" what you're here to create through those things. Whatever your beliefs are about the universe, when you explore and really know your core values and what you want from your life on the planet, you can live through the powerful knowing of that.

In order to develop your personal power you have to commit to it. You make conscious intentions about what to focus on, how you behave, what beliefs you hold, and what you include in your life. You commit to being centered in the truth of who you honestly are, even when you're afraid of judgment from others. You remember that you always have choice in *every* situation. There is a commitment required to remembering that truth. It means letting go of seeing yourself as a victim of others and of circumstances. Yes, there are certainly people who purposefully harm us and there are situations that can be devastating. The question is whether it serves you to see yourself as a victim or as a person who somehow, through it all, makes a positive difference.

Another way you restore your personal power is by trusting your own journey. You're in one of the most highly competitive businesses in the world. There is a challenge to being an actor beyond getting the roles you want and that's remembering you're not in a race with anyone else. You're simply here to be creative, to make a positive difference somehow, to serve others, to grow, and to be the most resourceful you can be.

Feeling you belong in the business requires looking at whether you've been blocking yourself through lack of self-worth; it requires knowing if you've had a strong vision for yourself of belonging or if you've chosen to look at it from the outside. It also takes looking honestly at whether you're simply not meant to be in the business because you have another path somewhere else. One thing to consider is that when something brings out the best in you, chances are you're where you're meant to be. If it doesn't, it may be time to move on.

Real personal power comes out of love, self-esteem, trust, and confidence in oneself and the process of life. When you trust yourself and know your unique worth you can relax and be open. When you're in your power, you don't attempt to have power over others, you move toward the possibility of power *with* others. You serve others. You encourage other people's inner strengths and self-knowledge and you inspire them to live out the truth of their uniqueness. This has to come out of the knowing that your journey is between you and something larger.

The Source

Scientists believe there is a direct link between happiness and a belief in something greater than the self. This *something greater* is what some call "the Source". The Source can be thought of as a manifestation of divine care that creates and sustains everything. It directs the universe with wise benevolence and is considered to be *omniscient*, which means having complete or unlimited knowledge, awareness, or understanding, perceiving all things. It is also considered to be *omnipresent*, present everywhere at the same time. As mentioned, scientists call this the *Unified Field*, and religion or spirituality calls it *God, Allah, Spirit, Nirvana*, and *Great Soul*, as well as many other names. In essence it is *consciousness*.

Everything comes from and returns to this Source. The Source is not only out there in the world. It's also within you. After all, it created you and you are part of it. When you "tap into" the Source you become aware of this. You become conscious. Your connection to the Source then means you understand the vast abundance in this universe and know that the only real power existing is the eternal power of good. When you remember this you're liberated to exist in a place where everything you deeply desire is possible.

Each one of us has various ways to tap into the Source. We have ways to align with the Source and ways to express and be a conduit of that Source.

In numerous studies, both religiosity and spirituality have been linked to increased happiness. *Religiosity* is defined as a relationship with a particular faith tradition or doctrine about a divine other or supernatural power. *Spirituality* has been defined by three researchers— Peter L. Benson, Eugene C. Roehlkepartain, and S.P. Rude—as "the intrinsic human capacity for self-transcendence, in which the self is embedded in something greater than the self, including the sacred" and this motivates "the search for connectedness, meaning, purpose, and contribution." Religion can be a way to tap into the Source. Spirituality is, intrinsically and in its highest form, a channel to the Source. One doesn't have to be religious to be deeply spiritual.

Scientists believe there are several possible reasons for the link between happiness and the Source. There is a social component to spirituality and religion. Churches, synagogues, mosques, temples, and other spiritual meeting places create opportunities for like-minded people to socialize, take part in community service, and make friends. As we know, social engagement is currently recognized as being very strongly linked to happiness. However, religious service attendance had the least effect on our happiness levels compared to the beliefs themselves, as well as our personal devotional measures. It turns out in a 2003 review of thirty-four studies with mainly adult populations that the strongest links to happiness in regard to spirituality were personal devotion measures, spiritual practices (like some of the things we have already been exploring), prayer, and meditation. Both spirituality and organized religion connects us with the Source and can provide us with perspective, hope, and a deeper sense of meaning. When we get beyond the dogma, judgment, and separation that some practices can contain, we tap into why they are so important to our deepest selves.

As an actor navigating all the fears and doubts that float around in our business, you will find that connecting to a higher purpose (one that transcends the life purpose of an acting career) will give you tremendous perspective and detachment from outcomes. That is only going to be empowering and uplifting. The higher purpose for all of us is to become more conscious and to align with higher consciousness (to tap into the Source) however that is experienced by you and whether you are religious, spiritual, or nonspiritual. There is no right or wrong way to the Source. Whether it is through religion or a deep belief in the goodness that lives in the universe, or anything else, you will have your own unique and personal relationship to the Source and your own beliefs and experience of what that Source is for you.

So, how do you, personally, tap into the Source? How are you conscious of being connected to the whole? Is it through prayer, meditation, writing, or caring for others? There is a part of you that knows the infinite wisdom of that. Aligning with the Source in your life, however you do it, will bring forward the answers and the happiness you seek. It is a journey that encompasses the whole being as a sacred spiritual entity experiencing this human journey, and that brings more than happiness. It brings bliss.

Life offers us many teachers and there is a lesson in every encounter. All we experience is a mirror reflecting back what is within ourselves, and every meeting is a glimpse at a part of ourselves that has become available to be noticed. Our responsibility is to open to that. Our journey is to become aware of the parts of ourselves that are love and the parts that are fear, and to invite the heart to expand. We enter this world with the ability to shed light on darkness and to love where there is fear. Let us remember together, dear one, the place this needs to be expressed first is within ourselves.

CHAPTER 4

There Is One of Us

This is my simple religion. There is no need for temples; no need for complicated philosophy. Our own brain, our own heart is our temple; the philosophy is kindness.

~ HIS HOLINESS THE DALAI LAMA

The Business of Relationships

Originally tribal beings, humans have grouped together and become like one for the purpose of survival since the beginning. We can catch dinner in the wild more easily, for example, when we are all in sync. What is known as *group mind* can be felt in any situation containing two or more people if we just "tap in." Just think of times when you've been acting in a play or scene and suddenly, as a group, you find you all move in a certain direction or the energy goes somewhere, not through the individuals but through the collective. The improv exercise "word-at-a-time story" is a fine way to experience the power of group mind. Standing in a line facing out, one by one the players tell a story by going along the line, each contributing just one word. The object is to create a coherent story with consistent characters, point of view, and plot. The players concentrate on reacting specifically to the word said right before them, so preplanning is useless because the other players don't know what's coming right before their turn. It's all in the moment and the game will only work if the actors are willing to be team players and agree to the objective of the game, which is to *create* something together. What's usually found is that, because the individual actors are unable to preplan or think for any length of time about what word they are going to say next, the group mind takes over and a story begins to emerge all by itself. It's a fun and quite extraordinary exercise!

You're in a business of relationships and whether you're an actor or not, other people are essential to your happiness, health, and ability to function and grow. As human beings, our loving connections (from breast-feeding to kissing and making love) secrete the hormone oxytocin, the chemical that brings us feelings of calm and comfort. Oxytocin plays a large role in the formation of our brains. If we are held and loved as children our brains form well, and if we are not they don't. Love affects our very ability to function mentally, emotionally, and even physically, because our entire biology is affected by our social interactions, not just as children but also throughout our adult lives.

A psychologist named Harry Frederick Harlow did some painful, but significant, research on baby rhesus monkeys in the 1950s. In the trials the baby monkeys were taken away from their mothers at a very early stage and placed in separate isolation chambers. Two mother substitutes were placed in an adjoining cage, both shaped roughly like adult monkeys. One of these substitutes was made of metal wire and had a milk bottle coming through it so that the baby could feed. The other had no food, but rather a soft warm covering over it that the baby could hold onto and cuddle. Time and time again these baby monkeys went straight for the soft warm cuddly "mother" and showed no interest in the wire mother with the food. These were cut and dry results. The babies would rather starve just so they could cling onto a warm, soft surface! Unfortunately these babies were also shown to suffer for the rest of their lives with emotional and psychological damage. They became severely disturbed and the footage of them is just heartbreaking. Being deprived of real love destroyed these little creatures' lives.

Looking back on this sad experiment, psychologists believe that the same thing is true for us. Since the 1930s there have been many cases of human babies adopted from eastern European orphanages. Because of over-crowding in many institutions, and the lack of time nurses had with the babies, they were not held, talked to, or looked at except for the few times a day when they had their diapers changed and when they were fed. The rest of the time they were left alone in their cribs. Many of these children died. Of those who lived, many spent the rest of their lives institutionalized. These children were shown across the board (whether they were adopted or not) to have significant emotional issues, communication problems, lack of empathy, and an inability to bond with others. Again, this sad and terrible situation only serves to show us what we fundamentally need to be healthy, whole, and sane: the love of others.

Further research has shown that some of the poorest people in the world, those who live in Calcutta, India—their homes tiny patches of mud under tattered sheets with little to eat and just the clothes on their backs—are generally happier than those living in California, America. This is due, in great part, to the fact that there is a stronger sense of community in Calcutta than there is in California. We simply need each other!

As we take this further, it's evident that the *quality* of our relationships is what's paramount to our ability to be happy. Successful, loving relationships are a huge source of happiness for human beings, and relationships that don't contain those elements can be a source of profound misery. Just as a plant in the soil will blossom and grow if it has light, fertilizer, and water, so will we, if we are given the nutrients of respect, connection, and the caring attention of those around us.

Successful Relationships

To have healthy, successful relationships with others, specific elements have to be present. Mutual respect, emotional transparency, conscious communication, sharing, honesty, trust, encouragement, compassion, loyalty, validation, acceptance, need fulfillment, support, and taking responsibility for one's own part in a dynamic are all essential. Good communication has also been found to be one of the most important parts of a successful relationship, and empathy is required for that communication to be effective. Empathy is not only essential in our interactions, but it is also a sign of good emotional and psychological health. Many of the psychological disorders like narcissism and psychopathy have a similar element missing in their descriptive profiles, and that is the ability to share and understand another person's feelings. In other words, there is a lack of empathy. The cultivation of empathy is a keystone to our own happiness and health, as well as the happiness of those around us.

Scientists also believe that a big factor in sustaining successful relationships is the ability to be relaxed. Stress can destroy not only our health but also our most treasured relationships!

Because we can't ultimately change other people and their behavior, we have to focus on our own growth areas. This means to have better communication we have to become better communicators, and to have more relaxed and happy relationships we have to become more relaxed and happy. That makes sense, yet it's something so many of us forget. We often expect people to come into our lives and be everything we want them to be, yet we don't think to *first become what it is we want others to be*.

Life has its built-in challenges. You are faced with losses and disappointments as part of life, and only you can control your state of being. Your state (meaning the condition of your mind or feeling / how you *are*) has a huge influence on how you respond or react to the people and situations in your life. An actor's life is very unpredictable. One minute you're working at a fast food restaurant and the next you get a call that you booked a television pilot. This means that things can go from dull to exciting in a second, and if there is a lack of consciousness about your own state of being it can get in the way of your long-term happiness.

Cesar Milan, also known as the Dog Whisperer, teaches dog owners to relax, to avoid getting excited and instead live in a state of calm assertiveness, and to encourage their dogs to also remain calm. It is a useful practice for all of us. Excitement is meant to be experienced in short bursts and then be over. The body often doesn't know the difference between excitement and fear because they are extremely similar physiologically. In both cases adrenaline and norepinephrine are released, your blood pressure rises, your heart rate accelerates, you breathe faster, your mouth becomes dry, your pupils dilate, you sweat, and you may become queasy, flushed or pale, and shake or tremble as blood is pumped into your muscles. This is known as the "fight or flight" response and it happens even when you are simply excited about something.

If either excitement or fear become a habitual, long-term state of being the body can no longer function well and the brain's higher level thinking shuts down. To be in that state of emergency long-term can really get in the way of making good decisions and being clear about things, and life can start to become dramatic and chaotic. Certainly, when positive things happen, celebrate! Sing out, holler with joy, jump up and down, and feel the goodness of life run through your being, *and* know that it's meant to pass fairly quickly, unlike the long-term, sustainable happiness we are focusing on here in this book. When that wonderful something comes into your life, after the initial high, you will naturally return to your baseline state. This happens for all of us no matter how hard we might try to stay elated or excited. I watch actors, especially younger ones, wanting to feel that rush of high again and again, pumping themselves up into a frenzy as though that will give them the energy to keep going and stay inspired and motivated. The thing is, it's like a sugar rush. It may create a big high for a while, but it's not nourishing, it doesn't last, and there will be the inevitable crash. There is also the natural need for the system to create balance by going the other way at some point and collapsing, which can cause mood swings and depression on the other end of it. All kinds of behavioral problems can come out of self-induced, long-term excitement.

When it comes to your happiness, you will find it's far more sustainable when it's developed through a calm and present state of being, dog owner or not. In a relaxed and centered state, for example, you will be far more likely to *respond* to other people when you communicate, rather than *react*. Reacting is fear driven. Responding comes from love and trust. When you're relaxed and centered you can more easily detach yourself from whatever fear is in a situation, whether it's yours or someone else's. You will be less likely to try to analyze the situation, but rather use your higher self to assess and observe and therefore be more able to find solutions. You will be more likely to have empathy and compassion. Incorporating daily stress-reducing practices into your life is the key to that. As mentioned, meditation, yoga, and breathing techniques are well-known (not only in many of the spiritual communities but now also in scientific arenas) to be all-around beneficial activities, especially when it comes to happiness and well-being. At the very least they help develop a much more relaxed state which makes the success of relationships far more possible. You will also find that your ability to remain present when you're acting and auditioning, when you're in meetings and on stage, is increased. You become a master of your own state.

So, have those moments of excitement and elation, let them pass fully through your body and heart, and then relax again into a grounded, present state. Make that calm, solid, and centered way of being your default baseline state and you will ride the rollercoaster of life as an actor far more easily.

Yes, And

When I was an actor and was thrown headlong into working full-time on a television show back in the late '90s I had not spent any significant amount of time working in groups before. I had not played any kind of team sport in school, been part of any club, had a job (be it acting, modeling, or catering) that had lasted more than a week or two, nor been trained in any way to communicate in or work in any sort of group system. Truth be told, I was a bit socially inept, and to top it off, I had no idea that I was! My childhood had consisted of moving from school to school and home to home so often that I never felt I belonged anywhere and never had the time to become part of any group of peers. I was ignorant, not only about how to communicate effectively in a group, but also that I was going around offending people and hurting their feelings when I thought I was being perfectly nice and reasonable. It wasn't that I was a mean person; it was just that, with the tools missing from my belt, navigating through the ins and outs of daily group communication was really out of my skill set. There was no lack of desire to be kind and loving or to be connected to others (in fact those things were deep desires for me), I just didn't know how to fit those into a good communication structure, so it just kept coming out wrong. The television show I was on happened to be full of other people who didn't have particularly good communication skills, so we were quite the group! It was a tough situation for everyone and, needless to say, things broke down pretty quickly and the general happiness factor took a nosedive.

Learning effective communication skills is a really important part of being happy as you navigate your career as an actor. You never know what situation you will suddenly find yourself in and what sort of skills you might need. Stakes are high on productions and people are often stretched thin due to the long hours, time crunches, and massive amounts of work. Becoming good at listening, responding, validating, reading emotions, having compassion, and being clear in your own feelings and needs and then communicating them is just a part of that. Just as I did, you will find there are tools out there that can change everything. I made it a priority, once I realized they were missing from my skill set, to take on those communication tools and all my relationships dramatically improved. Being prepared for a sudden shift in your career, like landing a role on a show or a movie and finding yourself with a new production family, is going to require you've got some really strong relationship skills already in place.

One specific way to gain relationships skills is with language. Words have a profound effect on our own experiences and the experiences of others. We have the power to be either a healing force or a crushing blow as we speak. Just as the universe around us responds to and is affected by what we focus on in our language, so do other people. Using our words consciously is part of being a responsible, caring adult. When we criticize or berate others we are dumping our hatred and fear onto the scars that they already have. We reopen the wounds of the past by the use of our words. In fact, it has even been found that subtle facial expressions of contempt have a harmful effect, both physically and emotionally, on the person that's the object of that contempt. We can affect the health and well-being of others, negatively or positively, in more ways than most of us might know.

There is a wonderful rule in improvisation called "yes, and." For a story to be built in an improv sketch, whether in short or long form, the players have to agree to the basic situation and setup. The *who*, *what*, and *where* have to be developed and agreed on for a scene to work. For example if one player says, *Hi, my name is John, welcome to my bar*, and the other player says, *This isn't a bar, it's an airplane, and you're not John, you're a crocodile*, then the scene has nowhere to go. The second player has basically blocked or denied the first player's offer. It's an absolute no-no in improv. Even "yes, *but*" is a scene stopper and will feel like an argument. Actors who find "yes, but" easier than "yes, and" do so because they don't have to listen to their partner or use their creativity and are stuck in an argumentative mentality. This is the number one reason most scenes in improv don't work. Any time you refuse an offer made by your partner, your scene will almost instantly come to a grinding halt. This works the same way in conversations in real life and, therefore, in relationships. We humans invalidate each other out of sheer habit and either say the equivalent of "yes, but" or simply "no" to other people's opinions with great regularity. "Yes, and" is more collaborative, agreeable, inclusive, and creative. Happy, healthy relationships thrive on lots of "yes, and" responses. As long as you honor your own needs, responding to another human being with "yes, and," ready to play and with your heart and mind open, you can create tremendous synergy. This one simple shift, this one adjustment of attitude, catching yourself from saying "no" or "yes, but" and switching it to "yes, *and*," will probably have a great impact on, not only your acting skills, but also your life and career!

I have known many people in the industry who are in fight mode, ready to be taken down or taken advantage of, seeing others as competition and as a threat. To have an attitude that others are the enemy will only create conflict in one's life. For an actor, a mentality of competition will stop you in your tracks. The truth is, no one is your competition. Despite how it may seem, you're never reading *against* other actors and no one is ever *better* or *worse*. The person who landed that role *was just right for it*. You're a unique expression of life and you're on your own unique journey. A big key to success is trusting that. There are great benefits from learning to trust life and others a bit more, deciding that perhaps no one and nothing is against you, and instead being open to the possibility that everything and everyone is *for* you. Research shows that people with high levels of social trust are happier and physically healthier, so it really can't hurt. You can either live in competition (which is fear and doubt) or collaboration (which is love and trust), and whatever you choose is what you create.

If you're going to serve a higher purpose in your life, make it include a contribution to the healing not the harming of others, and speak to them with respect and kindness. That takes finding a compassion in yourself that, even if it's the hardest thing you've ever done, is essential to your happiness and the happiness of everyone you will encounter!

Inspiring vs Impressing

Probably the most unique thing about being a performer is that you are the product you're selling. A lot of actors I coach talk about how, when they go to auditions and meetings and on sets, they want very badly to have positive feedback and validation. When it comes to what they are looking for in their careers, applause, accolades, and attention are right up there on top of their list. It's a real focus. This makes some sense considering their product is on the line, and because that product is *them,* it's pretty close to home. It's hard not to take it all really personally. Walking into a room can feel quite daunting when the onus is all on the actor. You really can't blame a product "out there" if things don't go well, so getting positive attention and being liked is often extremely important. The silent question you have in your mind when this is a focus is, *Will they like me?* and that can be really disempowering. It can feel like giving your power away.

One fact often not considered by actors is that many other people around them also want to feel understood, "got" by others, or at least accepted and heard. My clients include directors, producers, writers, and people in many other industries and positions in life, and I can vouch for the fact that it's not just actors who, at times, ask that silent question, *Will they like me?* We are all human and deserve to feel we are appreciated and that we matter, and we tend to get that through feedback from others—feedback that who we are and what we are putting out is interesting and valid.

Here is the thing, though. If we are all busy wanting that from each other, where's the room for the *giving* of it? How can we ever be powerful *for* each other?

What if there was a room full of people and all of them were busy hoping to be liked. After a while someone walks into this room silently asking the question, *How will I make a positive difference here?* and this person takes a genuine interest in the people there. They find ways to help these people feel understood, "got," and validated. This person speaks in their language, from their place, in their arena. They use instinct and awareness to connect with what these people are interested in and what inspires them. Who do you think will be the most liked person in the room? Ironically, the one person who is least concerned with being liked!

This person, at the very least, was creating what's called *rapport*— harmonious, sympathetic connection with others. "Yes, and" is one instant way to create rapport with another person. When you learn how to create rapport with others, you get out of your own way and begin to serve a greater good. You help others to become more comfortable, and you assist a situation in becoming more positive. To create rapport with others you first have to be open to understanding how *their* world works. You become curious. How do they experience the world? Do they mostly experience it through images, sounds, or feelings? Are they prone to rapid movements and fast speech, or do they take their time? What words do they prefer to use? What tonalities? What gestures? What expressions? What positions do they stand and walk in? And how do they like to be approached? What sides of their body would they prefer you stand or sit at when you visit with them? And how do you find these things out without asking them? Can you tell how they are breathing, how they might be feeling, what their energy is like? And can you then mirror these things back without them knowing or feeling self-conscious, and instead help them to feel safe, heard, understood, "got," and validated?

Making a positive difference is not about helping others in ways that *you* think they should be helped or, even worse, "fixed." It's about becoming aware, more than anything, about what a positive difference might mean to *them*. It's about empathy. It's about connecting in a profoundly conscious and intentional way, which even becomes about serving the good and well-being of others.

I studied with a well-known acting coach in Hollywood for many years when I was an actor. She was a powerful influence on me and my success. Back then, one of the many things she taught actors was to "win" or "top" the other characters in scenes. This technique certainly created an intention and drive in my work. The only thing was, it didn't align with my values or the way I wanted to evolve as a person. My acting became dynamic but I never felt quite right about it. I had a two-year break from working with my acting coach and when I returned, having grown into my own sense of values and voice, I decided to address this important concern. I let her know what my dilemma had been. It turned out that during our break she, too, had grown and had shifted her technique. She was encouraging actors to think more about empowering the other person. Suddenly I was so much more inspired to engage the other actors in our scenes and my work became layered, warm, and far more enjoyable for me. It also bled over into my life when I began to practice empowering others more and, not surprisingly, found my relationships improving. It was a great acting focus and a wonderful focus for life in general. Empowering others takes us away from being needy and combative to being generous, supportive, and validating.

Let's return now to the notion that many of us want others to be impressed by who we are and what we are doing. So often actors think they have to get others to hire them for roles by impressing them. It's really hard work trying to impress other people, especially when we usually have no idea what it is that they want in the first place. The irony is, they usually don't know what they want either, until they see it. Second-guessing what a casting director, a producer, a director, or a studio executive might find impressive is a lot of work and is, ultimately, futile. It's like standing in the dark trying to paint a picture of something someone has not dreamed up yet. The good news is there's another way forward that creates flow and movement in the universe, in your life, and the lives of those around you, and that's through *inspiration*.

As mentioned earlier, the word *inspire* means "to breathe life into." Inspiration is the very source of life, which is breath, and people feel it as a tangible force in a room. People ultimately want to be inspired, not impressed or motivated. Being inspired touches the core of who we are, expands us into our greatest selves, and connects us with our essence and with the great power of the creative universe. *And* before you can inspire others you first have to be *inspired*.

Becoming inspired, as we have established, requires getting to know what your core values are—what's deeply important to you, what your passions are. When you get to understand and know these elements—and therefore who you are deep inside—you become more grounded, confident, and self-sufficient. It means you no longer look outside yourself for validation from others, but rather find a steady knowing within your own being. The importance of others' opinions of you drops down from the top of your list. It may even leave your list. Your deepest values, the fingerprints of your soul, make up the foundation of your purpose in life. When you understand your purpose you know your mission, and that connects you with why you're even here. There is then ample room to feel that not only are *you* more than enough, but also that there is more than enough good to give to others. You live in a consciousness focused on making a positive difference in those around you.

The most successful, powerful, and essence-connected people I know fill the room when they walk into it. They don't arrive with concerns about getting attention, being famous, or acquiring money. They are brimming with something to give, something to offer, something to share. They are rooted into the truth of their own purpose in life and are deeply inspired by it and the responsibility they hold to serve others through it. They are fulfilled and filled full. They inspire others simply because they live *inspired*.

Walking into any situation with the intention to create rapport, safety, and validation for others, and living inspired by a higher truth about what you're here for, will change your life forever. You will find a power within yourself that you didn't know was possible. This power you have is not power over anyone. It's power *with*. It's a power that you channel from a great source. You become a conduit for something profoundly good and generative. You know to simply step out of the way and humbly serve. You elevate everyone you come in contact with when you learn to live through these intentions. Meetings, auditions, and work environments are transformed into places where the conversations, creativity, trust, and connections are raised, and then raised and raised again, and everyone becomes happier.

Author Frederick L. Collins said, "There are two types of people. Those who come into a room and say, 'Well, here I am!' and those who come in and say, 'Ah, there you are.'" Can this journey of yours become about conscious service to others, about having them feel seen, heard, validated, loved, understood, and perhaps even inspired? Can you imagine screen or stage acting being a spiritual practice for you? Can it be a vehicle for creating greater good in the lives of others?

How to Be an Adult

As an actor you will be asked at some point to be a leader. We all lead. We lead events, households, gatherings, groups, and teams in all kinds of situations. If you are going to be a lead actor in any sized production, for example, you are meant to step in and be a leader. This does not mean you are the boss, or that you tell people what to do. It means you take responsibility for yourself and for inspiring the group toward the best outcome. Leadership is a very important and often ignored part of being an actor, and leading requires being an adult.

Being an "adult" is really another way to describe someone who is emotionally mature, loves fully, is kind, is respectful, has great boundaries, doesn't take things personally, and can communicate effectively. An adult is someone who is also willing to take responsibility for his or her own part in a relationship dynamic. As I am sure you've learned, we don't automatically become adults when we turn eighteen! It's an ongoing journey.

There are many, many ways to become an adult. One of them is to remember this: *No one can make you feel a limiting emotion without your agreement.* Think about that. No one can make you angry unless somewhere in there you've made the choice to be so. No one can make you sad without your permission. Certainly, some terrible things can be done and said by others and we really do affect one another in many ways, yet ultimately we each have the power to decide how we *respond.* Having good communication skills doesn't mean you won't have feelings about something. It doesn't mean you will never express anger, for example. Anger is an important part of being human and can be a healthy response to something that doesn't feel okay. It's healthy as long as it's not an excuse for drama and abuse.

A person's actions can hurt you tremendously and it can feel devastating. The choice then becomes what you do with that. How do you proceed and how do you continue to feel and act? Healthy anger includes a consciousness that you have a subjective interpretation of the other person's behavior and that you're responsible for the feelings in yourself. Healthy anger is generally brief and informs the other person what change is wanted from you, with an acceptance that the change might not actually occur. Healthy anger is nonviolent and works to keep the other person emotionally, physically, and psychologically safe.

Drama and abuse, on the other hand, show up as being entitled, controlling, and invalidating of the other. There is blame and retaliation. Demands, aggressiveness, intimidation, and sometimes violent and out-of-control behaviors are displayed. Drama and abuse also show up as punitive, vengeful, contemptuous, and mocking. You obstruct the feelings and opinions of the other and insist that the other person agrees or sees that you're justified. What happens is held onto until it becomes resentment and bitterness. Drama and abuse also show up as a belief that the other person is the cause of the anger, even though the truth is that no one can make you feel anything.

If you have an issue with something someone is doing, it's just that, *your* issue. That doesn't mean what they are doing is your fault or that it's okay, or even that you need to take it on or get mixed up in it. It just means that your reaction to it is the only thing you can control. It's your work to make adjustments to resolve and complete your reactions within your own being. You can't control what other people do or say. If you continue to believe others have the power to make you feel or think in ways that limit your ability to be peaceful, rational, and kind, then you're agreeing to be powerless. This is where you agree to sign on for the role of victim.

If there is anything that's most responsible for how any of us feel, it's our beliefs, our values, and both the wounds and the soft spots in our hearts. The emotions we have tell us when something is okay or not okay in relation to how we are organized inside. The key is to ask whether you want to make any changes to that organization or not. That's where your power lies.

We all act childishly, dramatically, and even abusively at times, some of us rarely, some of us often, some of us in small ways, and some of us in large and irreversible ways. The important thing is to take responsibility for the times we are, and to decide to make a shift right now into adulthood. We do that by getting healthy and practicing relationship skills.

Effective communication skills help us become constructive and open and encourage the idea that the other person is whole and complete the way they are. The language used in good communication can be learned. It always respects the other person's view even if you don't agree with it. When contempt and lack of respect are present, effective communication is not possible. Respect is considered by many research psychologists to be the number one key to relationship success. Whether that's true or not, it's certainly an essential ingredient! This may all sound overwhelming, and just know that there are many resources out there now that teach us to become better at relationships, no matter if they are personal or professional. Think about what you would like to learn and improve upon in your relationships and seek resources that will educate and heal you into a higher place. This way you can step into being an inspiring and effective leader in any situation.

Your Choices

With relationships, as we've discovered, you can't change the other person's behavior, only your own. So the choice you have is to shift your own responses, patterns, and behaviors. Working on your own part in a dynamic is the only real change you can instigate. It will, by default, change the relationship. How it does that and to what degree is something you will find out as you grow. With any situation (personal or professional) you are in, you will find that you always have at least three choices. You can change the situation, accept it, or leave it.

Acceptance is when you drop judgment. You just let go of the need to control what someone else is doing. You say, *Okay. I accept.* In some cases, as with primary relationships, acceptance means you love them, support them, and stand by them no matter what. That doesn't mean you don't have boundaries. You *must* have boundaries. They are essential to your happiness and the happiness of those around you. Acceptance also doesn't mean you give up your own needs. They are essential to your life force. Acceptance just means you stop trying to control what you can't control, like the things other people do. You can only control what *you* do.

Acceptance is a big growth area for most of us. If you decide to accept a situation, you have to fully accept. That's not easy if the behavior of the other person goes against your needs and values. Your self-worth must be held intact. If the person is not honoring your value as a person or they are abusing you, accepting the situation is probably not going to be the best choice. No matter if it's in a personal or a professional relationship, if you're being physically, mentally, or emotionally dishonored or abused you have the profound opportunity to question what you feel you deserve, and then decide how you would like to better take care of yourself. Acceptance is more appropriate in relationships where there is at least some safety to communicate and you feel the other person is taking responsibility for their behaviors and doing what they can to grow. If that *is* the case, then learning to focus on these truths rather on what the other person is doing "wrong" is where acceptance emerges. Criticizing someone else repeatedly for not meeting your expectations can be extremely harmful to them, no matter if they are family, friends, or your team members. It not only doesn't stop the unwanted behavior, it then means *you* are moving into the role of behaving abusively, and that serves nobody.

Acceptance is not *tolerating* someone. Tolerating is a grudging, judgmental defeat. Most of us tolerate what we are not happy with about another person, and that leads to resentment. For many years I was very practiced at tolerating in relationships. This included my friendships, my romantic relationships, and most specifically my career representation. I had managers and agents that I felt treated me disrespectfully and dismissively and I tolerated them because I felt it would probably be too hard to find other representation. *It's tough out there*, I thought, *and I need to just suck it up and take it.* However, I was sending myself, as well as the rest of the world, a message about my worth, and that reflected back on how my life was unfolding at the time.

Then there is a third choice, and that is to leave. Sometimes walking away is necessary, perhaps forever. Leaving is a type of boundary setting. A *boundary* is a limit that promotes integrity. Like our skin, it holds in what is needed and keeps out what is harmful.

Years ago, when I was beginning to work as an actor in Hollywood, I auditioned many times for a particular casting director. She was quite old at the time and a legend of sorts in the industry, yet each time I met with her I didn't want to go back. You see, she had a tendency to bark and snarl at actors, making negative remarks and barely looking up from her desk as we would read to her. She had a reputation for this, so it wasn't just me, and I would dread her casting calls. One day I decided that I was done dealing with her behavior and I told my agent that I didn't want to read for her anymore. I thought that was a perfectly reasonable boundary to have. To be discerning is important, and I was learning about what kind of people I wanted to be around. My agent, on the other hand, had a different idea. "Who do you think you are?" my agent asked sharply over the phone. That was a great question, and one I'm not sure I could answer at the time. Who *did* I think I was? Actually, it turns out I was someone that I was just learning to take care of. I stuck to my guns and saved myself from any more of the casting director's behavior.

Boundaries mean that we can honor our values and needs. Any part of our life that's not working can be improved by setting healthy, specific boundaries, whether it's because something is harmful, or simply because it no longer "fits" you.

When it comes to harm, the truth is that there are people who take pleasure in hurting others. It took me a long time to accept this about the world, having had a deep and unshakable belief in the fundamental goodness of human beings, and I now understand that the human condition also includes a dark side that wants to destroy. The entertainment industry attracts all kinds of people. Sometimes you will find yourself in the path of someone who enjoys the suffering of those around them, for whatever reason, and you will need to take action beyond defense. The only real defense in a case like this is removing yourself from harm's way. In fact, with good boundaries defense is not necessary. Sometimes getting out is the most loving thing you can do for yourself and everyone else.

When a relationship simply doesn't "fit" or serve the highest good for you or your life anymore, the adult way to set boundaries is to do it with consciousness, grace, and respect for the other person's needs. To exit a relationship in this way requires communicating compassionately.

A few years ago an old friend of mine, renowned television director and producer David Nutter, told me that he had just fired his agent.

"How did it go?" I asked.

"Not great!" he said.

It turned out that *how David handled it* actually went really well! He had called his agent and told him he was leaving, and the agent went off on an angry rant. David, instead of defending himself or arguing about any of the accusations the agent had made, silently let the agent go on with his diatribe until he was done. Then David thanked him for all he had done and said his goodbye in a calm and respectful manner. He had communicated what his reason was for leaving, expressed his gratitude, and set the boundary around what he was willing to engage in.

I learned from David's story, though not before I fumbled around in my early learning process. By the time David shared his agent-firing experience with me I had already taken the leap and fired the agent who had asked "who do you think you are?" Firing her had been about much more than just that question. The agent had really, I felt, dropped the ball on a number of responsibilities and had shown me over the years that she had little respect for me. I'd had enough. The fact that I *had* had enough was really good news for me personally. The only thing is that I had also been afraid to set that boundary and when I finally did, I did it weakly and clumsily via a fax, which was not very classy. I felt bad about it (which didn't do much for my happy factor), but the good news is, I learned from it, and along with that learning, hearing David Nutter's story had inspired me and helped me grow.

At that time I happened to be on the brink of leaving my manager too, for other reasons. She had been absolutely fantastic for me in many arenas and I was tremendously grateful to her for that, yet she really had not been representing me and *who I am* out there in the world. I'd had repeated feedback from producers that she had been aggressive and rude in their dealings, almost hysterical at times, and that really had not changed despite my requests that she shift her tactics. It was time, obviously, to make changes across the board. Besides, my life was about to take a big turn and none of this was fitting in. So, I left my manager with a bit more class than I had my agent. I called her and thanked her genuinely, telling her how much I appreciated her and what she had done for me. I informed her of my reasons, but stayed away from any debate she wanted to get into about the whys and wherefores. I did my best to treat her with gratitude and respect and worked to set a boundary around what I was willing to engage in. It didn't mean she liked it or responded well to it, it just meant that I did what it took to be as kind, adult, and responsible as I could be. I will always be sincerely grateful to all the people who have worked for me, believed in me, and who have spent time and energy enhancing my life or building my career. This particular person will always stand out in my heart and mind as someone who deserves an enormous amount of gratitude from me, and she will always have it. We must always consider what people have done for us, not so much what they have *not* done, even as we move on.

So, as you move on from relationships, you have an opportunity to focus on *who you want to be* in the world and to do that no matter how other people behave or react to you. You then find your behavior begins to take on an adult quality, your emotional intelligence grows, and your relationships improve. Whatever choices you make, if you make them from a loving, adult perspective you will be making them with clarity of heart and you will be far happier in the long run. Conflict comes when both people feel that they are right (and that may be the truth as sometimes both people *are* right), and then the only thing you can control is who you want to be and how you want to respond. If we would each take more responsibility for our reactions to outside influences, what a powerful and connected world we would be in! Being a loving, forgiving person with healthy boundaries for both you and the other person (respectful and kind, nonjudgmental, patient, and responsible) is all you have control of. How another person responds to you is up to them. The opportunity is there for you to grow into being who you would like to be. That's the gift. What may come of the relationship is bonus. If the relationship has to end then that, in itself, is also a gift. Only good can ultimately come out of honoring health and love, even if the circumstances may not seem that way at the time.

You have choice, always, and your choices in every moment about what to accept, what to tolerate, and what to refuse either support or sabotage your greater mission. Getting to know yourself and what's important to you is the key, and then building a good fence around that will make good neighbors and a happy you.

As we each remember that we are in a position to make choices—making the commitment to step deeper into adulthood, owning our feelings, reactions, and responses, asking if they serve the outcome that we ultimately desire, and then shifting accordingly—we inspire others to step up as well.

Judgment and Rejection

Most of the actors I've known and coached have found that being judged and rejected are two of the things they fear the most. Understandably. There is a whole lot of both in the world, and most especially in the entertainment industry!

A casting director friend once told me that his job every day, all day, is to judge people, which I thought was an interesting perspective. I was expecting him to say something like *to discover talent*, yet *judging* is what he quite proudly feels is his valuable role. And he has been very successful at it, discovering many, many wonderful, talented actors, singers, and dancers over the years. He has also had to reject many hundreds of thousands of actors during his years as a casting director because, naturally, there has to be a weeding out of the people lining up hoping to be the next star.

Of course the word *judge* has different meanings at different times for different people. We need to be discerning, evaluating a situation, looking at *data*, and deciding what choices to make in life. If we didn't do that we would be considered unable to fend for ourselves. *Judging*, in this context, is needed. Then you look at the talent shows out there and the panel of judges—that's their title, *judge*, and that's what they are paid to do. Ultimately, no matter what the meaning of the word, it's *how* judging is done that makes the difference in the experience of both the judge and the recipient.

The judgment I am referring to here, and the type I believe we are most afraid of, is the black-and-white, quantifying interpretation that decides if something is either good or bad, clever or stupid, pretty or ugly, or terrible or fantastic. This type of judgment is based on thinking habits, old beliefs, and cultural, social, and religious ideas held up against something or someone, and done *without empathy*. What that leads to, when it comes to feedback, is something that is either idolizing or condemning and belittling.

The dynamic in this business of ours is to swing from one end of that spectrum to the other, and that can feel like an unsafe place to live. Some of my clients who have been very successful as actors, directors, or producers, delivering fabulous work for many years and winning awards for it, have found that one moment they are being idolized and adored by the media and the studios, and the next they are on the "out," being criticized, vilified, and—sometimes worse—simply avoided or ignored. These are talented, wonderful, complex human beings who never promised perfection, and yet one or two "wrong" moves and they are no longer invited to the party. For actors who are still auditioning, just walking into readings and meetings can feel like that kind of judgment, and after a while because of all the no's it can feel like a sea of rejection. It can build up and become a legacy of rejection in one's own mind.

The truth of it is we don't really know whether someone is judging us negatively or positively unless they expressly and clearly tell us they are, yet the dynamic out there tends to convince most actors that it's the former—as an assumption. So, how do we all navigate and handle the cultural dynamic of judgment and rejection? First of all, just like in any relationship, each of us needs to take responsibility for our own part in it.

We return again to the realm of self-esteem. Building that foundation within yourself takes the power out of what others think of you, and brings the power back to who you *know* you really are. You can't take what other people say or do personally. When others condemn you and you're in your own power, you detach from it, knowing it's not the truth. Equally, when others begin to idolize you, remaining in your own power means you detach from it knowing it's also not the truth. You don't buy into either because, at the end of the day, your value stays consistent no matter what judgment is occurring.

Feedback can be very valuable, of course, when it's constructive and informative, and when you're in a powerful place you can take that feedback and turn it into an opportunity for growth. As an actor you will get a lot of feedback about your work as well as your appearance, personality, and opinions. Take what you get as gifts for your own expansion and then let it go. When feedback is simply belittling, however, it's not worth taking on, and those who consistently, overtly do that may not be the sort of people that are resourceful to be around. They are certainly not going to be adding to your happiness factor, and this is when you get to be discerning about whom you have in your life.

When it comes to actors (and you may or may not relate to this), much of the time the *imagined* judgment is what the real issue is. The voice inside you saying, *I screwed up*, or *I'm bombing*, is very often the real obstacle to happiness. What you imagine others saying about you is more often than not a projection of what you're saying to yourself, therefore judging *yourself* is the first act. That needs to be transformed into compassion and a willingness to step into your best self. Condemning yourself, or even idolizing yourself, has no positive outcome; healthy self-love and self-esteem does.

An actor, "Christopher," had been in the industry for many years without having worked very much. He had done a handful of low budget films in a span of twenty-five years in Hollywood. Despite the fact that Christopher said he couldn't make heads or tails of why he had never "made it" in the film business, I asked him, nevertheless, to think about what might have held him back. He described a number of factors in the business that he believed to be the reason he had not made any headway. One thing that stood out in his story was how many times he felt he had been treated as though he were not important or of value. Christopher told me about the casting director who would not shake his hand every time he met her, and the other casting director who barked at him to take his briefcase off her desk when he had thrown it down for effect in the middle of his audition. He also felt his agent had shunned him because she had asked that he not call her during pilot season. He felt he had been judged and rejected over and over.

One of the things that every one of us has the opportunity to *decide* is whether to take things personally. Taking things personally generally leads to no good. The reason for this is that we are making judgments and assumptions based on our insecurities, and the lens of that kind of fear will only create more fear in life. We all do what Christopher had done to some degree or another. We see another person behave a certain way and we make it about us. We hear something and we decide it's an affront or an insult or we get our feelings hurt. We assume that our value is being measured. In reality, most of the time, it has nothing to do with our value at all.

As you can imagine, I invited Christopher to look at other possibilities. I have talked to many casting directors over the decades and know that a number of them don't like to shake hands with actors (or anyone for that matter) especially during flu and cold season, as they want to protect their health. If they shook the hand of every actor who came in they would be washing their hands or pumping hand sanitizer all day long just to keep themselves germfree, and there just isn't the time for that.

When it came to the casting director and the briefcase, she may have had papers specially laid out on her desk that were disturbed, or fragile items that may have become broken by the briefcase. The suddenness of his act may have scared her. She may have simply not wanted Christopher throwing his bag violently down into her space! It was her right to say what she would like, and in that case it was for Christopher to remove his briefcase. It was a boundary issue.

When it came to Christopher's agent she was probably (like most agents in Hollywood) completely inundated by calls and e-mails during pilot season and, again, wanted to set boundaries. She probably felt she would be able to do a better job for her actors if she was not on the phone with *them*, but rather with producers and casting people during the busiest time of the year.

None of these alternate possibilities are about Christopher being devalued. In fact they are all mostly about other people's boundaries. Whatever the real truth behind any of the interactions, the fact that Christopher had taken them personally meant that he was filled with tension, insecurity, and resentment, and that's how he engaged the people in his life and business. That got seriously in the way of him showing up well and doing his best work, and *that*, perhaps, was more likely a significant reason that he had not gone very far in his career. What he imagined other people were thinking or saying about him was likely a projection of what he had been saying to himself, so judging and rejecting *himself* had been the first act.

A direct path to your happiness comes when you take things less personally, and that includes when you're not cast in a role you wanted. Casting director Mark Teschner shared, "You might be not considered right for the role or you might not have the right essence, the right sensibility, and that's nothing you can control. You can only control your artistry. There are only two things an actor has: their talent and their dignity. Everything else is really out of their hands."

A way to begin taking things less personally is through the friendly, compassionate, nonjudgmental relationship with yourself that we have already explored. Again, when the product you're marketing is you (as it is when you're an actor) that's especially important. The judgmental and rejecting voices in your head are likely ones that you heard as a child, coming from a parent or guardian. When you place them back where they belong, with the original judge, you begin to set boundaries between you and limiting or belittling beliefs. You then create space for your own, more loving and resourceful beliefs about who you are. They become the voices that begin to speak to you more often and judgments from the outside have less impact.

Another way to take things less personally is to have a perspective on the business other than that of just being an actor looking for the next part. Many actors I know who have become directors or producers suddenly get the process from a different angle and stop taking it personally, just because they know what it's like to be on the other end of it. Christine Lahti is an actor who also directs and understands both perspectives. "One of the most important things is not to take rejection personally, and that's a really tough thing because we are called upon to be so open and vulnerable and raw and available and sensitive. That's our job. And yet we have to have a really tough skin . . . we have to really try to not take all those inevitable rejections personally . . . Being a director I know how subjective it is. It's based on nothing but how I envision the part for casting. And yes, it has to do with talent, but it could be brunette versus blonde, tall versus short . . . the kind of laugh of a person . . . it's so subjective and to take that to heart and take that personally, it's a waste of time and can be self-destructive."

Risa Bramon Garcia told me how she gives her acting students an opportunity to gain a new perspective for this very purpose.

"I do a mock audition in the class," Risa told me, "I set up a situation where a group of people auditions another group of people. I cast it, like, *Who would be the best director in this group?* because I want it to actually come alive. I've only had a couple of times where there's been a bit of a dud, but I also identify that for them. *Okay, you're the director but you weren't as vocal as the person who was playing the writer, and the writer then took over the room.* Someone will ask, *Who has the most say?* and I reply, *The person who has the most to say and is willing to say it! It's just a bunch of people here, making a decision about a bunch of people here.*"

"I think that's fantastic," I told Risa. "It gives actors the insight that people—directors, producers, and writers—are human beings and are all living it out in the moment as well as everybody else."

"That's right," Risa agreed. "Sometimes what I hear people on the other side of the table say is, *I didn't realize that someone could be a great actor but they're just not what we're buying that day!* If you're selling apples and they're buying oranges . . . You can have the best apples in the world and people will always remember, *when I want a great apple, I go to so-and-so.* It's like a brand. *But, right now we're buying oranges . . .*"

"What a great exercise for actors to have another perspective." I smiled.

"Yeah." Risa smiled back. "And sometimes, it's like, *We're buying oranges today, but man, that **apple** was really . . . let's see the apple, let's do that.* You never know. There are no rules."

Being open to the perspectives of the people who are hiring can be powerful and empowering, and as an actor you benefit from imagining what their process might be like as often as you can.

The other part of navigating judgment and rejection is to remember that what you put out into the world is what you get back on some level, and what you desire from others you need to *be* first. That means reviewing how compassionate, inclusive, and nonjudgmental *you* are with others. Again, it's important to be discerning and able to separate out what feels congruent to you and your values, yet when you judge situations and other people out of habit, fear, or the need to blame, exclude, or feel better than them you've fallen into a miserable trap. Judgment won't help you to feel any happier. In fact it will probably do the opposite.

What is the cure for judging others? Consciousness, empathy, and compassion.

Many years ago I decided to try an experiment in nonjudgment where every time I felt the need to judge a person, thing, or situation, I stopped, took a breath, dropped into my heart, and simply said, *it's just different.* I chose the word *different* because it helped me to move into something neutral. I began to notice the things I had been assuming and interpreting so automatically in my life. Why had I decided that rain was *bad* weather? What made me so sure that thick traffic was *terrible*? Why does that lady's blue hair have to mean *ugly* to me? Why can these things not be beautiful or peaceful or spacious or cute or touching or just different? I became aware of how often I had been judging situations and other people and had not even known it! Where was my compassion and openness for possibilities? How would I see anything beyond what was in a small frame? Through consciously catching myself and questioning my judgments, that frame, then, was what I decided to expand.

If you think about it, as we point one finger forward at another person there are three fingers pointing back at ourselves. This may well be telling us that we are either judging something in someone else that we've been judging in ourselves, or we have actually missed that *we are* the ones doing what it is we don't approve of. Either way, it comes back to ourselves, not necessarily in context but in dynamics. When we judge others it says more about us than about the people we are judging.

When we sit in negative judgment about anything or anyone, we are not being loving and we are not trusting life to be as varied as it's meant to be. We are in fear. Sometimes that fear is simply about our *own* worth. The great Indian guru Paramhansa Yogananda wrote in his book *Autobiography of a Yogi*, "Some people try to be tall by cutting off the heads of others." Judgment creates constriction around our hearts and actually attracts to us more of the things we are judging, so it's not constructive, nor does it make life better. We can be tall and enjoy others being tall too! There is room for everyone to flourish.

Judgment can also be about ignorance. Very often when we don't understand something we judge it, we call it crazy. Just thinking something is crazy doesn't mean it is. We may simply not yet see it for what it is. We don't really know the full story, see the whole picture, or grasp the entire truth. We don't know what someone else has been through or what his or her experience of life has been. We don't know the depths of someone else's pain or joy. We don't know how afraid someone might be or how hurt they are. We have filters in our minds that we interpret everything through, and these have been created by our beliefs and our past experiences, not always by real data or by seeing the present truth.

So, be careful with your thoughts and words (with yourself and others) and know that your judgment or rejection of others may only add to the suffering and confusion in the world. All you can do is stay open to the full picture, go into your heart, and have some compassion for the humanness of everyone.

Happiness Is Contagious

Not surprisingly it has been found that an important ingredient of our own health and happiness is the level of happiness in the people we are around. According to studies by the *British Medical Journal* both happiness and unhappiness are contagious. Being around unhappy people increases our chances of being unhappy ourselves by about 6 percent, and being around happy people increases the chance of us being happy by about 8–34 percent. Even having a happy neighbor can increase our happiness by 34 percent, according to studies done at both Harvard and UC San Diego!

When moving toward your own happiness, it makes real sense to be conscious about what kinds of people you spend your time and energy with and to look at whether they have been affecting you in limiting or resourceful ways. Who are your people? Are they relatively happy? Are they kind and respectful? Are they validating, encouraging, and able to empathize with you? Do they take responsibility for their actions? Are they relatively emotionally and psychologically healthy? Are they living out the life you're working to get away from, or the one that you're building *toward*?

Actors have a tendency to group together and "com-*misery*-ate." It's all too easy in the challenges of our industry to want to bond with other actors about how tough it is! However, this cycle heads directly toward more misery and unhappiness.

Research says that *you are a direct reflection of the five people you spend the most of your time with.* Your own income, attitude, and lifestyle are an average of all five of you put together. That's worth thinking about. On some level we are always taking on the energy of those around us. Actors are especially good at that. But the full truth is that we take on, not only other people's speech patterns and body language, we also take on their place in life.

When I was on that television series many of the actors were, like myself, quite pleased to be working steadily. There were, however, a couple of people in the mix who were very unhappy from the beginning and who chose to think negatively about the whole experience. I was tremendously grateful to be having the career success I was having and my positive attitude just didn't align with theirs. Because of that I become unpopular with them. They wanted to bond over the negative aspects of being on the show. Yes, a lot of what they were unhappy about was valid. The show was not always run well, the leadership team was extremely dysfunctional, the hours were often unnecessarily long, the writing was sometimes hokey and didn't make sense, yet there were also some real positives. We had the chance, as actors, to be creative with characters through many story arcs. We had money flowing in and therefore could afford to buy houses and cars and set up retirement funds. We could travel on our time off. We also had a community on set, a family of people we had the opportunity to get to know and live an experience with. These were blessings that I had wanted to focus on. It wasn't within my control to change most of the issues on the show, nor was it in the hands of the complainers, so to me it didn't serve anything to go on and on about the problems. I found out very quickly that I couldn't communicate with these particular actors because of my desire to be positive. We just didn't relate. The combination of this and my own limits concerning how to handle the situation made for a very uncomfortable film set, and the escalating negativity and anger coming from the complainers eventually led to destructive, even violent, behavior. Eventually, in order to protect myself, I made the tough decision to leave the show. I felt very loyal to the studio and yet, at the same time, unsupported by them in my own basic right for safety. I was also contractually obligated, so though it was ultimately worth it, having to make these changes put me in a very difficult situation. In the end it was a powerful move for me and I was able to take a stand for my own well-being and basic safety, as well as for my ultimate happiness.

So, in order for happiness to survive, it's essential to be a force of optimism and to surround yourself, as far as you are possibly able to, with other people who are seeing the good in life, who are positive and grateful, and who are living out the life you desire! If you have choice (which we usually do), even if it seems like it might kill an entire career, it's extremely important to weigh the significance of this. For you, if there is a situation where you have less complicated choices than I did, like changing the friends or the representation you have (and you don't have a concrete, binding contract that states you have to be around them), you only serve yourself by taking the steps you need to. Remember, on some level you're always taking on the energy of those around you, so it's paramount to look at the situation and make the necessary changes that serve your happiness.

There is a chance to move out of your tired old limits and surround yourself with more light, more love, and more creativity so you get to live the future you envision. What you surround yourself with creates your today and your tomorrow.

Who Is Your Tribe?

A few years ago my husband and I spent a weekend around author and speaker Mark Victor Hansen. You may know him from his *Chicken Soup for the Soul* books. He is an amazing human being. He fills the room with excitement, love, and humor, and he shares his heart like a river pouring from him. The weekend was brimming with other people like that too: successful, inspired, masterful, and generous. We immediately began to feel ourselves becoming our best. We got some exciting, new ideas and found we had loads of energy to make them happen. We got more focused, more energetic, and very inspired. One of the many things I learned that weekend was that we do very well around people who are more successful, more talented, smarter, more inspired, wealthier, and more evolved than us. It *elevates* us to take on the very best in ourselves. When we live day to day with masterful, inspiring people, we begin to evolve toward that in ourselves. We begin to manifest what we want for ourselves at magnificent speed. There are plenty of events like these, and we have been to many since, and each one of them has had the same effect. Imagine living in that all the time! My husband and I do what we can to create that sort of environment ourselves wherever we are and within our own events, and it's tremendously gratifying to hear that we have accomplished that for others.

So, what people do you want to be more like: the complaining, resentful actors you know, or the positive, grateful, and successful people you know? Take a look at everyone you are around. Whom do you have as your partner, your friends, your teachers, and your representation? Are they stuck or are they living out what you admire and desire? Are they fighting for their limitations or are they living in a flow of creativity, abundance, and personal power? Do they doubt and belittle what you've envisioned for yourself, or are they your greatest supporters? Are they your mentors, your teachers, your inspiration?

There are too many acting coaches, managers, and agents (at least in Hollywood) who treat actors in unkind and dismissive ways. In some cases even bullying, criticizing, and humiliating them. Do you believe that's deserved? If I were to ask you and many of your fellow actors that question the answer would likely be *no*, yet so often it's not only painfully tolerated, but accepted. Why is that? What is it about this industry that has created such a dynamic? How can so many people behave as though they are the gatekeepers to a hidden treasure and have actors convinced that they are privileged merely to be in their presence? How is it that there is a well-known phrase in the industry, *actor-friendly*, used in the context that someone like a casting director or an agent stands out of the crowd because they are actually *friendly* to actors, as opposed to the *norm*, which would be actor-*unfriendly*? And why does almost everyone take that as if it's par for the course? How did that become so accepted? No one deserves to be treated as though they are below another human, and it's not acceptable to dismiss or belittle anyone. It's a denial of basic human value.

Mark Teschner, one of those casting directors known for being actor-friendly, is well loved because of how he engages actors, and he is *conscious* about it.

He told me, "I try to be kind to every actor that I've met through twenty-eight years of being a casting director. I don't think I've ever in my life been rude to one, even under stress and limited time, because I always feel like that actor has spent money getting sides, they've done the work, they've travelled here, they've basically built their day around this audition. The least I can do is be present for five minutes."

I do believe his consciousness and heart have been a part of his great success.

On the flip side, it's also not fair to the many, many people who *are* perfectly friendly to actors and who are just doing their jobs when they are assumed to be scary, unfriendly ogres before they even have a chance to open their mouths. Have you ever had someone approach you with a preconceived idea of who you are and how you might behave or think, and then react accordingly to you? I have, and it's not great. There is no chance to be seen or heard for even close to who you are when the person in front of you is so caught up in their own "stuff" and their own filters of fear.

I had the great privilege of stepping out of the entertainment world entirely when I left acting to take the turn onto my current career path. During that period I got to be in what one of my agents had called "the real world" for the first time since I was seventeen. I had entered the arts and entertainment industry at that age when I went to art college and then became a model in London, so when I did leave, *not* being in the industry was new to me. In my late thirties I was suddenly mingling with bankers, realtors, psychotherapists, academics, and business executives for the first time. What stands out for me most as I think about the outside perspective I got on the business, and what I learned as I then began to coach actors, producers, directors, and writers in the entertainment industry, *from the outside*, was that there is a kind of lulling of consciousness when you're smack dab in it. We can get really used to things. Even things as utterly bizarre and limiting as "actor-friendly" being considered a standout trait.

Of course every culture has its dynamics and many of them are similar, some rather unique. There are cultural agreements. In the entertainment industry it's a cultural agreement that actors are a certain way, casting directors are a certain way, producers are a certain way, and agents are a certain way. In my deep personal work with people on all ends of the spectrum in the business I've found that everyone is actually very human— even the "suits"! And almost everyone wants basically the same things: love, happiness, safety, peace, acceptance, connection. There is also *fair* typecasting out there. Lots of agents act very much like the stereotype we hear about, and lots of actors act like their stereotype too. Even so, it's tremendously important to be aware of the myths and the preconceived ideas we have and to be *open to what is really in front of us.*

The important things is, as you do that, as you remain open, you also remain discerning about whom you have in your life because, as we have found out, your happiness is directly affected by whom you spend your time with. Really look at the data presented to you by someone's behaviors, actions, and words. Do not assume. Listen and watch and use what you notice as *information.* As best you can, make the intention not to interpret through fear, but rather through trust. Trust in your own ability to know when something is supporting your journey or denying it. Do they drain you or do they expand and inspire you? The truth of it is, when it comes to people like your coaches, your agent, and your manager, they are people you've taken on as your team members and they are there to provide a service to you. They are meant to work *for* you and *with* you. If you are holding up your end of the bargain, and are being responsible and reliable, then you deserve respect and support as a basic requirement. If that's what you're getting, great. In most other businesses that would be the expected dynamic, yet so often these people treat their adult clients as though they are desperate, annoying, and badly behaved children who barely deserve their time. It's extraordinary.

So, as you consider your team members, there is an opportunity to ask yourself whether what they offer as a service is really what you want and deserve. Yes, they have an expertise you need—that's why you brought them on—*and* is the *manner in which* they provide the expertise what you really need? There are plenty of service providers in the entertainment industry who *do* treat their clients with respect, and those are the ones that will ultimately align with you when you know you deserve that. They understand that it's a business of relationships, and good relationships create good business. It's a win-win.

So, consider that when you assess whom you have in your life. If you're choosing a *mentor* (which is essentially what you're doing when you choose an acting coach, for example) decide how emotionally intelligent you want them to be. You will be learning from them. What is it you want to learn? Whom do you want to become? Make sure your coaches and mentors have your best interests at heart, not their own egos. If you're not working much as an actor at the moment, are you still treated as though you're of value to them or do they give you just the sparest moments of their time? If you're busy and working do they suddenly become your best friend and make you their star pupil or client, demanding to be your guest at movie openings and award ceremonies? Do they measure their success by the success of their students? In a business that can be so challenging and, at times crazy making, it's so important that you choose carefully whom you have as your guides and models when navigating through. Surround yourself with people who are as healthy, mature, honest, and kind as possible and who celebrate and validate you, not those who bully you, use you, or tolerate you. This includes your agent, your manager, your publicist, your coach, your hairdresser, your doctor, you name it, whomever you have as your team. *Your team represents who you are, and who you're willing to become.*

And so, dear creative spirit, I ask again, who *do* you want to become? We all have the capacity for everything: the capacity to love, to forgive, to be courageous, and also the capacity to be hateful and childish, to lie and betray. We each have the capacity to murder and also the capacity to save lives. Who you are in the world depends on where you set up camp. Are you living mostly in a place of loving kindness and gentleness, or in a place of judgment and blame? How far do you go in those places? The wonderful thing to remember is that you have the power to shift the ratio on which of these places you spend most of your time. What do you want for yourself, and for the people in your life? Being loving, compassionate, and respectful toward others is critical to the world we live in. We are living in very important, turbulent times with a growing need for some very big shifts. Those shifts start with each one of us individually making our own changes. If we don't have healthy regard for ourselves we can't give that gift to others. We might *think* we are being a nice person, yet the war we have raging inside will always come out somehow and others will feel it. Peace, a healthy planet, and everyone having enough food, abundance, and happiness all starts with each of us being conscious about what is in our hearts and minds. If we each say, *Oh, I can't change the world,* then so it is. If we each ask, *How will I make a positive difference here?* then seven billion people are being conscious, responsible, and adult, and the world is profoundly shifted. Even if a small fraction of the world grows up and gets kinder, it's going to make a huge difference. Studies show that positivity spreads hundreds of times faster than negativity, so it may well go viral!

So, when you have team members who are good to you, let them know how much you value and appreciate them and *treat them with great respect and kindness.* When you have friends and partners who are patient and loving with you, *be grateful!* When a casting director, like Mark Teschner, treats you with kindness and respect, *let them know you appreciate it.* Goodness must be acknowledged in the world for it to expand and flourish.

For your happiness to thrive it's really, truly essential to be conscious within the relationships you have with your partners, friends, coworkers, and with your local and global community. In the realm of primary relationships, if that means therapy, coaching, and studying better ways to communicate then those must be committed to. It's essential to take responsibility for your part in the dynamic of any relationship. You are a part of it happening.

The answers to the questions you ask about your relationships are a map. The choices you make from there will manifest the landscape you live in.

When a person is clinically dead for a period of time and has an experience of being conscious, yet in another state or realm, this is called a *near death experience,* or NDE. Very often people who have NDEs, no matter if they are surgeons, politicians, housewives, or artists, see their lives flash before them, see or are pulled through a tunnel, and experience a warm, brilliant light and a feeling of blissful love, as well as a sense of "coming home." Many have a connection to the divine in some form and a profound spiritual awakening, even if they did not have spiritual beliefs prior to the NDE. Upon returning to physical life these people say that during the NDE they were not aware of their money, whether their houses were clean, how good their car or their casserole was, or what their neighbors thought of them. Many of them do, however, think about the people in their lives, and find that what it all boils down to when the end arrives is love.

Understanding your power comes not from ego, but from your deepest and highest self. It comes out of both love and knowledge. When you connect with your personal power you connect with the love inside you. You begin to understand that, not only are you created out of that love, but that it is really all that exists. You become aware of what that means for you and how you hold others, and you begin to create good for all.

The spiritual journey is to awaken from the illusion of separation and remember that there is just one of us here.

CHAPTER 5

Training Your Brain

Whether you think you can, or you think you can't—you're right.

~ HENRY FORD

Energy Is Everything

Science is aligning more and more with what our spiritually conscious communities have understood for centuries—that everything is *energy*. That energy is made up of particles so tiny that we are still discovering them as we go along, and as we do that they continue to defy our previously held beliefs about the universe and how it works. For example, we are discovering that the building blocks of nature (protons, photons, electrons, and so on) thought previously to be particles also behave like waves under certain circumstances, and that it depends on the observer which character he or she sees at any given time. In other words, the result is determined by which characteristic one is measuring: particle or wave. The *observer* determines what's observed! That's a pretty extraordinary concept for us to grow into.

So, how does that relate to you, the industry, and your happiness? Not to get too heady here, but as you recognize yourself as being a perfectly organized, yet chaotic and mysterious cluster of particles (many of them particles of light), you begin to understand your connection to the universe as a whole. Your *being* is part of this huge energy system, while at the same time it contains numerous individual energy systems throughout it. These systems each have different roles in the health and functioning of your entire being. Many people who have exhausted physical or emotional healing possibilities with traditional medicine have had great relief, if not full recovery, when they have chosen to work instead with an *energy worker*. Energy medicine and energy psychology are fast-growing areas and are thought of by some to be the health modalities of the future. This is understandable considering our scientific communities now see the universe on a quantum level and are becoming far more open to the existence of these energy systems, simply because as technology advances, they have been able to detect some of them. The meridian system (which the Chinese based acupuncture on), for example, is now accepted by some scientists simply because they have found their proof. They can measure the energy lines in the body and their effects with the latest equipment. Eastern medicine has had its own proof for over five thousand years with countless results of healing and recovery.

Some of the other energy systems are the chakras and the aura, among many more. Everything that has ever occurred to you in your life is processed through your various energy systems. Your experiences have been stored as cellular memory within the body and as patterns within the energy fields. When you take that further and consider that what you focus on gets bigger, you also know this sets up a vibrational frequency around you that mirrors the very patterns that were originally set in. This means that you can experience again and again the dynamics that you experienced as a child, unless and until shifts take place within your energy fields. These shifts are easily done if the right tool is used, just as with anything. This is where personal growth comes in. Through psychotherapy, coaching, meditation, contemplation, visualization, and energy work you can make the shifts that will clear out old, limiting patterns and fortify the naturally health giving state you then get to enjoy.

As Within, So Without

What's also understood now, as we look closer and closer into the world's inner spaces, is that everything vibrates. We usually can't see that happening with the naked eye, of course, though it can sometimes be felt. Depending on the vibrational rate or frequency of something, we experience it as anything from solid matter, which vibrates more slowly, to a subtle feeling, which may vibrate more rapidly. Even *thinking* is an energy that has its own measurable vibrational frequencies. When something vibrates at a particular frequency it has been found to affect the substance around it, which leads forward-thinking scientists to understand that our thoughts, our states, and our beliefs actually affect and transform the world around us.

With that in mind, imagine yourself for a moment as an old-fashioned film projector in a movie theater. The thoughts, beliefs, images, and states you consistently tend toward are the pictures, sounds, and stories that the frames of the celluloid film itself contains; and the movie you watch out there on the screen is the world you live in, the outer manifestation of that internal footage. In simple terms, the external world is an *out-picturing* of your internal world. Now, this doesn't mean that when you watch someone suffer or something devastating happens to them that you then say, *Well they're just creating that reality.* When we decide we are all individually creating our own realities we are buying into the illusion of separation. The truth is we create our reality together and, *at the same time,* we each have the power to manifest our own experiences. We have a responsibility to focus on the positive for ourselves and the world, and must remain connected for our species to continue. Our reality is ever-changing because of the changes in our collective mind.

If we take all this further we also find that most of what we humans experience as "life" is actually an internal *interpretation* on external data. William Shakespeare wrote, ". . . for there is nothing either good or bad, but thinking makes it so." With our thinking we place judgments and conjecture on everything we see, hear, smell, feel, and taste, which means one person may have a completely different experience of exactly the same event than another person just because of this interpretive filter. This interpretive filter has been affected by what we have been taught by others, by our past experiences, by our personalities, and more than anything by what we have chosen to focus on. We decide that life is a certain way (which is an interpretation) and that in turn creates our beliefs. That then affects how we respond to external events, which in turn affects outcomes and responses from others and the world around us. And because of the energetic vibration of those interpretations we then create more of the same type of circumstances and events that back those beliefs up, until we are stuck in a cycle of the same movie playing over and over! This is one reason we find ourselves stuck in career, financial, health, and relationship patterns, and this is why happiness is essentially an inside job.

If you think about a pattern of rejection (and as an actor, you've probably experienced that) it's likely that it started way before you became an actor. The pattern of rejection may have turned up in your life differently before, but it would have been set up early in your life and perhaps even been part of what attracted you (unconsciously) to the business of acting in the first place. That's not to take away from what else attracted you. The creativity, the interest in the human spirit or psyche, the freedom to express, the possibilities, whatever else you love about acting, are all valid and important reasons you may have decided to choose this path. We are exploring vibrational patterns for a moment.

When "Janel" was a child, her father used to spend a lot of time at work and in the garage building things—by ratio more time than in the home with the family. Janel pulled that particular data out of the overall picture of her childhood, highlighted it, and ignored the data that Dad did actually spend *some* time with her and the rest of the family. Janel then made meaning of the selected data, interpreted it as her dad rejecting her, and used that interpretation to create beliefs—beliefs that men will reject her, that she was unlovable, and that the world didn't want her. She then behaved accordingly. She could have chosen any number of behaviors and many of them would have told the world that she wasn't worth much. Shyness, over-apologizing, people-pleasing, and being shut down or overbearing are just some examples of possible behaviors Janel could have adopted because of these beliefs. As it turned out Janel became what she called a *show-off*. Part of why she went into acting was to get the attention she felt she had not received as a child. Then the sheer number of *no's* as opposed to *yes's* Janel got, just like most other actors starting out on the auditioning trail, then triggered the same vibrational frequency that was created as a child, and she found herself in a cycle of interpreting the no's as personal rejection. That, then, had her creating more beliefs that she was unworthy and unlovable, and so the show-off behavior escalated, which was off-putting to the people who might have otherwise hired her. She got caught in a vibrational frequency of rejection.

In order to stop any pattern that's not working for you from running on a loop forever, you have to make the shifts inside you first, changing out your inner footage before the movie itself out there will ever change. The more you build an internal environment that allows happiness to exist and grow by healing, clearing, and transforming the interior of your own being, the more the world around you will respond with fulfilling experiences, making way for the natural state of joy to come through. Ultimately what you think about, how you think, what you believe, and what you say are great influences on your reality and your experiences. You not only can become very good at being happy, but also can become very good at being *un*happy by having limiting and constricting thoughts, beliefs, and language patterns. When it comes to your happiness those patterns determine what life is like for you no matter what your circumstances. Some actors are not happy no matter what positive circumstances or opportunities turn up, and there are some very happy actors who are not yet making money acting and don't have that television show or movie career, yet they have fulfilling lives and are moving along on their path "on-purpose".

The power you have is to train your brain to be more resourceful, to focus on the things that serve your happiness and that contribute to your success as an actor as you take the journey. It's always going to be a journey no matter where you are on the road. The *facts* about what happens to you in your life are not what will determine if you're happy or not, it's how you *feel* about what happens that will. That comes out of your interpretations, your beliefs, and how you hold it all in your consciousness. One of the most powerful keys toward raising your happiness set point is to take the actions that free you from limiting thinking patterns and to replace them with new ones—those with the highest and most positive vibrational frequencies.

Thoughts Are Things

You've probably heard of *cause and effect*. When you focus on something, you have the thoughts, the images in your brain that then affect how you feel and behave, and that in turn affects the world around you and how others respond to you. You then attract more of what it is you've been focusing on. You've probably noticed that when you're ready to perform, audition, or start a scene and you're thinking about whether you're going to mess it up, you inevitably do. Rarely will you find that your best work comes after a moment of imagining things going badly! On the other hand, when you imagine things going well and you focus on the intent your character has in your upcoming scene, the outcome is far more likely to be one that you (and everyone else for that matter) enjoy. Thoughts are the cause and the effect is your current reality. Change your thoughts (the cause) and you ultimately change your reality (the effect). It's also interesting to note that happy, wealthy, successful people *do* far less than you might expect. Whether they know it or not, their success in life has come out of how they habitually think and what they focus on, more than what they have done.

Some of the world's top scientists have done controlled studies to prove the effects that thought has on physical reality. It has been found that human thought can change how machines operate, how plants grow, how water is structured, and how cells behave. These and many other findings continue to unfold, suggesting that we have the ability to change the very structure and signaling of our physical reality from anywhere in the world by using our thoughts. The idea of mind over matter is now going from spiritual to scientific thinking.

Thinking positively has a direct link to what happens in our lives. The Dalai Lama, an expert on happiness, said, "Choose optimism, it feels better." Well, not only does it make us feel good to be optimistic, studies have found that optimistic people even live longer than pessimistic ones.

Positive thinking is a habit that gets practiced and built. As you can imagine, it goes along with positive emotions, and in order for these emotions to have a transformational impact they must be genuinely felt. Forced or fake positivity like "putting on a brave face" or "faking a smile" can do more harm than good if it's a habit. Realistic, optimistic thinking that leads to a heightened sense of possibility is what makes you feel inspired and enthusiastic about what you are doing. In a business that can be daunting and disappointing, optimism will be necessary to keep you going!

If you think about it, we need positive thinking now more than ever. We need it because we are much more resourceful people when we are under its influence, and in order to go through current global changes in the way we are being called to do so, we must be our best selves. Positive thinking makes us more creative. It helps us come up with solutions and compromises, and makes us more resilient and able to build more skills. Therefore positive thinking is not only going to help you as an actor, it's important for you to survive as a human being in a rapidly evolving world.

Positive thinking is focusing on what *is* working for you rather than on what *isn't*. It's imagining what you want to happen rather than what you fear might. You remember what was good about something or what you can learn from it, rather than what was terrible or what mistakes were made. These are just some examples. Positive thinking doesn't exclude taking time to admit mistakes, hurt, defeat, disappointment, or regret, it just doesn't allow for wallowing in them for too long. It's all about where you choose to *live*, remember? We cannot and must not deny the pain of life. It is inevitable and must be accepted for happiness to be sustainable. We just have to remember the good and live from there first. Focusing realistically on the good that came out of a meeting or an audition, rather than on what didn't go well, will serve you in the short and the long run. It will allow you to learn from it and install confidence for the next one.

Be mindful that, as you discover any limiting or negative thinking, judging yourself is *not* the key! Simply noticing, becoming a detached observer, and then finding another, more positive thought would be far more useful to you. Saying the new positive thought out loud can also anchor it in more strongly.

Another thing to observe in your thinking is *how* you're motivated to make a shift in your life. You may find that you make changes by moving *away* from what you don't want. You find you're consumed with the desire not to mess up that audition, you wish you were not in debt anymore, you want to lose that ten pounds, or you don't know if you can stand being a server for one more thankless day.

Getting clear about what's not working has its benefits. Back in the early '90s I had had enough of living hand-to-mouth, serving rude partygoers, and being chronically late with my rent. I knew I wanted to work full-time as an actor. That was my passion at the time and I just wasn't living it out. So I quit my catering job, declaring to my friends, "I'm not a plate-scraper, I'm an actor!" and therefore I was going to be only that. That was a risky move. There followed some tight times, yet it had me draw a line and it changed my life. However, that alone would not have been enough to set the universe scurrying to put me on a prime time show if I had not put the other very important parts of the change equation into the mix. Anytime you're driven to make a change through what's called an *away-from motivation*, you've been focusing on what you *don't* want, and you can tend to get stuck right there. What you put your thinking on gets bigger in your life. As the Hawaiian Huna principle puts it, "energy flows where attention goes." The great news is that when you put your attention on what you *do* want, that, too, begins to show up in your life.

One of the vital ingredients of creating positive change is getting clear about what you desire and moving into creative and positive thoughts about it. You also stand to benefit from moving into a *feeling tone* of those thoughts. What I mean by that is, you imagine the physical experience of what it is you want to move toward. Before I walked away from that catering job, I had spent many hours in my little bachelor pad thinking about what I desired and what my life would be like if I had those things. I would imagine in great detail the way it would look, feel like, sound like, taste like, and smell like. I would then literally get up and step into it as though I was stepping into a movie. I imagined I was right there living it out, that wonderful new life already true. I kept the feeling with me as much as possible and before long things began to shift. My auditions became more powerful, my interactions more confident; I felt different and therefore life was different. Yet it went further than that. Because I was using my five senses to "think" about what I desired, the universe began to build matter (solid reality) to fit that.

So, make sure you notice the *away from* and *toward* parts of your thinking. Then let the vision of what you want to move toward soak into who you are today. Make it real for yourself, in your thinking as well as all the way into your body.

When I was offered the female lead in that network television show I was no more talented than the next actor or actress out there. It wasn't luck. There was no hidden reason that this happened for me. It was about my thinking.

Your thinking is the ticket to the ride you will take. Yes, make sure you know what you don't want, *and* if you're going to linger anywhere or get really specific, make that about what you want to move toward. How *do* you want to feel in auditions? How much money would you like to have? How much do you want to weigh? What would you love to be spending your time and energy on? As you take it out of the unreachable future and place it right into the "now," watch what happens!

The Power of Words

There is an old saying, "Sticks and stones may break my bones, but words will never hurt me." This couldn't be further from the truth. Words can be destructive and painful, and they can be creative, healing, and positive. They have an extraordinary power, one that many of us have forgotten. There is another old saying, "From your mouth to God's ears." This describes an intelligence in the universe that's constantly listening to what we speak and then creating the experience of our lives accordingly. Not only does thought affect what happens in our reality, so do our words. Yes, words—written, spoken, and heard—have their own vibrational frequency depending on the meaning and origin behind them. Language patterns affect how we experience the world as well as the experiences of those around us. They also mirror our mental world and show us what is happening inside our own human systems. Our habitual language shows us what our relationship is with life.

I recall having a way to get Microsoft Word to automatically find and list the keywords in a document. These words showed up enough to be a pattern, and in listing them you could get a gist of the tone behind the text. I was reminded of this during a visit with a relative who used the word *annoying* in almost every exchange: "it's so annoying," or "that was annoying." I thought about what my computer would have produced out of his dialogue. And, of course, though this person is probably not conscious of his verbal habit, he would be the first to admit to an unhappy string of stressful and rocky relationships. Not only has he seen much of his life through the filter of annoyance, he has also attracted things, people, and circumstances that are perfectly set to grate on his nerves!

There is a palpable power of *intention* behind each and every word we speak, passed down through generations, and that intention is a creative force. We literally create our lives as we speak. The energy of what we put out creates more of that same energy in our experiences. If we habitually use words that describe fear, lack, or limit, we will very likely create more fearful, lacking, and limiting experiences in our lives. If we tend to use words that describe love and abundance, we create more love and abundance. You paint a picture of your life with certain colors and the painting will have a particular tone to it. Words create our present and therefore our future. They even create our past by coloring it with the meanings we use. Language creates our world; we then describe our experiences accordingly, and in turn create more of the same. Though we may not be conscious of our own language patterns, our subconscious is fully aware of the collective meaning in the words we use and it takes that as a template to interpret everything. We respond and behave according to that template, and then draw more of the same to us.

Our words are powerful clues as to why our lives are the way they are. They can trap us in misery or liberate us into whatever we desire. Words can be a pathway to raising our baseline state of happiness in significant ways!

There has been some wonderful work done by a Japanese researcher, Dr. Masaru Emoto. I first heard about him in 1998 from my mother who had met him at a crop circle convention in England. Dr. Emoto has spent years dedicating himself to his experiments with water crystals, finding that when positive words like *love* and *gratitude* are spoken near or written on paper and wrapped around a bottle of water, and that water is then frozen, the crystals that emerge under a microscope are consistently beautiful and complex. On the other hand, when words like *hate* and *resentment* are used, the water forms either incomplete and jagged crystals or no crystals at all.

Sound has a vibration, and apparently so do our words, no matter in what language. Emoto's experiments show us that thought and words themselves have enough of a specific vibration that they affect the very structure and purity of water, one way or another, depending on what type of thought. Considering that our bodies are made up of 55–78 percent water, depending on our age, weight, and gender, the effect thought and words have on our own bodies is likely profound!

Here's the part that I find really striking. Dr. Emoto has said that it takes about twenty-four hours for positive words to energize water and half an hour for music to do the same. Prayer, though, sent over any distance, creates stunning water crystals *instantly*. Not surprising, therefore, that recent scientific studies have shown prayer to have a dramatic influence on our health and well-being.

In 1996 I was studying the phenomena of words and their power, and I made it a year's experiment to change my language to support my goals. I began to speak about the things I desired in the present tense and the things I didn't want in the past tense. This way I was claiming what I desired, bringing it into the "now," and distancing myself from what I didn't want, giving myself the opportunity to begin anew in any given moment.

Additionally, instead of judging other people, situations, and experiences (as mentioned before), I would simply say, *It's just different*. I also began to eliminate or lessen the use of the words *try, can't, but, have to,* and *hate* from my language palette and to use more words like *intend to, get to, open to, grateful,* and *blessed.* My life began to shift in *big* ways. Because of this, and other factors, I went from being so broke I was about to move into my car, to earning a substantial income, living in two apartments, and having a very exciting career.

So, I invite you to listen to your own language patterns, without judgment, just noticing. What do you notice about the words that you tend to use? What do you want your keywords to be and what kind of a palette would you like your life to be made up of? Do you want to "awful-ize" and limit, or would you like to comment on the positive and expansive things that you intend for yourself, for the world, and for your loved ones? Do you aspire to vocalize what you appreciate and are grateful for? There is a great opportunity to become more conscious and discerning with your language, and therefore to be awake to the creation of your life. Your levels of happiness are dramatically affected by the words you use and the intentions behind them.

This is part of the amazing power each of us has to manifest lives for ourselves that fill us and the people around us full of happiness and the things we love.

Let Go of Limits

The human condition is one that, when seen from a distant perspective, can sometimes seem extraordinarily funny. We so often argue heatedly, *doggedly,* for our own limitations. The thing is, whenever we do that, we win the fight! What a silly victory of human folly, and one that belongs in a sitcom perhaps. Yet, ultimately, when asked if we *really* want to keep our limitations, the answer is often a resounding *no.*

So, what's the big conflict? It's probably a number of things, but simple language habits are one part of the conflict that can be easily shifted.

You know how some characters on television or in movies have catchphrases? Those catchphrases become the de facto trademark or signature of the character. And, rather like our "it's so annoying" person, have you ever noticed how someone you know has one or two limiting phrases that they tend to say over and over, like, *Hey, life is tough,* or *I'm always late?* Well, chances are you have your own habitual phrases, many of which you may not have noticed yet.

Your happiness levels are dependent on exploring what you say. Language habits can show you how you've been limiting yourself. They can also, in changing them, have a really big impact on whether you're going to continue doing that or not. As you let some limiting habits go, you empower yourself just that bit more to be expansive, creative, and resourceful.

Again, on your journey into higher levels of happiness, the key is to simply *notice*, not to be hard on yourself or give yourself an excuse to feel bad. It's an opportunity to be curious about what you've been doing and then decide what you would rather do instead. The fabulous news is that you have choice!

One thing you may benefit from noticing is what I call "should-ing"— that is, using the word *should*. When you use the word *should* to make a particular choice about something, you're probably using it to *make* yourself do or feel something even when your deeper self may not fully align with it. If "should-ing" on yourself becomes an unconscious pattern it can make you very unhappy. Your happiness is dependent on making choices that come out of your core values and desires. If those are overridden by "shoulds," you're not honoring the very deepest essence of who you are. The word *should*, when it concerns making decisions in life, tends to come from the head rather than the heart. It's generally based on assumptions, unexplored beliefs, or on other people's values or needs. Fear is very often a driving force behind "shoulds." It is the fear of not being enough, of not doing the "right" thing, and of making choices that other people won't approve of. This doesn't leave room for gut instinct or deep desire to emerge. This is not to say that it's the best choice to ignore the "shoulds" that do come up and only go with "wants" or deep desires. That, as a default, might be irresponsible and may not take others' needs into account. The idea here is to take notice of what your head is telling you to do when it says *should*, paying attention to what the heart and gut desires as well, and evaluating the best choice from a fully informed place. If you recognize the "should-ing" strategy in yourself and choose to let it go, freeing yourself from the misery that brings, you can learn a new strategy that aligns with your deepest values.

Right now you can explore this by thinking about something you believe you *should* do or feel, and then identifying something you get to *choose* to do. When you think about the two different items, notice your feelings with each. Which choice feels heavier or full of pressure, and which choice seems lighter and more expansive? This difference will help you to become more aware of when you're aligning with your true self, your essence or not. Anytime you have a decision to make you can check in with your feelings and identify whether the choice you're making is a "should" or an "I want to because it aligns with my values and my deepest desire for myself and others." Let yourself explore the two possibilities. It may not be cut-and-dry to you as to which is which. This is simply an opportunity to take a step back and observe so that you get to know yourself and begin to trust your feelings more.

As an experiment, you could take a week and decide to avoid using the word *should*. If it pops out of your mouth, be kind to yourself and just consider for a moment whose voice it was. All you need to do is notice. You're not here to fix anything, nor to "should" on yourself about "should-ing"! Noticing and taking a moment to make a conscious choice of some kind is enough. Again, awareness is the greatest agent for change.

Another habit many of us get into is using *catastrophic language*. It would stand to reason that many actors are naturally dramatic, and that can create dramatic results. When you use catastrophic language like, *I am devastated!* or *I bombed!* or *You ruined my life!* you send a message to the universe, to others, and to yourself that there is an emergency, a catastrophe at hand, and everything else then follows suit. Your own body will respond accordingly by becoming stressed and sick, and your relationships will become more dysfunctional, dramatic, and even emotionally or physically violent. In fact what shows up in most of the rest of your world will mirror the catastrophe you've claimed with your language. Catastrophic language is used to describe feelings that are extreme, but that doesn't necessarily describe the situation in accurate proportions. The feelings have come, not from your essential self, but from your past and your fearful thinking. It has little to do with who you are when you trust the process of life.

Another example of how we can create catastrophic language is with *universals*. Universals are a big part of our language in the Western world. Examples of universals are the words *always, everyone*, and *never*. Universals affect our self-esteem. They put us in the role of a victim, of life and of other people. They can disempower us tremendously. When we say things like *I am always late for auditions*, or **Everyone is competitive with me**, the question to ask is, *Really? Always? Everyone?* The answer will likely be, *Well, no, not everyone*, or *Okay, not always*. When you can admit that, you can start to take your power back by saying instead, *I have had a tendency to be late for auditions at times and I am open to shifting that and being on time from now on*, or *I have interpreted other actors as being competitive at times and am open to noticing when they do seem to be friendly to me.* The language in the latter examples is just far more empowering and open to the possibility of good. Instead of *I never win anything*, you can think of times in your life when you have won something, even if it was a game of Trivial Pursuit or a little plastic toy from a cereal box. This way you remember that you've won at times and will therefore be far more open to it happening again. Remember, *what we focus on gets bigger.* In knowing there are no absolutes and that there probably *have* been positive experiences in most areas of your life, you will bring more of them to you!

Additionally, it's also only fair to avoid using universals when it comes to other people. Saying someone *always* or *never* does something is usually totally unrealistic and serves nothing to create success in your relationships. Happiness will come out of recognizing and respecting the truth about yourself, others, and the world around you.

Negations are another kind of limiter and are simply negative statements. Examples are *do not, not, won't,* and *can't.* When we talk about what we *do not* want or what we *can't* do we are putting attention on that. Remember again, "energy flows where attention goes," so when we use negations in our language we actually create more of what we don't want. For example, when you have an important meeting, audition, scene, or task ahead of you and you say to yourself, *Don't screw this up*—you focus on *screwing up.* Your entire system is braced for the possibility of that occurring, which will put you in fear, and fear is not a place to create the best outcome. There emerges the self-fulfilling prophecy!

Right now as you read this, take a moment, and whatever you do, don't swallow. Take all the time you need to notice what happens when you tell yourself *not* to swallow. Do you find you were compelled to swallow? Now try this instead: relax your throat and jaw. Notice the breath move gently through your nose and into your open throat. Did you notice the difference? In the first instance you were focused on *not* swallowing, and swallowing was therefore what you were likely compelled to do, or at least there may have been some sort of conflict about it. In the second incident you were focused on relaxing your throat, and in doing that you probably didn't feel compelled to swallow. Do you see the difference in what you're drawn to depending on what you focus on? This is the same principal as the *toward* motivation versus the *away-from* motivation explored earlier in this chapter.

I often like to give new talent a shot and I had heard about a young headshot photographer in Los Angeles who had some interesting photos in his online portfolio. Rather than recommending him to any of my clients right off the bat I decided to have some pictures taken by him of myself, and to bring my husband along as well. My husband needed some publicity photographs for his latest book release and this seemed like a good opportunity to test-drive the young artist. His studio was a loft in downtown Los Angeles, and the lighting and atmosphere immediately seemed hip and fresh. We were all enthusiastic. My shoot was up first and I got into place in front of the camera. The first thing I noticed was the photographer's language. Almost every sentence was a *don't* do this or that. Fortunately I've been in a lot of photo shoots over the decades, so despite my growing discomfort I was able to translate much of it and come up with my own version of what might work better. On the other hand, my husband had not had his picture taken professionally more than a couple of times prior to that day, and he needed and deserved to feel fully supported and relaxed. That turned out to be almost impossible with all the negations flying around! The photographer became increasingly negative, saying things like *don't turn your head that way, don't smile, don't frown, don't lift your head*, etc., and my poor husband became more and more nervous and utterly confused as to what to actually do with himself! It was a prime example of how paralyzing negations can be. I asked the photographer if he would give my husband some instruction as to what he *did* want him to do, but his habit was so set in that he continued the way he had started. Needless to say (and please excuse the negations here) the photos were not the best and he is not one of our recommendations!

So, when it comes to your words, the happiness of others is also profoundly important. With language, when you talk about or affirm what you *do* want, you expand it. If you focus again and again on what someone else is doing wrong or what you don't like you will likely create more of that. *Do not, should, try, never*, and *always*, as mentioned before, can be harmful not only to you, but to those in your life. In situations where you're unhappy with someone else's behavior, rather than complaining or criticizing and saying, *do **not** do (that thing you don't like),* or *you **always** do (that thing),* it's more effective to think about what it is you would *rather they do* and then ask them in simple, positive terms if they would do it. Saying, *please do (the thing you would **rather** they do)* gives them a place to head *toward*. It opens up *toward* motivation. Besides, the "do not's" in our language give little information about what we really want and very often have people defending themselves and digging in their heels. That serves very little. No one gets to be very happy when walls are up and defenses set.

A far more positive and effective example of language when it comes to communicating what you need is to be clear about what that is, and then thank, or at least acknowledge, the other person when they take the actions to fulfill your request. That creates positive reinforcement. In relationships people won't always move toward what you want, or they may just forget. For example, say your manager doesn't want to call a producer you've asked him to contact regarding a certain role; a simple and respectful conversation is in order so you can understand his reason. If your manager says he is willing, however, and still doesn't make the call, the move might be to simply ask him again. Sometimes you may have to repeat yourself or let something go that doesn't work for the other person, and either way it's important in relationships to keep calm, be respectful, and stay constructive, keeping the channels open to a dialogue in friendly terms.

Not only is your happiness dependent on being compassionate, patient, and loving with yourself, dealing with other people's fears and egos in the same fashion is going to be part of that, and your language contributes profoundly to that path. You get to create greater happiness for yourself and for others through your words.

Those Tricky Affirmations

Affirmations are a powerful way to begin creating what you want and therefore increasing your happiness levels. An affirmation is the assertion that something exists or is true. They serve you if they are positive, powerful, personal, and in the present tense, and are more effective, even, if spoken out loud. If used well they can align you with the divine flow of the universe. However, something many teachers and coaches out there fail to recognize or pass on is that affirmations can be rather tricky. What if there is a part of you that either doesn't buy it, or doesn't want what the rest of you wants? Wording is very, very important for the success of your affirmations. Statements like *I have a million dollars in the bank* (when you actually have seven dollars in the bank and are two months late on your rent) are going to make a part of you jump up and say *bull!* And quite rightly so! You may also find that you affirm something like *I am the lead in a TV series*, while a part of you says *no!* because that would mean you would not be able to see your family as much because of the hours involved. You can feel the conflict in your whole being when that happens.

The key to affirmations is to get clear about the overall feeling or good that you want out of something, rather than the *thing* itself. You then affirm that being in your life right now. It's vitally important to take a position of openness, using words like *I am open to . . .* Some examples of powerful affirmations are these: *Right now I am open to good and abundance in my life, I am available to the vibrant health in my body, I embrace myself exactly as I am right now,* and *I am grateful for all the ease and joy in my life; I am so blessed.* This way you open yourself to the source of abundance and good that the universe is constantly providing.

Language patterns affect how we feel. Our language also mirrors our mental world by showing us what's going on inside. We want to learn how to talk to ourselves as a good friend would, and that friend would want the very best for a loved one. It takes some consciousness on our part to shift patterns in language, and the effects can be profoundly positive. It's a process, and a privilege, that we can do this at all. Enjoy increasing your happiness by learning a powerful new language!

A Secret? Not So Much

We have been exploring what some people call the *law of attraction*, which in its most simple state is the idea that "like attracts like." Basically, our thoughts create our reality. This knowledge has been readily available for centuries, yet recently there has been a surge of interest in this law, partly because of scientific understanding that correlates with ancient spiritual knowledge, and partly because our new technology has allowed the information to move more quickly through the masses via the Internet and film. The general masses have now suddenly become more open to the law of attraction and its principles again, not because it has come out of some secret vault, but because we are ready, collectively, to regain our power. We must in such changing times as these.

The fact that so many people are now open to understanding this universal truth is, in itself, very positive, yet there is a real concern that people are taking the new messages about this as a quick fix for their lives. In a world where many feel powerless and unsure of their future, that's understandable; however, it has to be known that to simply close your eyes and imagine what you want is not necessarily going to manifest it. If that were so, we probably would not be in a world where there is starvation and war.

The law of attraction works for *everyone, all of the time, with no exceptions.* It produces exactly what we hold in our minds and with our feelings. In order to tap into the benefits of the law, we need to understand the nature of our individual and collective thoughts and feelings. The mind is a slippery thing. As soon as we try to control our individual thoughts, we remember that *the mind has a mind of its own.* Feelings can be equally slippery. There are hidden beliefs within us that drive our thoughts and feelings. For example, though the conscious mind may say, *I want a loving relationship*, a hidden belief may say, *I don't deserve love.* If you have wanted a different career than you've had and you have imagined it, talked about it, and even written about it and it hasn't happened yet, it may be because you have beliefs inside you that still aren't aligned with it. That, then, will manifest an outcome that reflects the unconscious belief.

The key to any kind of positive manifestation is a really strong sense of self-awareness. This is absolutely essential to creating a clear channel between mind and matter. Manifesting what you desire comes out of resourceful states, clear intentions, what you pay attention to, and what your goals are, and all of these must be supported by your beliefs. You must dedicate yourself to knowing how you are *organized* inside and how to transform unresourceful beliefs into resourceful ones before you can effectively use your mind to create.

There are some simple tools that cut through what it can otherwise take years to accomplish. Amazing new technologies of human potential are arising. We are in an exciting time. There is no fix. There are, however, ways you can powerfully connect with the law of attraction. I urge you to look for the multitude of resources out there and not rely on only one or two to give you the answer. Read, watch, and learn. Get to know yourself. Get creative. Nothing is ever a secret from you if you are ready to see it.

Your B.S.

B.S. is a pet name some people have for our belief systems. Many of our belief systems are very valuable and we want to keep them, and some are a bit of BS that don't serve us or anyone else. The idea is to sift through what's what!

As a coach to some very successful actors, directors, writers, and producers I've been interested in some of the belief systems that have emerged in our explorations, and have noted how, without fail, resourceful beliefs create resourceful outcomes, and limiting beliefs create limiting outcomes. For example, one of my actor clients had some very strong beliefs that he fit the genre of television in certain roles and therefore he became very successful in that particular realm. However, when he decided he wanted to branch out into film, he came across tremendous fears and just couldn't make heads or tails of his sudden lack of confidence. He had had a history, after all, of feeling pretty self-assured. He had reached a roadblock within his subconscious. With the right kind of questions we established that his resourceful belief (the one about him fitting into television in certain roles) also came with a limiting belief, and that was that he didn't fit into *film* and wasn't seen by others as convincing in roles other than the ones he had been playing. There was really no *evidence* that his limiting belief was true. It had been built primarily from assumptions. So, we explored the possibility that there was another, more resourceful belief due.

First, though, *getting rid of* the old belief wasn't going to be the answer. Every part of us has a benefit, and it is essential to find out what that is so we don't throw the baby out with the bathwater. We established that his old belief had a benefit to it, which was one of protection. His belief had been protecting him from the roles that stretched him, and from the parts of his own personality his family had had judgments about—the wilder, more spontaneous and dangerous sides to him. As an adult, he was now ready to let the bonds of that judgment go and free himself to play in the realms of any role he chose to play in from now on, knowing that his mom and dad would probably, realistically, be just fine with it. That cleared the way for him to then choose a new belief, knowing that he would still be protected from anything that wasn't going to be okay because he was now an adult and able to discern in ways he couldn't as a very young man starting out. He created a powerful new belief about the genre of film for his craft and the roles he was able to play, and, as you can imagine, his film career began to take on interesting and expansive new colors.

It is our beliefs that can shape our thoughts and, therefore, that co-create our lives. Yet very often our limiting beliefs are unconscious, so it requires the kind of exploration that coaching provides to recognize and then transform them. Our beliefs come in great part from what we have been taught by other people. These are called *introjected beliefs*. We are given data, someone around us reacts to the data, we interpret what that reaction means, we come to conclusions about it, and then we begin to act accordingly. We have then set up a belief system around that particular data. As an example, a small child might be crawling around on the living room carpet having a wonderful time testing out her new "space suit." She may notice a small, harmless money spider on the ground in front of her and in curious joy reach out to touch it to see what it would feel like. Then mom comes in and, because of her own experience some twenty-five years ago, she suddenly lets out a bloodcurdling scream, "No, no, no, that's bad!" scooping up her shocked child and whisking her away to another room. The child interprets this outburst as meaning that all spiders are terrifying and life threatening, and she concludes that she must do all she can to avoid being anywhere near spiders again. This girl grows up to respond hysterically around spiders. She has no memory of the incident from her childhood and believes that her fear of all spiders is completely rational. Her behavior is severely limited by this belief.

This simple example illustrates how other people's beliefs about the world and about us can form the very ways in which we think! We may take actions and make choices, therefore, based on things that have very little to do with us or our own higher knowing. And because we manifest what we believe, even though we may not like or want how that presents itself, *we will draw to us the very things that will reinforce that belief.* Someone who has a fear of spiders may find that they are visited, and perhaps even bitten, by more spiders than anyone else they know! If you believe spiders are a deadly threat, then you might draw to you the experience that they are everywhere and your home is not safe. If you believe that you are not enough, you will draw criticism, failure, and limits to you. If you believe love hurts, then relationships will hurt. If you believe life is difficult, then difficult experiences will show up for you. What you believe, you expand.

The good news is that this principle also works for the positive beliefs you have. If you believe it's easy to make money, then you will draw money to you. If you believe you rarely get colds, you will rarely get colds. If you believe you're lovable, you will draw loving relationships into your life. As soon as you notice your beliefs or listen to your thought patterns and the words you use, you can then understand how you got where you are. The best news is you can change your beliefs.

Wherever you are in your career as an actor, at whatever level, you may have asked the question, *How will I become happier here?* One of the ways to do that is to take actions that free you from the limiting beliefs you've had about yourself and your world, and they can only be let go of once they are recognized.

Most of your limiting beliefs are unconscious. If they were conscious you would be more likely to have changed them. However, by just exploring what your beliefs are you can bring them to the surface and that in itself makes them conscious and changeable.

When you've identified and looked at the kinds of beliefs that haven't been serving you and your career, you can release them and then replace them with ones that do. It's the same process you go through when you clean out your closets. You keep the things that work for you, and you throw away, or let go of, the things that don't work for you anymore. Those limiting beliefs, just like your closet throwaways, came in at some point in your life because they were probably useful to you at that time. They may have even allowed you to feel you could survive in some very scary or dangerous situations. The important thing to look at is whether those beliefs serve you *now*.

When you find a belief that *does* serve you, you can then cherish it and give it a lot of attention. By giving what serves you attention and gratitude, you will expand the energy it draws to you.

"Nicole" had had some success in the commercial world, yet had not been able to break into theatrical television or film despite five years of "pounding the pavement" as she described it. Her frustration was palpable. After establishing what she wanted to accomplish, we talked a little bit about what she believed had been stopping her from working in film and episodic television.

"I think it's been not having the right agents, the right opportunities," Nicole said.

"Okay," I replied, "what else?"

"Umm, I don't know. Probably because I'm not really interesting enough to be in film."

"Not interesting enough?" I asked. We had very quickly arrived at a belief Nicole had been living with about herself.

"Yeah."

"That's interesting!" I said ironically. "Say more." Nicole laughed.

"Well, like when it comes to working in features, I'm not interesting enough. I'm likeable, but not interesting or watchable for more than a few seconds. I mean, I've managed to hold peoples attention for short spurts, and that's probably why I've done so many commercials!"

"Ah," I said, "you're not interesting according to whom?"

Nicole blinked at me for a few seconds looking for the answer inside her mind.

"According to me I guess."

"And what data did you use to come to this conclusion?" I asked gently.

"Because I haven't done any film or TV yet," she said as we both smiled, knowing what was coming next.

"It's the chicken or the egg isn't it?"

"Yes, it is!" We laughed.

"It seems as though you started out doing commercials and had some success there," I said, "yet because film was going to come a bit later, you created a belief that actually limited your ability to imagine yourself doing film. And if we can't imagine ourselves doing something, it's very rare that we will end up doing it."

"Crap!" She exclaimed and slapped her hands on her thighs in frustration.

I encouraged Nicole, as she explored these areas, to be gentle with herself. It's important that we each know there is nothing "wrong" with us for having limiting beliefs. Everyone is taught some limiting beliefs to one degree or another and there are experiences that reinforce those beliefs over our lives. I reminded Nicole in that moment that there was probably a whole lot "right" with her for having the courage to face these things and do something to shift them.

As we talked more, Nicole discovered other limiting beliefs that had been holding her back, both about herself and about the business. She also found some positive and resourceful beliefs that I encouraged her to celebrate.

"Those resourceful beliefs are some of the treasures that have brought you the good things in your life."

"I am really glad I have them too!" she exclaimed.

"Yes, and as you discover the *limiting* beliefs you've had, just know that because you've believed something doesn't necessarily mean it's true. You get to decide, for example, whether it's true that you're interesting enough to be on film or not."

Nicole considered this. I continued, "Nicole, what have you been *doing* because of that old, limiting belief?"

"Like what?" she asked.

"Well, it might have been actions you've taken in your life, relationship or behavior patterns you've had, ways you've been treating yourself, how you've felt. For example, if someone has a belief that they are unattractive, they might wear a lot of makeup, hide their face under sunglasses, wear baggy clothes, go on extreme diets, cut themselves, avoid sex, or spend their savings on plastic surgery or clothing. So, what actions and behaviors have you led yourself to because of believing you're not interesting enough to be on film?"

"Haha!" she exclaimed with new clarity. Nicole realized through our continued conversation that she had been avoiding submitting herself for film roles. Her limiting belief had also stopped her from contacting the theatrical agents she would like to meet because she thought they would "laugh her out of the room." Her belief also meant that in acting classes she had raced through her lines, or chosen really short scenes or comedy sketches, so she wouldn't have to "bore anyone."

As she discovered what actions she had taken because of her belief, Nicole's eyes began to well up with tears. She discussed a number of other behaviors and actions that had come about because of the belief she'd had about herself. It was a tough, yet valuable awareness of what she had been setting up in her own life.

"And how has all that affected you? What did you create though all those behaviors and actions?" I asked.

"I created being stuck! I have been feeling so stuck and frustrated and haven't known why and what to do about it all."

"Yes. I imagine that's been really hard," I said with sympathy. It had been hard. It's hard for us all when we have any kind of hidden limiting belief, because it has us behaving in ways that stop us from going where we want to go. We label ourselves *self-sabotaging* or *procrastinating* and feel helpless to stop it. When we discover, finally, through working with a coach or doing any kind of personal development, what the limiting beliefs have been that are at the root of it all, we realize that we have been setting ourselves up. That, then, can be liberating. And again, importantly, this is not about blaming ourselves.

"What you're doing here is looking at the effects this belief has had on your life so that you can understand how much it will benefit you to create a more resourceful belief. Please be very kind and compassionate with yourself here knowing that you've done the best you've known to do with the information you've had," I encouraged Nicole.

She smiled through the tissue against her face and nodded her understanding.

"What would you like to create for yourself *instead*, Nicole?"

"I want to create movement instead!" she laughed.

"Yes!" I said. "Movement."

"I want to make it so that I have a career in film! I want to guest star on TV shows. I would like to feel like I am worthy of being in this business and of doing film and television."

"Okay. What will you need to *do* in order to create those things?" I piped in.

"Well, first of all I will need to start getting in front of casting people for film and TV! I need to start submitting myself for roles. I need to get a theatrical agent. I need to get myself a new headshot. I also need to start taking myself seriously and doing meaty scenes in class and see myself differently."

"Well, yes, and that last part brings me to my next question which is, what is the new, empowering belief you will have to have in order to do these things?"

I explained to Nicole that really useful beliefs are usually not complicated and can be stated in simple language. It also helps to presuppose something resourceful about yourself like *Because I have . . .* or *Because I am . . .* and continue with a positive result of that like *. . . I get to . . .* Nicole's new belief was "Because I am interesting and unique, I get to be creative in whatever I choose to do!"

Nicole stood up and stepped into a space in the room we were in. She brought up the *feeling tone* of her new belief and tried it on.

The physical body is a very immediate and fairly easy route to freeing ourselves from limiting beliefs because it's made up of dense energy. The body is something we can see, touch, smell, taste, and hear through our more basic human perception. It is a tangible vehicle that we can learn to master and therefore work with much more easily than the mental and emotional selves. The mind, body, and heart are all in creation together. Stepping into the feeling tone of a new empowering belief, and then breathing slowly and purposefully, can be a powerful way to gauge if it's "right" or not. Breathing is a physical act, and it affects the ways we think and feel immediately. Your subconscious stores old memories, patterns, and beliefs, and with your conscious mind and your emotions involved you will be able to shift into what's more resourceful quite easily when you start through the senses of the body. You can begin with the outside and work your way in, as well as start within and work outward.

Nicole soaked the feeling tone of the new belief into her physical body, noticing how it felt to her, tweaking it as a statement until it felt powerful and right to her through and through.

This process can be repeated with all the beliefs we discover in our-selves. The journey for you now might be to ask what you've believed about yourself, the world, money, sex, life, death, other people, casting directors, producers, the studios, auditioning, acting, working, creativity, health, you name it, anything that's part of your life. And looking back through them, decide from your highest self which of those beliefs are useful and resource-ful for you and which are limiting. By doing this you will get to know yourself better. Sorting through the closets of your subconscious mind you give yourself the choice to either keep what you find, or let it go and replace it with something that serves your happiness instead.

Life says, I will treat you as you treat me. If you see me as difficult I will be dif-ficult. If you see me as painful I will be painful. If you see me as a miracle I will be a miracle. If you see me as a fruitful I will be fruitful.

Whatever you focus on expands. You have the power to decide what you believe about yourself and your world, and because of that, how happy you would like to be. Reminding yourself that you are a sacred and eternal being is the process it takes to reform your beliefs. Anything is possible when you return to the light.

CHAPTER 6

Yesterday Is Not as It Seems

Life shrinks or expands according to one's courage.

~ A N A Ï S   N I N

Lessons of the Lotus

The lotus has inspired people from all over the world for many centuries and has been legendary in both folklore and religious mythology. For the ancient Egyptians the lotus flower was a symbol of creation, renewal, and rebirth. For the Hindus it signifies beauty and nonattachment. Every part of the lotus has been eaten or used as a medicine. By all accounts it's a very special plant, yet to me the real magic of the lotus surrounds the story of how it unfolds into itself.

Let me share. This beautiful plant grows in muddy waters of ponds and lakes, and even in some of the world's most stagnant swamplands. Its roots begin way down in the muck, deep in the underwater soil. Its long, cylindrical stalk unfolds and passes through the darkness as it moves slowly and determinedly using every cell in its being, every part of its energy, to make its way toward the light above. As it moves instinctively upward, the water around it begins to thin out becoming lighter and easier to move through. Finally one day the plant bursts beyond the surface of the water, meeting its intent. The magnificent lotus blossom unfolds gradually, one petal at a time until full bloom the sun touches the flower, flooding it with warmth and light.

This is what I hold out as possible for each one of us on our own journey through life. We are each on an adventure of upliftment, *whether we know it or not.*

As the lotus reaches the surface of the water it becomes the courage we seek to continue, and the fragrance of love we seek in its divinity. The flower is a celebration of itself in a way that we are being called to celebrate ourselves. The lotus inspires us to move beyond the darkness of our past and continue to believe that the light is ahead, waiting for us to realize it, never having been gone despite the absence of it in our eyes. The lotus inspires us to excel, to reach new heights, and to believe in the potency that lies inside, ready to burst forth into the world. The lotus shows us, not only what's possible, but also what may be the very reason we are here. We each have the right to realize the truth of who we are and to live through that in everything we experience and all that we express. Each one of us has the intrinsic ability to create peace, happiness, and abundance. In the midst of your darkest places, new life is possible; you just need to take a small step in a new direction and everything begins to shift. Even if that means taking tiny steps to align and align and align. Every moment is bursting with the opportunity to begin your life again. The yearning in your heart contains a map to the treasure. Your guide is love.

The Past and Your Craft

As an actor you probably use your past as material for your work. Your history is full of feelings, memories, experiences, and knowledge that fill your characters and your performances with life. Even when you use "what ifs" for your work they are based on your beliefs and your own experiences, and those come out of your past. Your past has been useful to you in many ways, and chances are it has also been very limiting, or at least the ways in which you've been *holding the past in your consciousness* have probably been limiting you. Remember how that big elephant believed that he was still little and that the bracelet on his ankle could still hold him in place?

As a species we are very good at thinking about the past and the future. Not a lot of time is spent in the present moment, which is strange if you think about it, because the "now" is the only thing that's real in any given moment. The past is important for us to learn from. We get to look back and review how we handled something and decide if we want to repeat it or do something different next time. We get to make new choices, we can set new boundaries, find new ways of doing things, communicate differently, or move in the world more consciously because of hindsight. We gather information and become wiser by reviewing the past with a detached eye and an open heart. However, the truth of it is that when we humans are thinking about the past we are usually regretting something that happened and feeling bad about it.

Remember monkey mind? The mind is like a monkey constantly jumping from branch to branch. It jumps from past to future, from thought to thought, from regret to worry, chattering madly all the while. We all have this tendency to some degree. Monkey mind is basically the neurotic mind. It creates tremendous amounts of sustained anxiety and doubt, and this in turn creates lack of trust in the self and in the world. Happiness is not much of an option in that space; so for happiness to become more of a living, sustainable state we must not only become more connected with the present, we must also clean up the unfinished emotional "stuff" of the past.

But I have to have all these emotions inside me for my craft! you might say.

I understand seeing your emotional life as fuel for your craft. Some top acting coaches in Hollywood encourage their students to be "as crazy as the business," and to dig deeply and frequently into their suffering. I disagree with that way of teaching. If, again, you think of everything as energy and you think of the past (memories, beliefs, thoughts, and most significantly emotions) as being either stuck and constricted or flowing and expansive, then you can imagine that completing the unfinished, stuck, constrictive emotional business of the past and allowing it to become healed, and therefore fluid and expansive, will allow your craft to become more fluid and expansive along with it. Completing or healing the past doesn't mean you can't access your feelings about it. It just means you don't have to *suffer* anymore. It means you don't have to be a victim of it anymore. It means you don't have to be a prisoner of your thoughts and your feelings. It means you can learn from your past at last, and you can begin to create a future based on that new knowledge.

Time is an interesting thing. We humans tend to live in the narrow dimension of time that we have all agreed upon. The clock ticks, tells us a number, and we all decide together that it's a certain hour; yet it's really just an idea we have adopted in order to move at about the same pace as a species. We look at the sun going down and we act accordingly. Certainly the ebb and flow of hours, days, and seasons has energetic vibrations of its own, and there is a certain order and flow to the honoring of it that allows us to be a synergistic collective force. However, that's only a sliver of the vast aspects of the universe. Time has far more dimensions to it than we are normally consciously aware of, so much so that scientists have great difficulty explaining the ways in which time works. Time is not linear. It is bendable and multidimensional and has qualities that most of us cannot fathom. Even if we could, it would be impossible to describe with our limited language.

When it comes to our own experience of time, most of us think of the past as having tangibly occurred, set into reality almost as though it were filled with solid objects that got created as we traveled the path of our lives. In fact the truth may be that we are floating around in infinite layers of time and space all at the same time, with everything that has occurred just a dream and everything that's to come having already happened. Whatever the truth about time and space, we benefit from thinking beyond the narrow field of past and future so that we can begin to loosen our grip on the fear of both.

Some of us have really challenging lifetimes and some have easier ones. That's just the way it is. We all, however, have losses to face and lessons to learn, and we only benefit from doing what we can to heal and let go of the past. Gary Craig, creator of the Emotional Freedom Technique (or EFT), a type of energy psychology, has shown that this can be done quickly and thoroughly using the right tools. I have seen footage of him working with Vietnam veterans who had been suffering for decades from post-traumatic stress disorder. They had deep emotional and psychological issues because of the traumatic events they had been part of. Within minutes with his Tearless Trauma Technique (which includes telling the story while tapping on certain points on the body), he helped the veterans not only neutralize the feelings they had about the traumatic events, but they actually started yawning and saying they had become bored with them! Does that mean something like the life of a child in a Vietnamese village is not important anymore? No, it just means that the soldier who witnessed her death is not going to have to relive it over and over and suffer a living hell any longer. It means that his mind is no longer stuck in time somewhere that no longer exists. It means that the atrocity that happened gets to be in the past, and the man who is freed from it gets to live in the present.

Imagine your past as a filing cabinet that sits behind you just over your left shoulder that you can access whenever you want to. Now you can also imagine you get to pull out any folder and bring it forward in front of you to peruse for a while. When you're finished with it you then get to close it up, put it back in its proper file in the cabinet behind you, and close the cabinet drawer. Because you can do this, you can choose when and how you access your past. You're no longer at the mercy of your past jumping up whenever something reminds you of it. You're no longer walking with your past constantly in front of you, inside you, or around you. You no longer have to feel the past dragging you down a hole. You're free to be here and now, to create your vision of the future, and to know that your past has all the colors, shades, feelings, emotions, nuances, power, expression, wit, wisdom, moments, or anything else you might need for your craft however you want to access it, *whenever* you choose to access it. You have your power, and your past is under your command. It's *your* past after all! You're not *its* person. It does not own *you*. You own it and you can do with it whatever you choose.

When it comes to your craft as an actor, your filing cabinet is a resource for you, if and *only if* you need it. I would bet you have great human spirit and just being present and connected is enough. However if you need any extra color for a moment in a scene, this is a way to use your past and then put it away.

When I was still an actor, and before I knew how to do this, it would take me weeks to recover from a particularly dark or harrowing character or storyline. My acting coach would have me delve and wallow in the worst imaginable memories and then make them even worse by bringing them into the present and imagining them happening again, only in more horrific ways. This kind of work became a nightmare and it made me sick. I understand now that it actually retraumatized me, and the last thing I needed was that. It's neither necessary nor healthy to dredge up the past in this way, nor make the past worse than it already is. We are human and we can connect in a moment with our humanity without torturing ourselves.

I spoke to actress Christine Lahti about this very thing, asking her what she found had worked for her. "When you work and there's something that you're using that's really powerful in a painful way, is there anything that you do or don't do when you finish the project, to then . . ."

". . . close up that . . . *thing?*" Christine asked.

". . . come back to something that doesn't feel so . . . hurt," I added, nodding.

"Yes, I think I just store it way. I'm not wearing it on the surface of my skin. When I'm working it's much more available and accessible. Raw. And then it just gets tucked away and I no longer think about it."

131

"It sounds like you have a really natural ability to do that. Some people don't," I said. I described my filing cabinet technique to Christine.

"Yes, that's literally what it is," Christine commented. "It may take a few days. This particular pilot that I just did, there was a lot of vulnerability, a lot of real raw emotion, and it took me a few days to get over (the role). When she loses her husband of twenty-five years like that in a car wreck . . . you know the script."

"Unfathomable," I said shaking my head. Christine had just finished shooting a pilot for Warner Brothers and I had read through the script with her a couple of times.

"Yes. So, there was a lot of having to access a pretty painful place. As you say, you just put it back in the file folder," Christine said, "because I think otherwise then there's suffering . . . There are acting teachers who say . . . for substitutions you shouldn't use real life circumstances. Why not? But if you're someone who's going to hang on to it and suffer from it and not be able to put it back in the filing cabinet, I can see the wisdom in that advice. But I'm not someone who's going to hang on to it. Who needs it?" Christine said firmly.

I smiled, "And the fact that you don't is probably why you're still working and healthy, because a lot of people have to somehow numb it or destroy the . . . there's an 'acting out' that starts to happen."

"Exactly," Christine agreed, "you're acting out and you're walking around depressed. I think earlier in my career I would do that, especially if I was doing a play. I remember when I was doing *A Country Girl*—it was a long, long, long, long time ago—I just remember being depressed and tired while I was doing that because I would hang on to it. I guess there must have been part of me that felt that if I didn't hang on to it I might lose it."

"Right," I said. I certainly understood that one.

"So it goes," She continued. "I'd *stay* in that. The joke is that when an actor prepares before a play and they can't move because they're . . ." Christine clenched her body tightly and laughed, "*I don't want to lose it!*"

"Exactly," I laughed too. "But then there's a trust that comes with time and experience as an actor, isn't there?"

"Yes, of course, a relaxation. Otherwise you're not going to be able to allow anything to be real. Because if you're watching yourself and are rigid and trying to cry, you're never going to."

The actors I've coached through journeys of healing and completing their pasts have found that because of it their work as actors is profoundly expanded. They are able to flow in and out of their feelings and thoughts more easily and have a far greater ability to be present and empathetic. If anything, completing the past makes their feelings more accessible and their work richer. This, I believe, is because they have freed themselves from the *suffering* part of being an artist and entered the *creative flow*. The creative flow allows for great art *and* great happiness simultaneously.

At this time you're probably in some kind of transition. You're reading this book and you've come this far, which means you're willing to take a very important journey for yourself. You've called into your life a change that you've probably wanted for a long time. You are beginning to create a foundation you've needed in order to create that happier, more fulfilling life. Both scientific research and spiritual teachings point toward a probability that, in order for you to create higher levels of happiness, you must do what it takes to resolve and complete the unfinished business of the past. The incomplete past can hijack your thoughts, your energy, and your emotions, make you sick, and hold you in a place of weakness and regret. If you're stuck inside, your life will be stuck. To create flow and an open, clear path ahead of you in your career, your relationships, and your health, you first have to create flow within your own emotional, psychological, and energetic systems. Tying up those emotional loose ends will allow you to take your power back and liberate you to be the joyful, healthy person you are here to be.

Your Timeline

There are many avenues toward completing unfinished emotional business. Some come through the assistance of a therapist, coach, mentor, healer, or program. Some come when you connect with the higher purpose of your life, and your perspectives shift dramatically. Some come through intentionally identifying what's incomplete, taking the appropriate action steps to complete them, and then setting a boundary on what doesn't serve you.

In order to identify *what* is incomplete it's important to take an honest look at your life's events. Sometimes it helps to move back and take a bird's eye view. When you sit with a friend over tea, or with a therapist in their office, and you talk about an event that happened in the past, you may find that you get close to it, imagining yourself back in your body at the time, reliving it again. This can be challenging if the event was traumatic. Alternately, you might dissociate with the memory—meaning, you have the experience of being outside of your body watching yourself from somewhere, or you imagine watching it from someone else's perspective. A "bird's eye view" takes you even further back so that you can see your entire life as though it were a runway or a road. Although time is not linear but is simply something we use to navigate life in the human realm, this runway or roadway of your life can be thought of as your *timeline*. To get a perspective of this timeline you can actually stand up and walk around a room imagining it as running along the length of the space you're in. It extends all the way from your birth up until today, and even beyond and into your future. You can, if you like, imagine it going back and out far beyond this lifetime (and for the purposes of keeping it simple for now, it may be best to stay within the realms of your current human lifetime). As you look at your timeline on the floor, you can get a sense of the events you lived through at various places on the runway. Notice how you respond as you think about the past events. Take a few moments and just be gentle with yourself, knowing there is nothing you have to do right now other than notice.

After you've explored the space of your timeline, move back to the "now" section of your timeline, make sure to step into today and bring yourself back into your body. Feel your feet on the ground, your heart beating steadily, your breath moving gently in and out of your nostrils. Just be present for a moment. You just had a different perspective on your past. That brings new awareness. Take from that whatever serves you. If you like you can draw your timeline on a piece of paper and mark it with any significant events in your life, whether you consider them to be positive, negative, good, bad, indifferent, sweet, sour, scary, or happy, or anything else. Name the events with whatever two or three words best hint at what happened. You will know. As you identify the events and name them you will get a feeling as to whether there is incomplete emotional energy there. You will notice that there is tightness, tension, pain, constriction, or heaviness anywhere in your body when something is in need of completing. This is simply energy that's not flowing—it's stuck and you can feel that. Energy in flow usually feels pleasurable, tingly, smooth, light, vibrating, humming, or soft, and you will feel that too as you identify the events that are positive resources for you. Those are treasures and they teach you how you're able to feel when your energy is flowing. The events that you find bring in feelings of stuckness are the ones that you now get to complete. They, too, are your treasures. They contain within them gifts of liberation and expansion you have yet to discover and yet shall as you continue your journey.

Any event that still has energy held hostage within you is going to bring with it a combination of feelings, even if one of them is numbness and you can't tell if anything is there. Just remain in your body as best you can and accept whatever comes. This is an opportunity for you to be compassionate.

Most importantly now, as you identify the events that still hijack your thoughts and feelings, you will also get to identify the *people* who have been in your life that you're incomplete with. Whether you ever see these people again or not, it's going to be really important to your happiness to get complete with those relationships. List them, every one, even if there is just a little bit of stuckness there. What comes up may be resentment, hurt, anger, guilt, shame, or sadness, and those feelings (if they remain in your system long-term) will keep your happiness baseline state at a low. You deserve to heal everything that needs to be healed, to clear everything that needs to be cleared, to honor what needs honoring, and to complete what needs to be completed! Give yourself the gift of support as you do that with a therapist, coach, or mentor. Whomever you choose, make it someone who listens compassionately and who keeps his or her own agenda out of the way.

Missing Monologues

The people that you have resentment, hurt, guilt, sadness, or anger about may be very much in your life, or they may not be around or even alive anymore. Either way, it's very likely your mind believes there are some things that haven't been said by you or by them. The only thing you have control over is what *you* haven't said. You have no power to decide or control what anyone else will or won't ever say to you, about anything. That's important to understand. Hoping for or expecting an apology or forgiveness, for example, only puts you in a position of disappointment. Placing your own well-being and happiness in the hands of something that's so out of your control is like saying, *I will only choose to feel better if that person decides to do or say this particular thing that they most likely will never do or say.* It's a sure way to remain in the prison of powerlessness. You have the ability, however, to turn to what you *do* have the power to influence or instigate, and that, dear creative spirit, is your own personal inner workings. It is the places where all those monologues lay restless, silently shouted, perhaps hidden, unspoken, and maybe sometimes said aloud to the wrong person, at the wrong time, in another context.

In your script of life, if you feel there are missing monologues, you get to unearth the words that have been unsaid by you, move them through your body, and place them out into the world in front of you. Then, *and only then,* can you choose what next steps to take when it comes to engaging the other person. That is, if it's even possible. A way toward that is to identify one relationship that has felt the most incomplete for you. You will know who this person is as you feel what it does to your body when you think about them. It might feel tight or heavy or painful in certain areas of your physical being. Your body is that miraculous tool that tells you what's going on in your emotional and psychological world as you listen to it. Take a breath, and as you focus on this person, take a quiet, private hour for yourself to write a monologue to them. This is *not* a monologue you're going to send to this person or even tell them about. It's not recommended that you go out to find all the people that you need to get complete with and start telling them everything you've needed to say. That can get very complicated, especially if you go in with expectations of a certain response from them. In order stay where you retain your power and so that you are likely to get a good outcome, it's best (at least until you're fully complete) to do this without the other person or people involved. You're going to write your monologue as though you were able to just say whatever you wanted to say and never could. Tell them how you feel, what it was like for you, what hurt, what you're angry or resentful for, what you feel guilty about or sad about, what you're sorry about, what you're grateful for, anything that you haven't yet said or need to say again. Take between thirty minutes and an hour, no more, no less. You have a story to tell and it's important that you tell it, and at the same time this is not the time for it to become a full-length feature!

When you've written your monologue, take a deep breath, put it aside, and notice how that was for you. It may have brought up new thoughts or feelings, and if so, add them to your monologue. It may have been easier or more challenging than you thought it would be. Whatever the case, just be with whatever came in for you without the need to judge. This is simply for you to identify and express in writing what you've held. Notice the regrets and resentments that have been in your system and decide if you want to keep them or let them go. This knowledge, by itself, is a big start. Again, the gift of support is a powerful anchor through any storm of feelings that may arise and sharing your process with the right person can be a wonderful catalyst for healing.

There are many ways to complete your past, and as you commit to doing that, however you do that, you will find the script of your life is more surely in your own hands.

Your Script — Facts vs Story

Have you told your life stories? Do you have a series of scripts memorized about your past that you recite to new friends, dates, and people you meet on set and at readings? Have you shared these stories many, many times? Are they about your past woes, about how so-and-so did so-and-so to you, or are they about how great things were back then when you were so successful, or younger, or smarter? Did you find in sharing your stories that any sense of connection or relief was temporary, and that *long-term*, no matter whether someone listened well or seemed to be impressed or felt badly for you, you still didn't feel any better?

We can't be unhappy without an unhappy story. We often create a litany and an identity around events. We even do this when we are not verbally sharing the stories but just running them in our own heads. Either way, internally or aloud, we go over and over them, and by doing that we keep the feelings associated with them alive in us. The event is over, but we foster it and keep it alive with our story. We may even begin to embellish and create meaning and substories to back up our point of view. We make up stories about the other people's sides and what they must have been feeling or thinking. We build movies about it in our minds, fleshing out the characters from our imagination and our projections. We put them up on the big screen in high definition and play them over and over. And each time we play the movies we become miserable. Think of the energy it has taken to keep all those movies going in big screen, high definition, surround sound magnificence for all those years!

Many of us identify more with the past than with the present. We think of ourselves in terms of what has happened to us rather than who we are right this moment. In reality the past is gone, it no longer exists, and when we think about it we remember based on countless filters, impressions, interpretations, and perspectives. The past is actually not what it seems. Deciding on a story, freeze-framing it, and mounting it on the walls of our mind can limit our ability to be happy, and we become prisoners, not of the past, but of our old *interpretations* of it. This also means we have decided where our identity lies based on those interpretations.

For many years I thought of my past as a dark, terrible string of traumas. If you look at data there were a number of violations, breaches of my basic human boundaries and I take nothing away from the *facts* of what happened. However, when I decide what those facts *mean* to me and what I say to myself about them. I now know I have choice.

You can see anything in a multitude of ways. The perspectives you choose to see your past from will either serve your happiness or not. While still knowing the actual data, it's possible to decide what it's going to *mean* to you, and the most essential thing for your happiness is to make sure you get clear about what is what. For example, someone might see her past in terms of, *My dad abandoned me when I was three.* That's an interpretation, and probably a painful one with all kinds of consequences for future experiences. If you look at just data, however, it might sound more like, *My dad walked out the door one morning when I was three and, as far as I know, didn't return.* The facts are these: Dad literally walked out the door of the house she lived in, it was in the morning, she was three years old, and as far as everything she knows her dad didn't walk back into her childhood home. Those are all factual, tangible pieces of data. Beyond that the story could be interpreted in infinite ways. Somebody else who had the same data may decide to interpret it as, *My dad must have had an accident, lost his memory, and probably had to start his life again somewhere, poor guy,* or even, *My dad probably decided to escape a mundane life, go find himself, and make a difference in the world, and I applaud him for that!* It's all about perspective. Very often siblings, people who were in the very same situation growing up, have very different perspectives about what life was like. This is due to a combination of personality and interpretive filters. Chances are, your parents or siblings won't recall having the same experiences you do. The facts may be similar, and yet the experiences of those facts will most likely be varied.

An actress, "Louise," came to me one day with a terrible story and the headline was "I have lost everything."

"You've lost *everything*?" I asked with compassion. Remember *catastrophic language* and *universals*? Louise was using both of them for her story's headline. She had evidently been stuck in a very limiting place.

"Yes," she said through her tears. Louise didn't catch the question in my voice about her losing "everything." She was deep into her story and continued on, "I was fired from my role in the off-Broadway play I was in and the producer has spread horrible rumors about me. He's made my whole career go down the toilet, I've gone broke, and I've had to move back in with my mom."

"That sounds like a lot," I said.

"Yes, it's a lot. I've lost everything," she repeated.

"What do you want to accomplish from coaching, Louise?" I asked.

Louise stopped, seeming a bit stumped.

"Ummm, this guy, this producer, said I was difficult to work with and has poisoned my name. He's ruined my career and I want to know how to get it back!" she lamented.

"I am not sure how we would get your old career back. And besides, if it were the same as before it would include all the things that got you to where you are now. And it doesn't sound like you're enjoying where you are now."

"Uh, okay," Louise said in surprise.

"I could support you in building some new, more resourceful things into your current career if you would like."

"Okay," she said as she blinked away her tears.

I continued, "There is one very important thing that would need to happen before you can move into a new place, though, and that is to take responsibility for your part in the past. The story you tell about what happened has a tone to it. What would you say that is?"

"It has a tone of anger probably."

"And what is the message in the story? What does it say about you?"

"Well, that I was screwed over I guess."

"That you were screwed over. It certainly sounds that way, your story. Our stories are our interpretations of facts. There are some irrefutable facts here. One was that you were fired from your job. What are the other facts?"

"The producer said I was difficult to work with."

"How do you know that for a fact?" I asked.

"He told me."

"Okay. I'm assuming that wasn't what he fired you for. Being 'difficult' is not legal grounds for firing someone."

"I was late a few times," Louise said sheepishly.

"Okay. You were late a few times. What other facts are there?"

"Well," Louise evidently wanted to get back to her story, "my career got ruined because of the producer spreading negative gossip about me."

"And how do you know he spread that gossip?"

"I heard from a bunch of people that he had been saying things about me."

"So it was hearsay. Those were rumors themselves. What *data* do you have that the producer spread rumors or gossip about you?"

"What do you mean?" she asked.

"Well, for example, data might be him telling you that he was going to spread rumors and then you witnessing him telling them to numerous people."

Louise took a moment and replied, "Well, data . . . I suppose I would have no data, per se, on that then."

"Okay. What data do you have that your career has been ruined?"

"Well, I haven't worked since!" Louise's anger gained strength again.

"Yes, what you just said is data. It's a *fact* that you haven't worked since you were fired." I nodded. "That your career has been 'ruined' is an interpretation of that fact," I then explained.

"Humph!" Louise pushed her lips out into a pout.

"What's that, 'humph'?" I smiled.

"I'm not liking where this has gone." She smiled back.

"And why is that?" I asked.

"I'm not sure." She looked confused.

Louse had been so invested in seeing herself as the victim of her story that she had not been able to move beyond her own suffering. That meant she missed the opportunity to create positive circumstances out of what was simply a chain of events. Taking responsibility for looking at and knowing the truth about the data can actually be very liberating, even though at first the ego wants to hold on to the identity it has created, which in Louise's case was "victim."

It turned out that Louse had actually breached her contract with the production company that had hired her. She had failed to turn up to a number of rehearsals and had been late for two production nights. This, she told me, was because her brother had been going through some marital issues and she had gone to his side in, what she considered, times of need. She had not communicated these reasons to the production company, she said, in order to protect her brother's privacy. The production company was equally thin on the communication side and had not given Louise any warning that they were going to fire her, so it came quite suddenly and she had fought with them, both sides raising their voices and blaming the other. Afterward, Louise had felt ashamed about her behavior and had imagined that the producer would probably tell other people in the industry how she had acted. Paralyzed by her own fear, she stopped putting herself out there for other roles in theater and her career naturally dried up. This perpetuated her fear that the producer had turned the industry against her, even though it was actually she who had stopped her career by ceasing to engage in meetings and auditions! It had been a cycle to nowhere.

As Louise had created an identity of victim out of what were neutral events, someone else might have seen it all another way: *Both parties could have behaved better. I was fired. I've learned from the chain of events. I have learned to be more communicative and more respectful of other people's time, and have created a better career and better relationships since then because of it all. What a great opportunity for growth and expansion that was!* That would have created a very different outcome than the one Louise had created.

Every single one of us does what Louise did. This is part of being human. And yet every circumstance is an opportunity to observe our own human responses and to make a better choice. Life is not always fair, and there are some people who do set out to harm us. We are sometimes, literally, victims of people's intentional harm and violence. And still, even then there are infinite ways to create meaning out of data. We have the chance at any time to drop our stories and make something good come out of what life offers us. It's not the weight of the load that we bear, but the way we carry it that make the difference.

When it comes to who you are today, the past and your interpretations of it *are not you*. The past, whether it's recent or long ago, doesn't define who you are unless you decide that it does. You may have built your identity on some interpretations you had of things that happened many years ago that just don't make sense anymore. The only thing you can control beyond data is your decision about what something is going to mean to you. And that meaning will shape how you feel, what you believe, how you think, and therefore how your life unfolds. You get to define who you are right now in the present moment. You get to decide in your story, your movie of life, if you're going to be a victim or if you're going to be someone who rises because of it and chooses to serve good somehow. The past can be seen as a metaphor for lessons your deepest self is undertaking. The power you have is to pick a metaphor that creates something positive and expansive, the very stuff your soul needs to fuel you forward into someone you desire to be. Ultimately, can that be a part of your legacy of happiness? Again, I take nothing away from the experiences you had or the impact events may have had on you. This is not to condone any type of violation to your being. These experiences have been very real to you, and they get to be honored and validated. Then, perhaps, if they have been holding you back, limiting your ability to be happy and confident, you can decide to let go of them by choosing to experience them differently.

As you take another look at your timeline and your monologue, you get to notice how much is based on interpretation and how much is actual data. Feelings are relevant and valid and I am not suggesting you throw them out. This is simply an opportunity for you to notice what you may have decided many years ago, or even recently, and you can now question and can perhaps free yourself from it by doing so. Is it serving your happiness to put yourself in the role of victim of a person, of life, or of God even? Does it serve you to be cast in the role of villain, underdog, loser, failure, clown, child, nobody, screwup? Or does it serve you to just *be present* in your life? If you're going to choose an identity wouldn't you rather play the role of the spirit warrior, the complex, challenged, imperfect, growing, multifaceted, gloriously courageous hero of your movie? Can you stand and look at your life and feel yourself as the one who made it through to this place, to right *now*, doing the best you could in your humanness and being determined to not only survive whatever challenges you faced, but also to flourish despite them?

You have the opportunity now to rewrite your past from that perspective. You can start with the simple facts and say, Okay, those things happened. Those are facts. What meaning do I make out of them that will serve me and become resources in my life now?

As I looked back on my own life I found that instead of being the victim of numerous assaults, I was a girl and then a woman who kept finding ways to create healthier boundaries, to love myself, to be kinder to others, to trust my instincts more, to be clearer about my needs, and to make a better life for myself and those around me. Even when I made mistakes and came across badly I kept returning to the intention to live through my essential self. That took courage and determination with all that I had faced. I witness myself having turned the events that happened into catalysts to surge forward into greater clarity, maturity, and health. That's the meaning that I take out of what facts there are in my past. I choose interpretations that serve my present life. It's an ongoing awakening—never arriving at an end result—where I continue to reframe and reframe and reframe the past into something that nourishes me, rather than drains, and grows me, rather than diminishes.

Rewriting your history frees you. Interpretation is just that, interpretation. You can decide that you're a victim or a healer, and either way will give you a result. So why not pick a focus that feels good, empowers you, and makes you healthier and happier? Like the phoenix rising from its ashes, reborn to live again, you get to do the same. You have the power to be writer, director, editor, and producer of the movies of your past. You get to choose whether to be a prisoner of your wounds and regrets, or the inspirational, courageous spirit on a very human, sacred journey.

Forgiveness Is Freedom

Have you ever had someone ask you to forgive him or her? And did you feel as though they didn't deserve it? Whether they deserved it or not, forgiving them may have actually been the gift you needed to give *yourself*.

Despite misunderstandings of the nature and meaning of forgiveness, it's actually, foremost, an act of self-love. This is because it's not something you do for the sake of others; it's something you do for you. Forgiveness is a direct route to your own power and happiness. It's an act that frees you from the toxic prison of resentment and enables you to become the loving, clear, productive, and happy person you are meant to be. The love you are then able to put out into the world is going to positively affect, and perhaps even heal, others. Ultimately, forgiveness heals the planet and it heals our future.

There is increasing scientific evidence that forgiveness leads to greater levels of sustained happiness and well-being, and for you to flourish in the business you're in, being as free from as much baggage as possible will allow you to create the life and career you want.

First of all, let's look at what you are left with if you choose *not* to forgive. Resentment is there when you choose to hold on to the past, seeing yourself as a victim. When you don't forgive, you're saying yes to this resentment, and that's a toxin that harms the vessel it sits in. Saying yes to having a toxin in your own being means you're saying yes to harm that goes beyond the original event. This means that over time the resentment might hurt you even more than the past or any person in it ever did in the first place! That's worth being conscious about.

The thought that resentment is a *toxin* is not just a fanciful idea. There is increasing scientific evidence that holding resentment, grudges, regrets, guilt, blame, and shame all lead to health and emotional issues. In studies conducted by Dr. Fred Luskin, Senior Consultant in Health Promotion at Stanford University, subjects' blood pressure, heart rate, and arterial wall pressure all rose when asked to think about a grudge. In addition, muscle tension increased, stress levels increased, and discomfort and lack of control were reported. Resentment is related to anger. In other studies it was shown that simply thinking about something that makes a person angry for five minutes could depress immune responses as well as affect the heart's ability to respond to stress. People with high levels of anger have been found to be three times more likely to develop heart disease than those with low levels of anger. Resentment can also cause depression, and depressed people have a significantly greater risk of a stroke. The lists go on. The great news is that when people learn to forgive they also become psychologically and physically healthier. Forgiveness has been found to improve blood pressure, immune function, and heart and brain functioning. Dr. Fred Luskin also states that when people forgive they feel better, have fewer headaches and fewer stomach aches, are less tired and less achy, end up making better decisions, and are more confident and optimistic. All of these benefits are *for the person who has done the forgiving.* The person who forgives gets to be healthier and happier.

It's quite likely that there have been some things in your life that haven't gone the way you wanted them to go. Somebody let you down, they didn't do what you wanted them to do, or did something you didn't want them to do—someone betrayed you, lied to you, cheated you or cheated on you, didn't give you the job you wanted, stole your money, harmed you or the ones you love, or ended the life of someone you love. None of us can change the facts, the *data,* about what happened in our pasts. You can't change a devastating fact, you can only be right here, now, and turn within to see the love that needs to be exchanged there. You can be gentle and compassionate with yourself and begin to allow the healing, and you can, with great kindness and grace, begin to take responsibility for your own *present* reactions to what happened back then. Doing that doesn't mean that you're responsible for what happened. This doesn't mean that what happened wasn't devastating. This doesn't mean that the other person is not responsible for their actions or inactions. This doesn't mean that your pain or anger wasn't very, very valid. This simply means that you can take your power back. The other person doesn't have the power to make you feel any way at all, so don't give them that power any longer.

At the time of the event or events you may have been a victim of their actions or inactions. The event is now in the past. Do not let yourself feel like their victim now as well, in the present. Resentment is like picking up the weapon they harmed you with and harming yourself with it over and over again. Think about that. Have you, in fact, been victimizing yourself by holding on to the past? Can you choose to free yourself from that suffering? Have you had enough of casting yourself in the role of victim? Have you had enough of blame? As you take responsibility for your own current feelings and responses, you get in touch with your responsibility to yourself. This is where you get to take care of yourself.

Most of us haven't been taught about forgiveness and the real power that lies behind its meaning. Many of us have thought of it as a way to excuse bad behavior or to brush something away. When we get in touch with the most powerful meaning of forgiveness we understand that that's far from the truth. Forgiveness doesn't condone in any way what happened. It doesn't excuse the other person's behavior nor does it make the other person "right." It doesn't excuse the other person from lawful justice. It doesn't mean that reconciliation has to happen between you and them. In fact, it doesn't mean that you ever have to speak to the person or see them ever again if you don't wish to. Forgiveness doesn't mean that you didn't have a right to your anger or pain, and it doesn't mean that you will forget what happened. It also doesn't mean that you are inviting other events like the one that happened to ever happen again.

So, what *is* forgiveness? Russell Freidman, cofounder of The Grief Recovery Institute, describes forgiveness as "letting go of the hope that things in the past will be different, better, or more." As we can't change the facts of the past, letting go of the hope that we *can* liberates us to live far more fully and peacefully in the present. Gary Craig, the creator of EFT, said, "Forgiveness is the ultimate aim of all psychotherapy ... as long as one is open to true understanding. There is no such thing as an unforgivable act. There are heinous acts and regrettable acts and disgusting acts, and as long as one retains anger and unforgiveness about them, the result will be ongoing emotional and physical symptoms for the abused person. That has no value for anyone."

Forgiveness is freeing yourself from the pain of the past. It means that you can know the facts about what happened and not be a prisoner of them, or a prisoner of the effect it has had on your life. It's the gift you give yourself. It's for you and no one else. When you forgive, it means that you won't have to run the movie of what happened over and over in your mind. It means that you will be able to think more clearly and make better choices about your life. It means that your heart will begin to heal, your body will work better, and you will be healthier. It means that your relationship with yourself and with those around you will improve dramatically. Your old voices, your doubts and fears, may question and resist forgiveness, *and* you can just keep on forgiving until you're no longer trapped. What happens then is that you don't give away your power any longer. You take care of yourself right there, right then in that moment, and let the pain of the past be just that—the pain of the past—whether that was fifty years ago, or five minutes ago.

The hidden gift in every experience that feels painful is the reminder to return to love. We are given challenges in this human experience, some more extreme than others. Not only can we survive these challenges, we each have the capacity to thrive despite them, perhaps even eventually *because of them*. We have the capacity to turn from the unwelcome role of victim and become healers. We can take what has happened to us and use it as fuel to propel us. *Can we learn to breathe and soften when we are faced with them? Can we yield to the impact rather than brace ourselves?* Imagine being swept away by an enormous tidal wave, and instead of thrashing wildly and fighting the force, perhaps, in that sudden and horrifying moment choosing to relax into it. The odds of surviving may well become greater. A universal truth stands that what's rigid and hard will break when met with force, and what's supple and yielding will not. It will bend and then return to some kind of recognizable shape. That's how we can choose, at times, to be in our lives. Forgiveness softens us to the exquisite feeling of life when we most want to be hard. It brings us into alignment with the love that will heal us. When we forgive, we drop it. We drop the shield and the sword. We simply let go of the "stuff" that has burdened us, and in our new lightness we find that we can ascend. What an opportunity we have to be free!

The way to forgive others is simple. It's by saying the words *I forgive you, I forgive him, I forgive her*, or *I forgive them*. You don't have to say it to the other person, even if they are around. In fact sometimes you can't, or it's better not to. However, do choose to say it aloud so that it is expressed through your voice, and if you like, say it in front of a supportive witness, like a therapist, coach, or neutral friend.

It takes just a moment to forgive, and in that moment you've chosen to heal. Ultimately, forgiveness liberates you, and you may just be saving your own life.

Liberate Yourself

As you make your personal shifts and the relationship inside you becomes more loving and compassionate, you have a renewed ability to love others in a deeper and healthier way. That includes an ability to make amends. We are all human. We make mistakes, make poor choices, and sometimes do destructive things. It's important to be honest with yourself about the things you've done to hurt others. Making amends is a powerful and important ingredient to good relationships, both within your own personal system and with others. Being responsible for your own actions and making sincere apologies for them clears blocks in your life and frees you, as well as possibly others, to become happier. You bring consciousness and compassion into the world, and are able to grow and learn from your mistakes.

An important piece in the process of making amends is to know when it's appropriate to make them directly to the person, and when to keep them to yourself. It's not always beneficial to go to someone and blurt out an apology. It has to be done with consciousness and sensitivity. For example, calling an old cast member and saying, *I'm sorry I secretly made out with your boyfriend when we were working together on that play*, would only serve to hurt someone who otherwise may not have known about a betrayal. Confessing past mistakes to people who may be "blissfully unaware" is not what amends are about. It may be kinder and more respectful to let some things stay unsaid. If, however, you know you behaved in a way that some-one probably felt hurt by, it may be time to say you're sorry. Being willing to apologize is a basic characteristic of being an adult.

Real amends-making not only includes saying you're sorry in a sincere and heartfelt way, but it also means making sure you don't say *but* when you're doing it. Saying, *I am sorry I did so-and-so to you, **but** it was because of* ___ or saying, *I'm sorry, **but** I did it because you did so-and-so*, is *not* an apology. You might inform someone separately about your own personal reasons for your behavior; however, adding an excuse or turning it back to the other person and making your reason because of something *they* did will only perpetuate the conflict and hurt between you. Some "apologies" are not apologies at all but rather need to be in the "forgive" category. When you hear yourself saying, *Sorry that I did this, but you did that*, you can bet you need to face the truth of your own resentment. Similarly, if you find yourself saying sorry for something you're not really remorseful about (for example, *I'm sorry that I couldn't take your crap anymore*, or *I'm sorry you were a terrible agent*) you know that's not an apology but a chance to, again, clear resentment from your system. Both of these examples are opportunities to do some forgiving first. Your deeper wisdom will let you know when you're purely apologizing to someone or not.

Powerful amends also include making up for your past mistakes. That means either doing something to rectify the situation you may have put the person in or helping them out in some other way. If neither of those seems appropriate, you can always help someone else out in their honor.

Beyond amends, what will ultimately serve you and those around you is being compassionate with what you've done in the past. This is because what you focus on about yourself, you will very likely repeat. If you focus on having a flaw through guilt or shame, it will keep showing up in your experiences. If you focus on the times you are kind to someone or bring something positive to a relationship, you will encourage yourself to go there again, and that creates esteem and ultimately happiness for everyone involved. It will allow you to grow and start living as the person you want to be from that moment forward.

Additionally, what you do to *yourself* will project outward and then come back again, somehow, to be done to you *by others*. This not only applies to harm, it also applies to forgiveness, compassion, acceptance, and encouragement. It's a universal law. This is why, in order to receive love from your experiences, you must first be loving with yourself.

Author and speaker David Icke writes, "If we have imbalances that lead us to act negatively toward others, it's those imbalances that attract us to a physical experience, a 'mirror' of what we think of ourselves. In this way what we do to others will come back to us because we will still be holding on to the imbalances, the lack of self-love, that will attract those experiences."

In other words, if we hold a picture of ourselves (even a subconscious one) as a bad person who has done something "wrong," we will keep setting up experiences that reflect that through "getting what we deserve." That is, unless and until we recognize that inner belief about ourselves, let go of it through forgiveness and compassion, and replace it with a new belief—one that includes the truth that we deserve love and happiness in our lives no matter what the past has held.

To emerge from a cycle of negative experience we first have to clean house right where we live. We have all done things we regret. No one is perfect. Every one of us has the capacity for everything. We make mistakes, acting out of fear and terrible doubt at times. We have to make room to admit that we are sometimes impatient, mean, selfish, and arrogant. I know I have been. I can't count the number of things I've done that I know hurt others or myself that I would never, ever choose to do again. I lived with great shame and regret for many years over some of my own behaviors, and I still acted "badly" at times even then. There were occasions when the shame was so great that I couldn't stand myself. I felt that the harmful things others did to me were deserved because of it. So the cycle continued. Yet ultimately, eventually, I chose to heal and emerge, and I did that by forgiving, making peace with myself, and learning from my mistakes.

When we haven't forgiven ourselves, shame is left standing in our hearts, minds, and bodies. Shame is an energy that can't be expressed. It's a form of emotional violence against ourselves that has nowhere to go. It's a dead–end street. It keeps us in a place where no solution feels possible. Shame initially comes from others, and then we take it on as our own. It creeps in and diminishes our sense of self and disempowers us. It hijacks us when we least expect it. Shame tends to create still pictures or short films running on a loop that get hung on the walls of our minds. They get put on display as terrible "evidence" of our lack of value. Shame makes it hard for us to create healthy boundaries in life and it very often leads to shaming others. It also often leads to addictions.

Shame is different from feelings of remorse. Remorse is a healthy way to learn about what we value, about what's really important to us, and about whom we want to be in the world. Remorse comes from within, from our own value system. A decision arises from there to not repeat the actions in question and to find different ways to behave in the future. Remorse adds to a person's character. It empowers. It also passes over time because it's processed through the system. Remorse helps us to create healthy boundaries and it leads to better choices and therefore better lives. We can shift from shame to remorse through forgiveness.

Just as in forgiving others, forgiving yourself doesn't excuse your past behavior. It doesn't make it "right," and it doesn't mean that it has to happen again. It doesn't mean that the people your actions or inactions harmed are obliged to reconcile with you or ever be around you again. That's up to them. Forgiving yourself doesn't mean they don't have a right to their anger or pain. It also doesn't mean that you or they will forget what happened.

However, forgiving yourself *does* mean that you can be free from the pain of the past. It means that you can know the facts about what you did or didn't do *and not be a prisoner of them, or a prisoner of the effect it has had on your life.* Forgiving yourself means that you won't have to run the movie of what happened over and over in your mind. It certainly means that you will be able think more clearly and make better choices about your life, and it means that your heart will begin to heal, your body will work better, and you will be healthier. Forgiving yourself means that the relationship you have with yourself will improve dramatically. Your old voices, your doubts, and fears may question and resist it, *and* you can just keep putting your hand on your heart, forgiving yourself until you're no longer trapped. What happens then is that you become empowered, you take care of yourself right there in that moment and let the pain of the past be just that—the pain of the past—whether that was fifty years ago, or five minutes ago.

Forgiving yourself is saying the words *I forgive myself.* It takes just a moment to forgive yourself, and in that moment you've chosen to heal. You may just be saving your own life. When you forgive, you've given yourself the gift of life as it's meant to be. Happy.

What if you finally get sick of the fear, and of the same old voices of doubt, judgment, and shame? What if you decide to let go and surrender the story? What if you take a leap of faith and decide that without it you will be free?

The soul is forever new. It recreates itself in every moment, advancing and expanding into the remembering of its source. Each one of us has the inherent ability to follow suit with our humanity. We can choose to die to the past in an instant and become reborn into the brilliance of a new present.

CHAPTER 7

Creating Your Future

You see things; and you say "Why?" But I dream things that never were; and I say "Why not?"

~ GEORGE BERNARD SHAW

How You Create

You are the co-creator of your life. You and the amazing universe you live in, with its eternal, positive power of life, are in co-creation at every moment of existence. There are universal laws that get understood through spiritual, philosophical, and scientific channels, and as we begin to understand them more through our own evolution, we begin to understand the power we each have to create what we envision.

Some truths are these: Your life experiences always mirror what's going on inside you. Your external life is an out-picturing of your inner life. When you change your inner programming the external results will change accordingly. If you don't have something in your life that you desire, it's because you're not yet aligned with it mentally, physically, and spiritually. If you *do* have something in your life, whether you want it or not, it's because you *have* been internally aligned with it. When you learn to consciously shift your functioning (mentally, physically, and spiritually) you will attract the results you desire. These truths work all the time, perfectly, consistently, and for everyone. No exceptions. And we are all on a journey of understanding this.

Many actors live with an idea in mind of their success without really understanding the most effective steps for getting there. When I say *steps*, I don't mean the typical *get new head shots, go to acting classes, find an agent* types of steps. Those are necessary logistical business steps, and yet they are only part of the equation. There are internal steps that have to be put in place before any of the logistical steps can be truly effective. It doesn't matter if you spend every day imagining yourself winning an Oscar if you don't have a specific and fleshed-out vision of your future and how to get there. It doesn't matter if you walk into an audition with the most beautiful head shots anyone has ever seen if you're not internally aligned with a successful outcome. It doesn't matter if you have the most powerful agent in town if you don't feel, in your intrinsic self, that you deserve an equally powerful career. Everything in your life starts with what's going on *inside* you. Having the desire to be a successful actor alone is not enough. A big key to making what you desire happen comes from being aware of how you tend to function internally and then organizing it so that it serves you.

To create a great life you have to establish what's important to you, what you really want, and how you're going to make that happen. Having a plan, in itself, creates confidence, and that will add greatly to your happy factor as an actor. You have the power to be writer, director, producer, and star of the movies of your future.

Have a Vision

Very often actors have an idea of the future that stays in the realm of *dream*. It's a lovely, vague, mesmerizing idea they have floating around in their minds that could be described as something like, *I'm going to be a successful actor,* or *I want a series regular role,* or *I see myself walking the red carpet and winning an Oscar.* These are great dreams to have, yet because they are not very specific and have little solid plan they don't often take actors on the road to success. The kinds of ideas or goals that will create success are grown out of robust and fully formed *visions*.

Some actors interested in the law of attraction have learned about vision boards, where they cut and paste pictures of the things they want for themselves into a collage of the future. Some actors make mock magazine covers or movie posters with their own faces pasted onto the bodies of the stars. These can be powerful ways to bring clarity to that general idea and to start manifesting something, yet a strong vision takes more than a vision board or a mock poster.

If you've studied the art of acting and have had the experience of really getting into the bones of a role, you will have learned to explore details—the details of what your character is seeing, feeling, hearing, even tasting and smelling. You will have entered the "self" of the role.

One of the origins of the word *rehearse* is *harrow*, which is "to rake or dig into the dirt or to weed out." When you rehearse, you are digging into your character's life, their reality as it were. You're making it real and specific for yourself. Actors spend a lot of time and effort on this essential and powerful part of the craft, yet how much time and effort do most actors put in when it comes to their own vision of the future? What about the dream you want to make real for yourself? Is that not as important, if not one of *the* most important things, when it comes to what you create? It's your *life*, not a movie, a television show, or a play after all!

How you see, feel, and hear the future will have a great effect on how it turns out. In order to create something you also have to know, in specific terms, what it is. Having a strong vision is essential to creating the future you desire. When you explore what you want, you also get to know who you are.

When I first arrived in Los Angeles in the early 1990s I was "hip-pocketed" by an agent, David Rose at Innovative Artists. *Hip-pocketing* is a term used when an agent or agency takes on a client, often one with little or no experience, but doesn't commit to signing with them. It's a way to get them out, get feedback from casting directors, and gauge if there's potential. There are mixed feelings out there about the practice, yet it can often serve to create some knowledge where there may not have been otherwise. David Rose was probably very smart to decide on this strategy with me at the time. I had been recommended to him by a hot young producer/director, yet I was very new to acting, having done only a handful of small parts in films and television shows. He was a young up-and-coming agent eager to get his career on the right path. I happened to book one of the very first auditions he sent me on (a huge pilot for Paramount Pictures) and because of that the other agents at Innovative wanted to meet me, presumably to consider drawing up a contract between us. Needless to say, I was very excited and nervous about the meeting and I thought long and hard about what I would wear and how I would impress them. I walked into a room full of people watching my every move, asking me questions, and listening to my every answer. I talked about wearing my "Sunday best" to meet them because I thought they would find that cute. I told them how much I admired Susan Sarandon when they asked me who I thought my peers were (even though I am almost two decades younger than she is). I tried hard to reach for the right things—the words that would make them love me. Then one of them asked, "Where do you see yourself going, Justina?"

That was a zinger. It was a question that went straight to the heart of the matter, and they got the information they needed right in that moment. I remember feeling as though I had walked around a corner and found myself standing face-to-face with a huge wall that went on forever. I couldn't speak or see beyond the short space in front of my face.

"I want to be a star!" I blurted out. That was *so not* what I wanted deep in my heart. I wanted to be an artist, to express myself, make a positive difference in the world, and yet those were the words that came out of my mouth in that fearful, ungrounded, disempowered moment—that moment of vague ideas and fantasy. Not only did I lack a sense of self, I simply didn't have a vision.

Without knowing who I was and what I really wanted to create, the agents at Innovative only saw a silly girl who (never mind that she just booked a pilot) was, by all appearances, not going to be a successful actress, let alone a "star"! Within days David Rose stopped "hip-pocketing" me and did so, I would imagine, in the kindest way possible. I was dropped. It must have been an embarrassing situation for a young agent at such a high-profile agency, yet thankfully that tiny moment in his life certainly didn't seem to hurt his career. It took me on another path, however, and though there are no regrets, one wonders what would have happened if I had had confidence, personal power, communications skills, a sense of who I was, and a clear and robust sense of my own vision.

So, where do you see yourself going? Really? And not only what it *looks* like. What does it feel like, sound like, smell like, and taste like? Though *vision* is a visual word, it's essential to also make it about your physical senses: how you want to feel, how it will sound, taste, and smell. Get into what you desire through *all* of your senses. Play with it, have fun, create a movie for yourself in every arena of your life. Not just your acting career, but also your relationships, your health, your spiritual life, your financial life, your environment, your home, your friendships, and your family life. Flesh out your vision and give it anchors. What car are you driving? Where are you living? Whom are you living around? When you say you want to have a great film career, what does that mean in reality? How does your day begin? Where do you wake up and what does it feel like to be there?

Whom are you with, if anyone? What sounds do you hear? What are the things you take part in during the morning? What does it feel like to be doing them? What are the colors around you? The light? The shadows and spaces? What are the voices, the conversations within yourself and between you and others in your life in this vision? How does your day unfold? How do you travel through your day? What kind of vehicle are you in? How does it smell and feel to drive? Or does someone else drive you? What does the set sound, smell, and feel like? What is it like to speak the scripted dialogue and live through the life of your craft? What are your interactions like with your coworkers, your friends, your lover, and your family? How does your body feel? How do your emotions feel? How does your mind work in this vision of yours? You can explore every detail of your existence and meander through your vision, shifting it until you make it just as you like it, and then change it again if you choose. You can write, paint, dance, and sing about it. It's yours to flesh out, and then yours again to step into as you would a role you're taking in so that you embody it entirely.

In my workshops I will often ask for a volunteer from the group to let me guide them toward discovering their vision. I suggest that the other group members make sure they can clearly watch this person go through the process, as very often it's enlightening and moving. One such volunteer, "Ally," became so connected with the specific experiences of her vision that her entire face and body began to light up in awe and she was moved to tears. She told us later that she had never given herself permission to be so detailed with a vision. She was deeply affected at how powerful the experience was. The closest she had come to formally creating a vision of her future prior to my workshop had been at another workshop given by someone else years ago. Ally told us that the facilitator had whipped everyone into an excited frenzy, insisting that the group move around the room shouting, jumping, and high-fiving. He had made sure everyone was tremendously excited about their vision for the future, yet without getting specific or going into what was deeply important for each of the participants. Ally said she had felt that there was something wrong with her because she had not been able to find her vision in that environment. She had felt set up, empty, disconnected, and compelled to hit the facilitator in frustration, though I was relieved to hear that she had refrained from doing so!

Many workshops and conference facilitators use techniques to stir audiences into highly excitable states. This is similar to the mass excitement created at large sporting events like baseball games. Yet these states of "high" are event-specific and the participants often find that whatever positive shifts they might feel at the time quickly dissipate as they return to their everyday lives. This is even more often true when the exercises are designed in broad, nonspecific terms and participants aren't able to get grounded in their own unique truths. By asking specific questions, however, Ally was quickly able to plug into a fleshed-out vision for herself. She was also very relieved to know there had not been anything wrong with her after all!

One thing to note in all this is that everything has the potential for extremes. Many coaches and teachers forget to tell their clients that specifics can also, actually, get in the way. It's possible to get *too* specific when it comes to the "who's" and the "what's." For example, if you've decided that your vision is about costarring with Emma Stone and Ryan Gosling on three movies back to back and they are all directed by Michael Bay, you're setting yourself up within some narrow parameters! If the vision turns up in a slightly different package you may even push it out of the way when it shows up—even if it's something spectacular. And all because you're so busy scanning the horizon for what looks exactly as you had imagined.

One of my NLP trainers, Tim Hallbom, told us a story about a client who really wanted to have a relationship, and yet just didn't seem to be attracting one. Through Tim's questioning, it emerged that not only had this client worked really hard on the specifics of his vision for a mate, but he had also gone as far as imagining her as blonde and blue-eyed and wearing a blue sweater. He even named his future bride "Wendy." Meanwhile a number of smart, loving, attractive women who would have been great matches for this man had been pushed aside because they were not "Wendy-with-the-blue-sweater-on"!

Creating your vision more out of *experiential specifics* and *feeling tones*, instead of contextual outcomes, gives room for the universe to provide. As you drop into your body and ask it what it wants to *experience* in your future life, you will get to know a bit more about who you are, what's truly important to you, and how those things are always, have always, and will always, be part of you.

Having vision makes you a visionary. One of the meanings of *visionary* is "one who has knowledge of things before they exist." The magic of life is that as soon as you create a vision in your mind it instantly does exist. One thing you can be guaranteed of, if you *don't* imagine something, it's far less likely to be created, so it's up to you to decide if you want to make it possible or not!

Set Powerful Goals

As we explored earlier in this book, getting in touch with your values is fundamental to aligning with what's deep within the fabric of who you are. As you now move into creating goals that are the building blocks of your overall vision, your values will come into play in a big way. You get to put the fingerprints of your soul all over your goals!

Some people love to set goals and some people won't go near them. Goals are *essential* to making your vision happen. Visions must be taken to action or else they are just that, visions, and nothing more. As Will Rogers said, "Even if you're on the right track, you'll get run over if you just sit there."

As you take your vision and move to action, what's most important to consider is *how* you make goals. If they are borne out of "shoulds" or old beliefs that don't align with your overall vision and core values, then you will be in conflict with your goals and not much will be accomplished. Happiness can't be sustained when there is that kind of conflict. The *why* part of your journey as an actor (what the passion and greater purpose behind it is), as opposed to the *how* or *what* parts (the intellectual reasons), will help direct you toward your *mission*, the infusion of your human purpose with your higher purpose. And when you set goals based on your mission, then you move through your essential self in a far stronger way.

Interestingly, an exploration of your values has the potential to reveal that it may not be acting that you want to be doing after all. You may find that the deeper meaning you've discovered in yourself can be better fulfilled in another arena. I've had the occasional actor client discover through coaching that their passion was elsewhere. When I was in my thirties, as my values changed and became clearer to me, I realized that being an actor wasn't my calling in life after all. Helping others find their destiny became my destiny. Helping others become happier and empowered turned out to be my passion. Whatever your mission turns out to be, no matter what life or career that leads you to, if you're on path you will be far happier than if you had not discovered it!

Speaking of paths, as you connect with your vision and get a sense of your mission in life, wherever you head you will need to create your path's edges. If your path doesn't have clear edges you may find yourself wandering around the landscape of your life, never really accomplishing much. Your path's edges are the parameters by which you live your life. Building those parameters based on your values, beliefs, and vision will help you make the tangible and powerful goals that will keep you moving in the direction you want to go—toward your vision. You first have to identify what those goals are, what it takes to make them happen, and decide how to break them down into manageable steps. Asking the right questions will also help you find out what the obstacles are (real or imagined) that might get in the way of making those goals happen. You then create what are called *well-formed outcomes*, meaning you cultivate an environment in your mind that expands the potential for you to create what makes you happy.

Christopher (the actor who had come in with a habit of taking things personally) quickly became clear on a number of new goals. Courageously he had looked at his own part in the dynamics of his past and had become clearer about what had been working for him and what had not. He began to explore a vision for his future and out of that began to identify some new goals.

"As you think about your overall vision, what would be five goals within it, just to start with?" I asked Christopher.

"Well, first of all I would like to not take things so personally!" he laughed.

"Yes, I can see why you would like that." I laughed with him. "So, if we start with that one, what might that goal sound like if you said it in the *positive* and in *present tense?*" I asked.

Again, when we focus on what we *do* want (rather than what we don't want) we are more likely to align with it. Additionally, talking about a goal in *present tense* rather than future tense brings it into the here and now.

After a few versions of the goal Christopher settled on this: "I know my own worth, know who I am, and can detach from other people's behavior."

"What other goals do you have?" I asked him.

"Well, some I can think of would be to feel confident in my acting again, get a new agent, do a guest star role on a network TV show, have a lead in a great indie movie, and get into the top five thousand on IMDB."

These were tangible goals. Some were more about Christopher's personal development and some his career development. It was a good mixture to start with and by getting specific Christopher felt more enthusiastic and inspired than he had felt in many years.

So, what are *your* dreams and goals? Is it to be the lead in a television show or to have a big film career? Is it to make a living playing supporting roles? Is it to spend your time on stage with a live audience or on a talk show? How specific can you get with your goals? As you edge into the realm of possibility, you get to touch on the good and happiness you want for yourself.

When you establish a goal for yourself, another question to ask is whether you can personally *initiate* the outcome or not. If the answer is *no*, then you probably need to find a new goal. This is simply because you have to be able to take the first steps to create it! If the answer is *yes*, then ask yourself if you can *control* the outcome. The word *control* can be confusing. Let me clarify how it's being used here. If you *can't* control this outcome, you're likely putting expectations on someone else. For example, *I wish my agent would send me on more auditions* is a goal that leaves the outcome, *and your power*, in the hands of someone else. You may even be hoping to control the uncontrollable with something like, *I want that producer to like me.* Remember that you can't control what other people do or feel. You can influence, inspire, or motivate them toward something, but you can't control their behavior, thoughts, or feelings. You can't control the end result either when it comes to *context*, yet you can control the journey. So make your goal something you feel is within your own power and that's not about something specific someone else might or might not do. Make your goal something that has you in the driver's seat, and that you can, at least, initiate!

Let me tell you about a client that explored this concept. "Sandy" wanted to feel more respected by her agent and have him respond more often. That kind of reciprocity and communication was big on her values list. Her agent, on the other hand, was less than interested in talking or writing to his clients unless it was about a job offer. Sandy came to me with a goal that her agent would call or e-mail her back every time she reached out. She was clear about that desire.

I first asked her if she really meant *every time*.

Sandy said, "Well, that would be nice, and okay, no, at least 85 percent of the time."

When I asked if she could control that outcome, she said, "Yes."

"How would you control that?" I asked.

"I can tell her she has to respond to me and that it's important."

"What if your agent says no?"

"I guess I'd have to put my foot down."

"How would you do that?"

"I would tell her that it has to happen. Maybe tell her I'd have to go elsewhere."

"Is that ultimately what you want?"

"Not right now, she's pretty powerful in the industry and I don't particularly want to move."

"Okay, so again, what if she says no?"

"Well, I don't know . . ."

"And if I said you *could* control your agent's behavior, that you *can* control whether a director hires you, or if your partner makes dinner on Mondays, or if your mother stops nagging you, what would you say to me?"

"I guess I'd say you're wrong," said Sandy, smiling through gritted teeth.

"Aha! And your truth may just set you free!" I laughed. "Okay, if we revisited your goal, what would be a desired outcome around your relationship with your representation? One that you can control the outcome of, at least in the majority?"

"Ummm. That they . . ."

"How would it be to start the goal with *I*, rather than *they*? This is about you."

"Okay, that I have a good flow of communication with my agent."

"Great."

What Sandy and I then did was to explore the *value* within that goal, what she wanted in the communication. Reciprocity and response were high on her values list. It meant knowledge, connection, and personal power for her. Her desire was really to have a reciprocal and fluid engagement with her team members and that became the new goal. She could then answer yes to the question, *can you control that outcome?*

When we want an outcome that involves another person or people, we need to look at whether we are hoping something will change in them. If you look at what you want out of it, for example, what the core value is in your desire, then you can find ways on *your* end to make that possible. You have to be creative.

Sandy then came up with new, more positive ways to phrase her e-mails and reduced the amount she reached out to her agent, all of which were simply ways to shift the old, limiting dynamic. She also made personal changes in how she generally reacted to the lack of response from others in her life.

Once you've practiced those new personal behaviors and responses, and it looks like the other person is really not going to engage in ways that you need, then it may be time to make a more logistical change. Sandy's agent had shown that his priority was to spend time communicating with casting people and making deals, not e-mailing and talking on the phone. So Sandy hired a manager. A manager's role is to communicate with a client far more than an agent would and Sandy found the sort of communication she valued within the relationship she had with this new team member. The new goal "to have a good flow of communication with my representative" was then met.

It was no wonder that Sandy's initial goal to feel more respected (and that it was dependent on her agent calling and e-mailing her back more) was driving her crazy. It was an unreasonable expectation she was putting on her agent and a guarantee of disappointment for herself. With powerful questions she was able to understand that, find out what the deeper desire was, and then create a well-formed outcome. Now, she may ultimately change her agent to suit her communication needs, and meanwhile, she opened herself up to what made her happy in the present!

A well-formed outcome requires that you've chosen a goal you can initiate and control the outcome of. This often requires getting really clear about the value seated way down in the bottom of it. It also requires that you make it about you. You are, ultimately, the only thing you can change concerning what you want, and you can always say yes to that!

The next step in creating a well-formed outcome is to ask, *What is the concrete evidence that my desired outcome has occurred?* This is a very important next step in creating what you want, because, just as it is with your vision, until you're clear about what your goal will look like, sound like, and feel like, it will be vague and unreal to your fundamental senses.

My client, "Jason," provides an example of the concept of concrete evidence. Jason had a goal to be more confident in auditions. That would be a major step in making his overall vision happen, which was to have his own television show.

"How would you know you were more confident in your auditions? What would be the evidence that has come true?" I asked him.

"Well, I would feel more grounded and sure of myself."

"Okay, what other 'feeling' evidence would there be?" I asked him.

"My heartbeat would be nice and calm."

"Great, and how about what you would literally see, for example? What will you be seeing around you as that's happening?" I asked him.

"What would I see? Um, I imagine my eyesight would be clearer. I would be able to focus. And probably the people in the room would make eye contact and smile and nod when I'm done."

"How about what you would hear as evidence that you're more confident?" I continued.

"My voice would be steady and strong. Again, my heart would be nice and quiet," he said smiling, "and I would be able to hear what the reader was saying. I could probably really listen to the other person in the scene!"

We both laughed. Not a lot to ask, you might think, yet how many times have you gone into an audition and been so nervous that all your listening skills went out the window? Being confident makes you more present and able to connect, and vice versa.

"What else?" I pressed.

"Okay, and maybe later from my agent I would hear things like, *We heard you did a great job and were really super confident, Jason. They booked you on the show!*" he added.

Jason imagined what other evidence there would be that he was more confident in his auditions: what that would feel like, sound like, look like, taste like, and even smell like. This meant his whole being could experience his goal as if it was already happening. It also gave him a chance to understand what his needs were and to shift anything that had been subconsciously blocking him.

In going through this process Jason discovered that he had not been clear on a number of things. He had not previously thought about the detailed aspects of his desired new reality. For example, with his career taking off, where and how was he going to relate on a day-to-day basis with his family as all this was going on with his career? This spoke to his entire vision (having his own show) and to the conflict this confidence goal might create.

Asking the right questions allowed him to explore how he would divide his time and his attention in a balanced way. We went through hypothetical hour-to-hour planning for this. He also became aware of what he would need to ask his family to shift in order to support him in his new career.

Jason also got very specific with the professional team he would need to have around him to make all this work. He began to understand the lifestyle that would ensue and the logistics that would come with that. He also got to understand himself a little more, and what values were driving the desired outcome.

So, taking your goals and asking these questions will bring you closer to them intellectually and logistically, as well as in your five senses, and by doing that you will bring the outcomes to you on a vibrational level as well. Each of these questions is important because they reveal your subconscious beliefs and feelings to you, which leads to greater awareness and therefore greater action.

Jason was ready for my next question. "What would the *benefits* be of having your goal happen?"

I suggested that he include the benefits that "more confidence in auditions" would bring to his career, as well as to his finances, health, social life, community, environment, living conditions, spiritual life, psychology, and family.

"I would book more jobs! That's pretty obvious," Jason said with a grin.

"What else?" I egged him on.

"I would have more money, probably be able to go out more with my friends, visit my sister in India . . ."

"Yes, what else?"

"Er, I would feel happier and more confident. I would probably attract a hot girl!" he laughed.

I laughed back. "A hot girl. What else?" I encouraged Jason to dig further. He came up with many more: increased energy, happiness, a great place to live, better relationships, love in his life, feeling stronger, a new car, traveling, seeing his family more, creative control, balance, the ability to buy bunk beds for the local homeless shelter, and so on.

"Wow!" he exclaimed happily. "I had no idea what all I would get from my little goal. Being more confident in auditions has a lot of benefits!"

"How does that sit with you?" I asked.

"Amazing! I'm so inspired to do whatever it takes to make that happen!"

Jason began to realize, most of all, what absolute abundance, adventure, and unbridled fun lay ahead simply because of having more confidence, and that gave Jason incredible energy and clarity to move forward in creating it.

When it comes to your own goal, ask yourself what the benefits would be to having that goal met. Perhaps the benefits to your goal are a specific dollar yearly income, a certain style and size house in an area you love, the ability to set up a charitable foundation for a cause close to your heart, or the means to pay for something your family needs. Whatever is important to you. As you think about the various areas of your life (your finances, your relationships, your social life, your health, your spiritual life, and your environment) and what positives would occur in each of those areas, you can imagine how those parts of your life would benefit from your goal happening. Chances are, you will discover some benefits you had not previously thought of. Lean into your own happiness as you do that. The benefits you identify in your goal happening are the things that will fuel you and get you inspired and passionate about where you're going. When you explore this, give yourself permission to make as long a list of benefits as you can. You are creating possibilities. You are connecting with some of the things that are most important and valuable to you!

It's also important to explore what the possible downsides, problems, negatives, or difficulties might be from having your goal met. Doing that will make you aware of the logistical items you may need to address so that you can find solutions ahead of time. This also means you can get clear about what your fears may be. For example, if your goal is to be a regular lead on a television series, you can imagine that you would be extra busy with those eighteen-hour days and might not have time to see your family as much as you would like to. You may have concerns about how to handle your newly expanded income, or be afraid that being in the limelight might harm your privacy or put you under scrutiny. Whatever your goal is, you will probably find a few potential obstacles (practical and logistical as well as emotional and mental) that may slow you down. This is important. As you really take time to think about these possibilities, you can get clear about what your fears are, conscious and subconscious, and then understand yourself more, ideally with compassion.

You now get the opportunity to create some solutions to these potential issues. There may be some perceived cost or real risks in your goal happening. The next step is to troubleshoot ways to minimize or address them. As an example, if your concern was not seeing your family enough, you may consider tweaking your goal a bit and making it (more specifically) a regular lead in a half-hour multi-camera show, a daytime soap, or a cable television show. These, after all, would take up less of your time than a one-hour network drama, and you would have the job and would *also* have more time to spend with your family. You might also build a number of family get-togethers and vacations into your vision of the future so you would feel more balanced in those areas. The underlying truth behind why you haven't achieved your goal yet may be because you have had legitimate, yet subconscious, fears or concerns, and your system has been protecting you.

Another way to reveal what may have stopped you from creating what you want is by asking *What would the benefits be of **not** having my goal happen?* or *What is the benefit of staying where I am?* These two questions are often some of the most baffling to people I work with, yet they are probably some of the most powerful. So before you jump to say *Nothing!* just think about it. There is always an answer if you take the time to ask and listen, and what you hear might be the clue to what's been holding you back. As you can only shift the things you're aware of, when you have that information it's like finding gold.

Every choice you make, whether it's conscious or subconscious, has a benefit. You wouldn't make those choices otherwise. If you've had underlying benefits to staying where you are, *you will stay where you are.* I often hear *But there are **no** benefits to **not** having my goal met! If there were, I wouldn't want my dream to happen!* The truth is, the benefit of the goal not happening doesn't stop you from *wanting* your goal. It simply creates inner conflict and keeps you where you are.

Jason discovered that one of the benefits to his lack of confidence in auditions had been "an excuse for not booking the parts." Again, this may sound crazy, yet it's quite a common answer. For actors, the odds of booking a part, unless you're already in the top two or three people being considered, are usually fairly low, and the disappointment can be challenging to deal with. Many actors take it personally, and, not understanding what a numbers game it really is, that makes it hard to find a reason beyond "I wasn't good enough" for not getting the part. Not being good enough is usually not the reason actors don't get hired. There are so many other factors involved like not being completely right for the role or for the ensemble cast that's being so carefully put together, or just not being at the optimal point in their career. Those things are not personal, and they have nothing to do with the actor's value. Continuing to come away from auditions with the experience of not feeling confident had been a way for Jason to say to himself, *Well, hey, at least it wasn't because I'm not good enough! It was because of my lack of confidence.* The fact that he could lean on that habit or belief, even if it was subconscious, meant that Jason avoided the pain of feeling "not good enough." To someone else, "not feeling confident" in auditions may have been a way to avoid the other things that may feel threatening in a successful career, like commitment to a contract that requires long hours, or time away from family, or suddenly being in the limelight where everyone will see your "flaws." You name it. I've heard many great benefits to not feeling confident in auditions! The mind is a slippery, clever thing that has very intricate ways of protecting us from things that really do feel like threats, and we may not even know it until we do this kind of exploration. The benefit, for example, of *not* being a regular on a television show (even with its substantial pay and creative opportunity) could be that staying where you are (which might be auditioning and looking for that big break) means you get to set your own schedule, get up when you like, go to the gym, and see friends all on your own time. It might mean you get to be in your comfort zone with familiar things and people around you without having to stretch or push yourself through the anxiety or risk of failure. These are just some examples. I understand your career may be at the point where you don't want a television series, but want a new direction in your flourishing film career instead. You can just plant your own scenario into these questions and explore accordingly.

If you think carefully about this question in regard to your own particular goal, you may find that some very important values will continue to be met if you stay where you are in life. Those benefits are valuable and your system is taking care of you. It knows what's important to you and it fulfills your needs wherever it can. If there's a hidden benefit to not having something happen, then you will subconsciously act in ways that prevent that change from happening. Once you understand this you can understand what has been compelling you to stay where you are and how you've been sabotaging the future you think you want. Simply having this information creates the opportunity to shift. You can now find ways to minimize the perceived threats within your goal and to shift previously unconscious beliefs, and the road becomes cleared of blocks that were not even visible before.

Now, once you reveal what the benefits are to not having your goal met, you don't want to get rid of them. Why would you? A benefit is something that's advantageous or good, and it increases your levels of happiness. The business you're in can be challenging enough and you deserve as much good as you can pack into your life, so keep as many benefits as you can! The opportunity is to find *other ways* to get them met, or else build them into the design of your goal.

For example, Jason came to understand that another benefit to not having confidence in auditions was to "live a quiet life with no major responsibilities." This is because, with lack of audition confidence, a busy, vibrant career would never take off. However, instead of just living with a failed acting career, Jason decided to build some quiet time into his goals—time where he would get to rest, relax, and have fewer responsibilities. He also looked at the overall plan and where he would need to delegate some of the work and responsibility. All that made it possible to have more of the benefit (to "live a quiet life with no major responsibilities") inserted into the goal *happening*, as opposed to *not* happening. He also looked at what his experience of "responsibility" had been in the past and if the meaning he held was still relevant. This gave him a chance to change his old beliefs about responsibility into something new and resourceful. By exploring in these ways his inner being became far more aligned with his goal.

If you have a goal and parts of you are not on board, whether it's because of perceived difficulties or unconscious benefits to having the goal not happen, the goal will remain unreachable. Your system is always taking care of you and your actions will come out of that. When you discover what the benefits have been to staying where you are, you're then able to find new and more resourceful ways to get those benefits without sabotaging your goal. You factor in the need that shows up in the benefit and it takes the resistance out of the goal. By taking this exploratory journey into your own consciousness and rearranging your plans accordingly, conflict is no longer an issue and the outcome becomes easier to reach. You're essentially making a truce, making peace. You clarify and eliminate many of the blocks that have been getting in the way of you aligning with, and therefore reaching, your dream.

There are many ways to create powerful goals. Another one is to make sure you know what resources you will need to make them happen, like information, training, money, support, community, or simply a shift in internal state or attitude. You then plan to introduce these resources into your life as you can. Get specific about where you will get these resources. You also have to take your vision to action and create a good business plan. A life coach is today's resource for many people to do just that.

In our coaching Jason and I did all of the above. We did some deep personal work to boost his confidence levels and used powerful tools to create new states, beliefs, and perspectives. We also created a business plan. I asked him when we wanted his goal accomplished and what his next steps were. He looked at what needed to happen between our session and a specific date, making the first steps small, doable, and easy to take. He also planned some behaviors and activities that were confidence builders for him. He chose a new acting class that would raise his confidence levels and decided to do a bit of improv at a comedy club to get him into his creative flow. He also realized his relationships needed to change to reflect his sense of self. He was committed to his confidence levels being raised, found resources that would support that happening, set a date, and took first steps. He took his vision to action and began to change his life.

Asking these questions is a powerful way to gain insight about your goals, discover where the resistance has been to reaching them, and determine how to rearrange your plans accordingly. By doing this you clear the path for action, and the outcome becomes easier to reach.

Step into Your Future

Confidence is not just a goal; it's a way of being. Have you ever watched a successful actor, someone who seems to have it all going on, and said to yourself, *How great it must be to have such power, to be so in tune, to have so much success!* Yet is it the chicken or the egg that came first? Consider whether the success some of our top actors have is what makes them seem so confident, or if it was the confidence, clarity, connectedness, directness, and decisiveness that made others say in the first place, *Who is that person? They are so interesting and unafraid. I want to put them in my movie/television show/ production.* Of course, success does increase our confidence levels and we feel empowered, then, to create more. On the other hand, lack of confidence and fear rarely inspires others to bank their time, money, projects, and careers on any of us! Right? So, again, confidence has to be there as a foundation before success can really occur. Knowing this, (beyond the exploration you've already done here) what can you do to create a level of confidence within yourself that you may not have a previous experience of, one that would inspire the confidence of producers and studio executives? You begin living in the frequency of what it is you envision.

Many of us see our dreams *out there*. We imagine our future lying ahead of us, and that's where it remains. *Ahead*. Yet once there's clarity about what's important and what the goals and next steps are, in order to actualize something we've imagined, we have to begin *living it out*. Actions, thoughts, beliefs, habitual states, focus, intentions, environments, and goals—everything has to support and fit that desired future. Those are the things that anchor us. As an actor you are better equipped than most other humans on the planet to do this because your craft demands that you step into other realities so much of the time.

If you have a robust vision for yourself and you *keep living the same way you've always lived*, you will remain anchored there and won't manifest that desired future, ever. It's no good wanting to live a life of elegance and serenity, for example, if you're living with a bunch of noisy, dirty room-mates and spending your weekends at the local dive. If, however, you let go of the anchors that don't fit that vision and introduce anchors that *do* fit and support the desired state, then you will find yourself anchored, instead, to your new, desired life. This way you're aligning with your vision. In order to create what you desire and then manifest it, you have to live in the vibrational frequency of it first. As an example, rather than going to the grubby coffee shop on the corner, getting your Sunday morning coffee at an elegant patisserie might allow you to live in the vibration of what you've been wanting. If that's not it, and you've been dreaming of a life surrounded by creativity, art, beautiful things, interesting people, and stimulating conversation, go and find them. You're living in a world where there are ample opportunities to either find the world you want to be in or create it for yourself.

How can I do that right now? you might say. *I don't have the money and I don't have the jobs I want yet. It has got to **happen** first before I can live it!* It may seem impossible to simply start living the life you desire when you have limited resources. Yet is it?

An actress (whom I will call "Michelle") had worked in some small movies and on a couple of television shows in supporting roles. Things had been moving a bit slowly for her and she was frustrated. She felt quite clear about what she wanted for herself as an actor and what sort of life that would entail, yet she felt stuck. So, when Michelle came to me for life coaching I invited her to share what her vision was in the various areas of her life. We started with the acting part.

"What I want is to be working a lot," began Michelle.

"How much is 'a lot'?" I asked.

"Well, probably nine months out of the year, so almost every day, and with time off to do other things and take breaks."

"Okay, and in this vision of your future, what sorts of roles and productions are you working on?"

Michelle described her detailed vision.

I then asked, "What sort of money are you making in this desired life?"

"Loads. Enough to be living stylishly!"

"How much money does that take?"

"I don't know. I guess a million a year."

"What does 'living stylishly' look like?"

"Well, I would have a beautiful house in the Pacific Palisades. I would have a nice car and lots of dogs. I will have lots of successful, creative friends and a great social life. I take time to travel, like hiking in Nepal and seeing the Great Pyramids in Egypt. I also take time to help other people. I go to charity events and I help set up an orphanage in Haiti."

Michelle and I got even more detailed about her house, her car, her dogs, her partner, friends, family, her charity work, and really established the emotional, physical, spiritual, and psychological impact and effect these things were to have for her. Once we had done this we explored how she could begin to *live that life*.

We started with Michelle's love of acting. She wanted to be "working a lot."

"How much are you working as an actor now?"

"I'm only *working*, getting paid to act, about ten or twenty days out of the year. I'm *acting* when I audition, about once every two weeks."

"So, if you were going to be *living the life*, you would be acting a lot. How would you do that *now*?" I asked Michelle.

"Well, I guess I could go back to class. That would mean I was acting more."

"That's one way. How else? What ways would you be acting and making money at it for example?"

"Plays. I haven't done many and not for a while because I really want to do film. I could do that."

"How would that be for you?"

"Fun probably!" Michelle laughed.

We established that Michelle had been missing out on being an actor on a day-to-day basis. The idea was in her head; however, she had not actually been living it out. With our coaching Michelle came up with ways to make her vision real today. She got some friends together to make a short film. She joined an improv class, taking part in their monthly public performances, which led to an invitation to join the cast of a play. Because she was spending so much more time actually immersed in the creative craft of acting (and in the part of acting that she initially valued), her work began to flow, her demeanor lit up, and her auditions got better. Inevitably she started booking more television and film roles. In fact, she found herself working a lot.

We found that Michelle was also able to live into the other parts of her vision for the future. She drove around Pacific Palisades, going to open houses to get a feel for what it was like to live there, what she wanted in a home, and what the prices were. Though at the moment she didn't have the money to buy a house, being able to touch, smell, and walk around those houses made it more solid and brought it closer. Michelle also cleaned up her current living environment, her apartment. She threw out some old things that were cluttering it and that didn't fit with her vision. With the proceeds of a yard sale she bought a beautiful antique trunk that would go nicely in her future house in the Palisades.

She also test-drove a few luxury cars to get a feel for what would fit her desired life. She went to low-cost charity events and free screenings where she met new, creative, successful people. Michelle volunteered at the local dog rescue to be around dogs. She sponsored a child in Africa and did some work for Habitat For Humanity. Michelle also took a camping trip to Yosemite and hiked the beautiful trails in readiness for her trip to Nepal! She let go of many of the old things in her life that didn't fit her desired vision, and brought the aspects of her desires for the future into the present *through literal, active, practical means.*

Pretty soon, as you can imagine, her life changed even further. Her reality began to take on the taste, smell, feel, and look of her vision. Michelle, at last, was manifesting what she had desired all those years.

When you wait for the future to happen and put things on hold until then, you will stay where you are. *Living the life* means finding what fits with your vision and adding it into your current life. It means letting go of the things that don't fit. It means bringing the future closer to you by having it around you in whatever ways are possible. It also means checking in every day with each action and decision, and asking, *Does this fit my overall vision?*

You can start living the life you love right now!

Release the Outcome

You've been on a journey here with me and have hopefully discovered some things about yourself that will help you become a happier person—things like what you truly want, what you believe about the world, and what really matters to you. As an actor you dedicate much of your time and energy to the craft and platforms for acting, so the assumption would be that it's one of the things that matters to you most. Yet, how you *relate* to what matters also matters. Being *attached* to what you find important is subtly yet significantly different from being *connected* to it. Let me explain.

Attaching can be described as "fastening one thing to another with ties." You might have found at times that you've become attached to things, to people, to outcomes, and then put the importance on *them*, rather than on how you feel when you're in or around them. At times you may have hung onto a picture in your mind of an outcome as though your life depended on it (like landing that great role you were up for) and when the picture changes (because someone else books it) it feels like your life is over. Ah yes, that old beast again!

Casting director Mark Teschner put it wonderfully when he said to me, "It's so tricky, because you have to be passionate about acting and passionate about loving what you do, but you can't become passionate about the result because that's out of your hands."

How right he is. So, I encourage *connecting* instead. Being connected is about joining. When you're connected to something that you've created, or to what or whom you love, you've connected to your values and what has deep meaning for you. You understand that it's about the *experience* of those external things (that great role, that relationship, or condition) that matters, and about your capacity to have those experiences through many, many different channels.

When you experience the loss of something like a role you had hoped to land, or even a relationship you had banked on, yes, of course you feel that loss to whatever degree. But when you are *connected* you understand that there is still the essence within you of that relationship, object, idea, or that acting role. The essence didn't go anywhere. It's part of who you are as a creative being. When you connect with your values, your purpose, and your passions, you're in touch with your deepest self even in the face of disappointment. You trust in something ongoing.

It's the ego that wants to control outcomes. It is attached to results. The ego focuses on a goal and then creates stress around it by making the outcome more important than the in-the-moment activity. One of the most valuable things you will learn in your craft as an actor is the ability to release outcomes. You can do your preparations, know all the lines backward and forward, understand the story, the wants, the obstacles, and the relationships, and the end result is not up to you. It's out of your control. The moment you try to control how a performance might turn out is the moment you're out of the present moment and in your *head*. You've lost the opportunity for magic. Remember the word *enthusiasm?* When you are enthusiastic, your enjoyment of what you're doing in the present moment is primary, and the outcome is secondary. When you let go and surrender everything, you're living in the moment and the results become art. When you're acting and in your creative zone, when you're fully alive and present, those are the times you connect with your consciousness. It's a type of *doing* that is a means without an end, without expecting anything back in that moment. It's not just the love of doing what you do; it's the love of *being* it.

This is also a calling in your life. As you move through your journey as an actor, working daily to create what you desire, there is an opportunity to practice being connected to it on an even deeper level and at the same time being detached from the outcome. You release it. You trust. And when you do, you may find that you *respond* to situations (like a role going to someone else) rather than *reacting* to them. You take things less personally. You let go of the way you think things "should" look. You keep the experiences, the purpose, and the vision that is borne from the deepest parts of you. Nothing can ever take those away.

Be in the Flow

Extraordinary as it may sound, many people have a resistance to receiving. The culture we have created is very prone to wanting, hoping for, and taking, yet receiving seems to be a lost art. Happiness increases as we become more open to the good in our lives, and we have to receive it to do that. It's an intrinsic part of what I call being *in the flow*. We allow the infinite abundance of good in the universe to flow into our lives, as well as through us toward others.

Receiving also requires that we *give* what it is we believe we don't have yet. In reality you already have what it is you desire. It exists within you, and the only way you will know that you already have it is by giving it to others. As you allow it to flow through you and from you, you experience it as already existing. If you believe there is something that has been lacking, then give it. If, for example, you want more response from people in your life (like your agent, your manager, or your friends), then this is an opportunity to look at being more responsive to others. If you feel you don't have enough support, look at who might need your support and give it to them. If you think you haven't got enough money, then give some of what you do have to those less fortunate. If you think you don't have something to give to others, *act as if* you have it and give it anyway. Then watch what happens. Being in the flow has you stepping into that which has no limits!

Another avenue to being in the flow is through gratitude. Acknowledging the good in your life is the foundation for all abundance. When you feel the universe owes you or that you're a victim of other people or circumstance, you're forgetting the truth—that everything is part of a divine plan. If you're in a mind-set of lack, and if you focus on that imagined lack, then lack will expand and you will have less. Very often getting back into alignment with the divine flow just takes being grateful for what it is that you've forgotten you already have.

Over the many years I have been involved in the television and film business, I've heard a lot of actors complain about lack of auditions, work, money, you name it. Yes, of course, it can be a tough, unpredictable business at times, *and* I would bet that those habitual complaints haven't helped any of them get what they wanted. I can also bet that when an actor (or anyone for that matter) *does* get what they want and they become what's normally considered successful, it doesn't necessarily bring happiness.

On a summer day in Los Angeles I checked in by phone with a friend of mine who was in the middle of directing a pilot for one of the world's top producers. Knowing where my friend stands with the studios I know he has a huge amount of creative control and an even bigger paycheck. He also has a mansion by the ocean, a family who loves him, his health, and an industry that would give him just about anything he wanted. Yet as I spoke with him, asking how he was, he answered in the dullest tone you could imagine, "Eaagh. You know me. I'm miserable when I'm working, I'm miserable when I'm not." When I asked him what was going on with that, he replied that it was nothing really, just that they were having trouble casting the roles and there wasn't enough time for pre-production and the script needed work. The usual things.

I laughed, "Well, you're in a wonderful position to enjoy the process. I hope you can do that."

We know that positive external circumstances can make us feel better about life, temporarily, yet if we are used to focusing on the negatives we will see them in even the most incredible gifts. Those external circumstances may not be a happiness booster, even temporarily, if we don't experience the positives in them. Certainly, there are things we have to navigate and overcome, and that's part of life. At the same time there is abundance and good everywhere even in times of great loss. We just have to see it for it to exist for us.

No matter how "successful" I've seen my director friend become, even with his increasing popularity, power, and income, he has not become a happier person. If anything he has become disconnected from his own sense of mission and purpose, and that (combined with his focus on lack) has made him a pretty unhappy man.

Another example is an actor I worked with many years ago on a television show. He initially seemed quite pleased when he landed the lead on his network television series, yet as time went on he returned to his habitual state, which turned out to be angry, ungrateful, and cynical about almost everything. The newly attained money, fame, and creative opportunity had been like a blast of cocaine, yet when the initial hit wore off he became as unhappy as he had been before the series entered his life. The drop in his mood happened so extraordinarily quickly that the producers and studio executives commented, on the very first day, how miserable and angry he seemed. Because of this I suspect he had been *excited* about his new circumstances, as opposed to *truly happy*. He went on to work in other series, yet never did seem satisfied with his lot. There are hundreds of thousands of actors out there who would give anything to have half the career this actor had, yet he didn't seem to enjoy it and his career dwindled, most likely due to his ungrateful attitude.

These two examples provide a lesson to anyone who has a dream. While you take the emotional, spiritual, psychological, and practical steps to make your vision manifest, it's just as crucial to acknowledge and be grateful for what you already have along the way. Then when things come into your life that you've worked toward, you will naturally be able to appreciate them as well.

It's also important to remember that, because you're reading this book, chances are you live in a society where becoming an actor is feasible and would not take away from your actual ability to survive. You're probably not a man living in the mountains of Afghanistan. If you were, you would not have the privilege of choosing *actor* as your vocation. You would be working to feed yourself and your family every day by tending sheep, living in the rugged wilderness for weeks on end, not seeing your family or friends, and certainly not watching movies, listening to music, or meeting girls. It's likely, too, that you're not a woman living in Saudi Arabia. If you were, the choice to become an actress would probably not be on your list of possibilities. In fact, you wouldn't be allowed to leave your own home without a male guardian, drive your own car, or vote. You're probably not a young woman living in Somalia. If you were, acting would not be something in your consciousness because you would be spending each waking day trying to survive the threats of starvation, rape, and murder.

It can be so easy at times to fall asleep to the privileges we have every day. Taking our freedoms and our safety for granted can leave us with a skewed perspective on life, and we are left focusing on the lack of a nice enough car or a fast enough line at the bank. The ungrateful actor on his television show was privileged enough to be safe, fed, and sheltered, let alone paid hundreds of thousands of dollars a year to be creative and to play.

To put things in some perspective; if your focus is being an actor, it's likely there are many things to be grateful for in your life.

When it comes to actually saying *thank you*, thanking others for what they do for you is a powerful way to create better relationships and raise happiness levels all around. When anyone does a good job, shares a resource or referral, gives you a gift, responds to an e-mail or phone call, lets you go first at a four-way stop sign, opens a door for you, smiles at you, serves you at a restaurant, or makes you feel in any way seen, loved, or cared for, look them in the eyes if you can and thank them. The kid who bags your groceries, the girl who buffs your nails, the person that takes away your trash, the casting associate who brings you in, the agent's assistant who gives you your audition information, your mother who keeps cooking for you, your friend who calls you even when she knows you're in a bad mood, the makeup artist who makes you look good—everyone you meet deserves your gratitude. When your spouse or partner opens the door for you or cooks dinner, never mind if they do it regularly, thank them each and every time.

Gratitude is a rich fertilizer for growing what you love. When you're grateful for the good in your life, you've added the ingredient that stimulates more to come in, and you're then able to serve others in more expansive ways. Being thankful for peace when you're stressed will awaken you to the peace that's already here. Being thankful for love when you feel alone will awaken you to the love that your life is made up of. Being thankful for abundance when you feel lacking will awaken you to the abundance that's always around you. There is a Chinese proverb that says, "Better to light a candle than to curse the darkness." Gratitude is lighting that candle in your life. This opens the energetic channels for you to receive what it is you desire. When you're in the vibrational frequency of abundance through gratitude, abundance will become known to you, and good will expand in your life.

So, next time you notice yourself with an attitude about the lack of auditions, bookings, or money, first of all, be kind to yourself. This is not about beating yourself up or denying what might seem challenging. It's simply an opportunity to be open to the gifts as well. Take a moment to turn inward and remind yourself of what it is you would feel from having the outcomes you desire. Become open to receiving them and be grateful. Decide to be in the flow. Acknowledging the good in your life is the foundation for all abundance. You have the power to be happy no matter what your outside circumstances are. The extraordinary thing about how the universe works is that the more you focus on the positive, the more you create what you desire and the more you can enjoy those gifts permanently. That, to me, is success.

Celebrate Your Successes

What you have in your system is what you will experience outwardly. You squeeze an orange and you get orange juice, not apple juice. If you have a sense of failure because of a repeated focus on the rejection, mistakes, or *no's,* then you squeeze out the juice of failure. You walk into a room and people there smell the scent of failure and they run. If, instead, you have an inner sense of success, then *success* flows from your pores and out into the world around you. A big key to being a successful, happy actor is having a habitual sense of success flowing through your system, and the way you create that is by celebrating your accomplishments and victories, no matter how small they might seem.

One of the many wonderful aspects of being a SAG-AFTRA member is the residuals checks you receive after the shoot is over. I have received many hundreds of them over the years, ranging from thousands of dollars to a couple of pennies, and I've made sure to be grateful and to celebrate every one of them, including those that are less than the cost of mailing them to me—those two, three, or four cent checks. The reason I do that is so that I am *in the flow*, and also to anchor success into my being and into my life.

At the end of a session with a client where we have come up with a game plan, whether it's strategic or personal, I often ask, "How will you celebrate when that happens?" The look of surprise on their face isn't unusual. So often the focus is on making things *happen* that the idea of celebrating an accomplishment is bypassed. A box is checked, an item on the list is crossed out, and the next task then becomes the focus. Imagine if you worked for someone and they gave you task after task and never acknowledged your accomplishments or efforts. You may well have worked for someone like that and I would bet you were probably not inspired to keep going. If you had an employer who noticed your accomplishments and then *celebrated* them, you would feel appreciated and inspired to do well again next time.

You would feel successful at what you do! That's how you can engage with yourself as well.

So, celebrate whatever it is you've accomplished, even if it's in part. Celebrate the small as well as the large successes. Notice when you were really connecting in a scene, got somewhere on time, did something for the first time, finished a project, made that phone call, completed a mailing, did that first interview, booked that role, hired a new representative, made that deal, or signed that contract. Get your whole body involved in the victory. Throw your arms up, jump up and down, and cheer. Get your loved ones involved, if they are so inclined. Be creative about your celebrations. They can be anything from doing a victory dance, to having a meal with friends, to taking a trip somewhere beautiful, to running on the beach, to getting a massage, to paragliding, to buying yourself a gift. Celebrations are about you taking the time to rejoice before you move forward again. Then, you get used to being successful. When you walk into a room, you smell of success to the people there and they want to be part of it. They want to engage with you somehow, whether that's to hire you or befriend you. When you celebrate your successes, you live out the experience of accomplishment on a day-to-day basis, the larger, more significant victories simply become par for the course, and happiness becomes the fiber of your being.

The universe listens and watches very carefully. What you speak, think, feel, and believe will be delivered to you perfectly every time. In knowing this, you know your own power. There is always choice and anything is possible. All that you dream of is always here, ready for you to step in. Say yes to the miracle of your life. It's time.

CHAPTER 8

Going Forth!

What the caterpillar calls the end, the rest of the world calls a butterfly.

~ *LAO TZU*

Your Anchors

Right now you're living your life with a particular set of anchors installed. Much of what we have gone over in this book has helped you identify some of these anchors, as well as new ones that will create and sustain the life you desire. Anchors are things like your surroundings, your thoughts, your beliefs, the people in your life, your habits, and the ways in which you engage the world, and all of them make up your experience of life. They literally and figuratively *anchor you to your life.*

You can't have the life you desire with the set of anchors you've been living with. It's not possible. You may have found in the past that a seminar, workshop, book, or travel experience changed how you felt about the world and life became new and refreshing for a while, but then you returned to many of your old ways. It's the old anchors that keep returning you to your original ways of living. In order to create a sustainably happier life filled with more of the experiences you desire, you have to permanently install the anchors that support that life.

Our planet is, right now, going through a massive paradigm shift that has been predicted for centuries. It is sometimes referred to as "the end of the world." The literal interpretation of this phrase has created unwarranted fear and plenty of disaster movies. It is, instead, more like the end of the world *as we have known it*, and it is, in fact, already happening. Technology, just one example of how fast this shift is occurring, has changed our fundamental day-to-day reality. This shift is occurring on an individual and collective level, as well as a universal level, and old anchors are being uprooted whether we like it or not. The old paradigms in communication, relationships, social systems, and the allocation of power no longer work and we are being called to create brand new ones.

When a caterpillar in a chrysalis begins its metamorphosis into a butterfly, there is chaos. Something foreign to the caterpillar begins to appear called *imaginal cells*. These cells carry different information than the cells of the caterpillar. They vibrate at a different frequency—the frequency of the emerging butterfly. At first the caterpillar's immune system perceives these new butterfly cells as enemies and attacks them. Conflict within the chrysalis between the old caterpillar cells and the new butterfly cells is intense, the *old* trying to devour the *new* in fear of its own annihilation. But the imaginal butterfly cells are not deterred. They continue to appear in even greater numbers, recognizing each other and bonding together until they are numerous enough to organize into clumps. When enough of these butterfly cells have formed to make structures along new organizational lines, the caterpillar's immune system is overwhelmed and its body then becomes a nutritious soup for the growth of the new butterfly. The butterfly uses its past as fuel to launch it forward into a new realm as it waits until just the right moment to emerge and spread its beautiful wings.

We are currently moving through a global awakening, a struggle between the old paradigm of the over-consuming and unconscious weight of the adolescent soul, into the freedom and higher consciousness of the adult soul. The chaos we feel both within ourselves and out in the world is part of this metamorphosis.

As an actor in an industry, not only hit by the economy, but also by years of union strikes and massive changes, you're living through times unmatched in history. You're being invited to think very resourcefully right now, riding these complicated, challenging times with as much consciousness as possible. The most important thing we can all do during this time is to continue bringing in and creating those "imaginal cells" (the new, resourceful, and positive anchors) that we will then, collectively, be able to create our desired reality with. The anchors you've discovered for yourself as you've read this book are a fundamental part of creating your own happiness, as well as a new paradigm for the globe. Those anchors may be meditation; being in nature; journaling; taking on new communication skills; having a support network like therapists, spiritual teachers, or coaches; regularly using books, tapes, CDs, DVDs, webinars and seminars to support your transformation; practicing positive thinking and gratitude; completing your past with forgiveness and amends; working toward meaningful goals that are consistent with your cherished values; being creative; having balance in life; forming good relationships and social connections; taking part in regular physical activities that nurture your body and spirit; and a belief in a higher power or purpose.

You may feel alone at times in your journey. Just know that there are many like you who are here to make a stand for a new way of living, bringers of the new dawn of consciousness, not only in the industry you've chosen, but also on this entire planet. One of your greatest anchors will be the connection you have with others who are of a like mind. Just like imaginal cells, as you come together, your vision for the future will be fortified and you will begin to vibrate at an even higher frequency together because of it. The old will no longer be able to continue destroying the new, and your past ways of living will naturally fall away as you, together, create a synergistic awakening. You go from *I* to *we*, into reciprocity, compassion, and unity, recognizing that at all levels we are part of a larger whole.

As your consciousness rises you become more discerning about what you have in your life. You may find that, as you grow into your own best self, there are things in your life that suddenly no longer fit. Your agent, acting coach, friends, and even your partner may appear to live in a dynamic that no longer works for you. Your living space, location, habits, old haunts, and typical activities may suddenly feel off path. It is important now to ask what does seem to fit. What serves your happiness? What serves the good of others? Does the structure in your life serve your purpose? Do the things you watch on television or read nourish and fortify you and your vision, or do they poison your mind and distract you? Does the food you eat strengthen you? Do your activities elevate you? Do your surroundings fill you with awe and gratitude? Do your friends inspire you? Do your day-to-day choices connect you with the Source?

As a creative spirit it's also significantly important to *create* every day. Being in the creative flow is what keeps you on path, connecting with your highest purpose. Whether you're acting, writing a play, videotaping an idea with your friends, singing dialogue in the bathtub, painting a portrait, or putting plants in the dirt, create something every single day. Go barefoot and dance the flow back into your life. You will inspire and be inspired. Spend more of your energy focusing on where you have control—where no one can tell you *you can't do it, you're not right for it*, or *you didn't get it*. Keep focusing on the passion, the deeper *why* you're even following this dream, as opposed to *how* it's going to happen. You have no control over the outcomes, just the steps you take and the energy with which you take them. Think positively, focusing on what you're grateful for and what you desire. Simplify, simplify, simplify. Take the deadwood and the complications out of your life and make things straightforward. Breathe deeply and consciously. Commit to being as kind and loving to yourself and to others as you've ever been. And remember, *there is always a new opening at the end of every tunnel you go through.* Perhaps the garden on the other side of this is more lush, more bountiful, and far easier to live in than you might imagine.

Have a Life

As you open yourself to being happier, you open yourself to avenues other than acting. Placing everything on acting can be limiting and puts tremendous pressure on one spot. Yes, keep the main thing the main thing, but don't limit yourself. If you bring a limited life to your work as an actor, it will be limited. If you bring a rich, diverse life to your work, it will be rich and diverse!

Mark Teschner said to me, "I think that for any actor pursuing this career, happiness has to be related not to your development as an actor exclusively. I think your development as an actor is always crucial, but your development as a person . . . If you're a complex and interesting person, that will inform your acting. If you're not, you're not going to bring that into the room. I hear actresses who have just become mothers tell me that it's made them better actors for two reasons: they are just much more emotionally present because they feel a sense of depth and love that they've never felt before. They also detach more from needing the job, because they have something they love so much outside of acting that they're no longer defined by just being an actor. I tell actors, 'Don't define yourself by your acting career. Find things you love, whether it's your family . . . Find something else that's artistic for you, find other ways to feel creative and alive.' If you're only defining your happiness by your acting career, you're going to be unhappy a lot of the time. I think you're a better actor when you come into the room with a fulfilled, happy life than if your life is defined by your acting. There's just a different energy. You vibrate at a different frequency when you're happy."

Risa Bramon Garcia said something along the same lines to me in the following conversation. "Having healthy relationships outside the business is so important. Having family. One thing that I believe very strongly for actors—and anybody in this business—is to make sure your juices are flowing creatively, emotionally, physically, and elsewhere, especially in Los Angeles where it's not as easy to find those outlets, to find that community. And, I think it's essential that actors, directors and writers find other ways to express themselves. You're so dependent on getting the job, but someone else defines that for you. As an athlete, you have to keep yourself tuned. I've seen so many wonderful actors become writers and directors . . . It doesn't mean you're not an actor anymore, it just means that you have other ways to keep yourself juiced, tuned, alive and connected."

"Yes. That way your whole identity is not on one thing that you have very little control over. You have many other things that you have at least some control over and that you can fully live through," I agreed.

"Right," Risa replied, "Really, its so vital. It will feed your work as an actor. It will also mean, when you walk in the room to audition, it's like, *Oh yeah, okay, I'm going to do this now.*"

"You're part of the flow," I piped in.

"Yeah. I always say to actors, don't ever go in the room to get the job. Ever. Go in the room to do your work on that character, in that scene. If you can be focused on that, you're sort of saying as an afterthought, *Oh, and you guys are here. Come with me on this ride. I have this great thing I want to do now. You can bear witness or participate. We're in this together.* Actors always look at me and go, 'Are you sure?' And I go, 'I'm totally sure.'" Risa laughed. "It can never be about getting the job. Yes, we all need to pay our mortgage . . ."

"And you can't bring that into the room," I added in agreement.

"You see this in pilot season. Actors come in and get taped. Then they come back in to read for the producer or director. Then they come in for them again. Then they sign the contract, and read for the studio. Then they have to go back in the next day for the network, and then finally sign their life away in the negotiations. They're up against four people, and they know that if they get this job they're going to be on a TV pilot that could change their lives. Well, it could, but it also couldn't, you know? And, who cares? You never know what is going to come of it. I've seen actors over and over again completely stop and suffocate. It's almost like they stop breathing. They walk into that room and they tank . . . Or they test for five or six things in one season. That's got to be debilitating . . . I don't have the answer for how an actor can go through a pilot season in Los Angeles and test for four, five, six different pilots and not get hired and be okay with that. I don't know. You have got to find a way to purge. There's got to be something at the end of that where you know where you're headed, so that you can clean out, because it's . . . that's a bitch."

"I was there," I shared, "and I changed my attitude. That sounds really simplistic, but I did, and then I booked a show."

"What did you . . . what was the shift?" Risa asked.

"I changed my perspective on the big picture and said, *This is just a part. It doesn't matter. I have all these other things in my life.* I felt like I was ready to make a shift anyway, or leave. It wasn't *everything* to me anymore."

"Right. That's it," said Risa. "But that's huge. So many actors are afraid of that, especially as they get older. There aren't going to be as many roles. We need to hear the wisdom of our experience and know that it doesn't really matter. If you do good work it will speak for itself and there will be a part for you somewhere."

"Yes," I said nodding, "and the stakes can't be made so high that it stops you breathing."

"I would say, take the stakes and put them into your character," replied Risa. "If you can walk into the room and say, *Today, my character has to get this guy to love me,* and then make that your mantra, then the people in the room are like, *All, right you guys, okay. **This** is what we're doing now.*"

David Nutter told me a story that illustrates how important he, too, feels life outside of the business is. He said, "The first episode of *ER* that I directed—this was when the show was at its height—it was a big episode. Sherry Stringfield was basically going to leave the show, so I walked over and met her. I said, 'I'm David Nutter. I'm really honored to be doing this show. I know it's your final episode. What are you going to do? Are you going to do movies?' This was a time when George Clooney was doing Batman. All the actors on the show were doing big things. Sherry said, 'No, I am just going to go back to New York, be with my boyfriend, make pasta, have friends over and just turn off for a bit.' I looked at her and I said, 'Life is not a race is it?'"

David's comment apparently described things perfectly for her. A short while later she quoted him in a *New York Times* interview as she explained her choice to leave the show and live a more "normal life".

David also shared, "I consciously *don't* work. Often that can just be dead time or down time, but at least I'm out of it, day trading stock, or I'm playing golf, or I'm just doing something else, something that's totally out of that world. I feel that if I worked too much, or all the time, then it would be just that: work. And the minute it becomes work for me is the minute that my heart's not in it." David continued with actors in mind, "What can you do that you truly love to do, where you're not hurting anyone else and you're not hurting yourself? What is it that you can do that can fulfill you outside of acting? Because then, and only then, can you come back to it with a perspective."

Yes, life is not a race, and it's not all about one thing. It can't be. Whether you're starting out or already established as an actor, your life has to be balanced and filled with many things. Your work will be fuller, and you will be far more fulfilled and happy.

Accept Healthy Support

What we all really want is for the source of our happiness, which is love, to become known to us again. We crave it more than anything, even if we don't recognize it as being what we want. Yet we can't *find* love, because love never leaves. Love is always present. It's when we forget that truth that we suffer, and it's when we remember love that we experience our deepest joy.

We each have ourselves as our own precious charge. We have the sacred responsibility to parent ourselves lovingly through this strange and mysterious human journey. We must take responsibility for our own lives, *and* we must also be open to support.

Many of us don't have role models for the kind of healthy, caring parent we need to be for ourselves as we go out into the world. So, how do we create something we have no frame of reference for? We have to build a picture of that healthy parent, and we do that with healthy support. Support is an important part of our happiness. It's connected to our sense of community as well as the fundamental need to be heard, valued, and cared for.

The kind of support that will do that—whether it's through a therapist, coach, manager, trainer, advisor, spiritual teacher, or mentor—does not fix something that's "wrong" with you, but rather nourishes the truth of who you are. Support is meant to be there to fortify the strengths within. It's meant to be there to help you find anchors for the things that work in your life. It may become a healing journey. At the very least, it's meant to provide a space in which you can grow.

Many actors rely on their parents to support them financially as they work to "make it" in the acting business, and as time goes by the relationship can become strained. The parents start wondering if their adult child is ever going to become self-sufficient and make a living as an actor, asking questions like, *Are you sure this is what you want to do? Why don't you just get a real job?* That can cause all kinds of conflict! The actor feels guilty or resentful, and because they are not independent adults yet, their self-esteem is affected by their lack of success. Financial support from a parent can be valuable and necessary at the beginning of a career-building phase, but it can get sticky if the relationship is not reciprocal. Many actors balance out the flow of support by helping their parents in other ways, like running errands, doing housework or yard work, helping out with projects, or planning family outings. They treat their parents with respect and gratitude and make sure they know their support is appreciated. They have a relationship agreement that works. Building and sustaining self-esteem comes from feeling good about who you are, how you treat others, and what your relationship dynamics are like.

Some actors are highly self-sufficient and independent. They have one or more jobs to support themselves while they work on their acting careers. They are highly motivated to make it on their own and don't ask for help from anyone else, sometimes even pushing support away. Opportunities can sometimes be missed by doing this. Again, it's about balance. Whatever your tendency has been in the world, taking care of yourself in the most loving way *and* being open to healthy support from others both must be part of the ever-changing journey.

As you know, an actor's career can go from plodding along to high gear in six seconds flat. I have experienced that myself, as have many of my clients. A career-changing role, whether it's a high-profile television guest spot, a series, or a movie role with a big buzz, brings with it a whole set of new things to navigate. You will find yourself suddenly needing team members to manage your money, your public relations, and your hair, makeup, and clothing for events. You will be expected to know *instantly* how it all works on the set, on the red carpet, at press junkets, in taped interviews, at photo shoots, at studio events, you name it. You will not only need to deliver the best work of your life as an actor, you will also need to play the newest role of your life: "star." And you will need to handle all this, possibly, without a shred of coaching or a bit of training in that realm.

If this career rise has already happened to you and you learned the hard way, you may look back and wish you'd had some help, training, and preparation. You probably still feel like you could use more support. If you haven't already had that leap in your career, you get to think ahead. Not only do you deserve support right now in your life, but you also get to start pinpointing what sort of support you would like to have when your vision of the future begins to materialize in the present. Rather than feeling lost, scared, and uncertain, the choice is to educate yourself on who is out there to hold your hand through a time that you will want to enjoy to its fullest. Wherever you are in your career or in the world, you deserve (after all the work you put into building your career) to feel excited, confident, prepared, grounded, and most of all *supported* while going through your magnificent rise. That way, you will be able to savor every wacky, sublime, fascinating, magical moment, and because you will be supported and sane, you will sustain.

Do your due diligence when it comes to picking people to support you. How long have they been in business? What are their real credentials? Do you know anyone who has worked with them? Establish up front what they expect from you. If they seem nervous and things don't quite add up, go with your gut and remove yourself. No matter if someone is an authority figure or they say they are a caregiver, a healer, a doctor, a therapist, a manager, a financial advisor, or coach, it doesn't guarantee that they are healthy emotionally, physically, or mentally. They may have a certification or a license to practice, *and* that doesn't guarantee they are professionals in the most essential sense. There are many people out there who are not evolved who want to "fix" or control the lives of others, and that can be profoundly damaging to those in need of real support. If you find anyone, no matter how convincing they are, telling you *only they have the answers,* they will probably not be a resource for you. (Of course, someone who knows tax law because they are trained in that field, for example, will probably know more than you do and it will be worth listening to their advice.) Gather information. Become knowledgeable. If someone tells you they ultimately have the right answers about your life, take a breath and consider this: *you are the expert on you*, and the support you deserve will nurture your ability to discover your own answers, to know your own truth.

When it comes to support from friends and family, focus on the people in your life who are really there for you, who take responsibility for their actions, who are emotionally intelligent, and who are adults in the deepest sense of the word—people who are respectful, empathetic, clear, and empowering.

Your job is to find people willing and able to be that support, team members who provide more paths to your higher self than you can discover alone. You may meet a few before you find the ones that you really connect with, and when you do, they then become your anchors. You can then pay it forward and be a powerful, healthy support for others.

Fill your life with what and whom you love and with what and who loves you, and life will love you back.

Ask What You Can Do

The world is changing rapidly and we have come to a tipping point. We have become a society full of competition. Most of our "reality" television is competitive and makes one person "better" than another. Award shows do this. Talent shows like *The Voice, American Idol, The X Factor, The Glee Project*, and *Project Runway* pit artists against each other. Certainly there is some collaboration on many of these shows, but on many there is rivalry and egoism and everyone is out for themselves. Competition can be useful for us to stretch ourselves as a species and become better at what we do, *and* it ultimately means there have to be "losers." If we are all fighting to be the best, then how do we come together to overcome life's challenges? Our old ways of living are no longer working for our survival and something has to give. Really, the person each of us most benefits from outdoing is our less evolved self. There is a Hindustani proverb that says, "There is nothing noble about being superior to some other person. The true nobility is in being superior to your previous self."

You can become part of accelerating the evolutionary shift that's already happening on this planet by asking those you meet, *What are you working on; what are you wanting to accomplish? What are your hopes, dreams, and needs? And how can I support or serve or help you?* Whether the help they need is a connection, a resource, a bit of information, physical support, or emotional support, you get to offer what you can toward that.

A couple of times over lunch I offered to help a casting director friend who was undertaking a non-casting project, one where I could probably be of use to him. I made my offer explicitly to help him as a friend with no strings attached. Both times I offered my support, his eyes glazed over, his face hardened, and he changed the subject. It's not unusual for me to encounter similar reactions from people in the business we are in, and I believe that's because so many people in it are inundated with their own needs as well as the needs of others. This goes especially for agents, managers, and casting directors who are barraged with actors wanting something from them: representation, an audition, a job, or a leg up in their career. This is especially true of actors, who are often in a habitual state or belief set of lack and need. So, when an actor or anyone else comes along with a collaborative stance and an offer of support, many industry people are immediately suspicious, expecting the other shoe to drop and the next thing to be, *Now here's what I want from you.* It's a sad state of affairs. However, if this is a response you receive, keep going without the need for something in return. The only way we will change our society is by staying with a stance and proving that our intentions are good and without a hidden agenda.

If someone does respond with a *yes, I need this or that,* or asks you to do something for them, make sure you let them know if you *can't* do it, and suggest something else you *can* do, even if that's to keep your eyes and ears open for someone who can do what they need done. If their request or need is something you can do, make sure you follow through and actually do it.

Another avenue toward happiness is getting right in there and helping those in need, either through a charity, nonprofit, or government shelter. When we enter the lives of those who have very little or who are suffering, and we take action to help them out, we connect with the source of life. The illusion of separation begins to dissolve and we remember that we are one. One species, one being, one mind, one soul. We look into the eyes of those who have lived in fear, pain, or sickness, and our hearts connect with theirs. In rolling up our sleeves, getting in the middle of their stuff, their humanity, and doing what we can to elevate their lives, we elevate ourselves. Serving others is a powerful way to create happiness on our planet.

Stay Grounded

You now have the tools to raise your baseline state of happiness higher than it may have been for years, or perhaps ever. As an actor, you have the opportunity to thrive in a business that can be challenging and uncertain. You've chosen to make some changes in your life. Reading this book is just one sign that you're ready for positive shifts to occur.

Change is an interesting phenomenon. It's the one thing that we know will occur. You may have found that you're often more comfortable in the familiar and become surprisingly afraid and resistant when change begins to occur, even when you've wanted it very much.

Opposition can come, not only from within, but from other people. You may have found that even those who love you and want your happiness have resisted your changes. Throughout history there has been opposition to change, especially when that change takes us down a road less traveled. The very people who have taken humanity into higher states of evolution by doing what feels right, rather than what the general collective has deemed normal, safe, or expected, have faced enormous challenges from the majority.

So, despite all the objections, you must return again and again to your truth, to what will ultimately nurture your evolution toward happiness. It's that mysterious gut feeling that must be considered with more weight, for your intuition can ultimately save your life. It's your birthright and your moral obligation to be open to the joy that awaits you.

In order to claim your happiness you must learn to embrace the change that comes with it, and being grounded will make the process easier. As an actor you will likely portray the violence and suffering of your characters at various points in your work. It's very important to find ways to process and clear those experiences, as the body, psyche, and emotional selves don't distinguish well between real life and acting. Violence, trauma, and suffering have certain vibrational frequencies, so, though your mind may understand the difference, your system won't. Clearing your "work" out of your system is vital to your overall health, as well as your happiness, and grounding is part of that.

While we are living on this beautiful planet Earth, all great foundations start in the ground. The ground supports you, and the energy of its gravitational pull keeps you in your body—an important place to stay while you're still in the human journey! Being rooted consciously in your physical being is especially necessary as an actor because it's one of your main creative and expressive vehicles. When you're grounded you're able to be more present, and that is where your happiness grows.

Without grounding, we humans have a tendency to be scattered and spacey. Ungrounded people give off an air that they are not really living in their bodies and are not quite sure of themselves. They may tend to laugh nervously, roll their eyes, and speak in a faltering manner. They may also tend to be accident prone, have numbness in particular areas of the body, and be disconnected from their own emotions and the feelings of others.

People who walk into rooms with a calm, yet vibrant, presence are usually the ones who have grounded themselves. They are like great oaks that have strong roots and are therefore able to grow far-reaching limbs. They inspire interest and confidence. People feel good around them. They tend to be the ones who have long-lasting and respected careers.

You may relate to the first example, the last, or one in-between. Wherever you fall on the scale, the fact that you're an artist and that you work in such an unpredictable business makes it that much more important to stay grounded.

The benefits of being grounded in your body, and in all of your various parts, are infinite. You can't be fully present in your life otherwise. You can't feel joy, inspiration, and aliveness in its greatest capacity unless you are grounded. As you explore different ways to do this you will discover what works best for you. One of the ways you've already learned to ground yourself is by understanding what's deeply important to you, what your values are. In exploring what's essential to you at your core, you find ways to honor that and root into an experience of what's right for you.

Another way to get grounded is to remind yourself to drop down into your body from time to time, bringing your conscious awareness out of monkey mind and into your physical being. I call that being "in your socks." There are many ways to do that. Being ungrounded can arise from the conscious self disconnecting from the physical self as protection. You may have experienced a time in your life when, because of real-life trauma, violation, or shock, being rooted in your body didn't feel safe. From the point of the trauma onward it felt impossible to allow a consciousness of the emotions stored in your physical self. The body stores all of our history like a little library, and as long as there are items unfinished or still not dealt with adequately, there will be some kind of discomfort, numbness, or disease, either in the body itself or in the emotional or intellectual self. A way to become grounded in the presence of your physical being is to remember that the past is no longer here. You have a different present, *even if it's only slightly different,* and you've changed. The past, as we've established, no longer exists. It's done, finished. The danger or pain of the past is no longer imminent. Make your amends, and forgive and complete, and give yourself the gift of taking up residence in the "space suit" you so carefully chose for your human journey. Practices like yoga, Chi Gong, and Tai Chi are powerful ways to diminish the pain body of the past and fortify the healthy body of the present. Something as simple as walking barefoot on grass or the beach can also be very grounding. Being in nature and having your hands in the dirt are ways to be more grounded, as well as to be happier. Research has found that even being able to see a plant on a balcony raises the happiness levels of people working in buildings.

Breath is also grounding. It puts things into perspective. The in-breath brings joy and energy. The out-breath brings peace and letting go. Life itself breathes. Everything expands and contracts like our breath. The seasons breathe. Ocean waves move back and forth like breath. We have times when things feel stuck and dark, and that's contraction, and times when there is a lightness and ease, which is expansion. Perhaps right now, in this very moment, you can connect to that rhythm and return to your physical being with one small action. As you read this take a slow and steady breath through your nose, down through your lungs, and release it slowly through your mouth. When you've done that, take another one and let the breath move deeper this time into your lower belly, releasing it slowly, this time through your nose. With the next steady breath take the oxygen into your pelvic area all the way into your lower organs and then down into your feet, releasing the air slowly again out through your nose. As your breath returns to its natural state simply notice now what seems different.

The people who hire you, the performer, want to experience *you.* You are entirely unique, and there is no *trying* in that. As you move along on your journey, being aware of your feet as they plant themselves on your path will bring you a consciousness of the moments as they *are.* It's simply a matter of breathing, being in your body, and connecting with your heart and your gut. If you think about it, filling your toes may bring more to your craft than filling your head!

Enlighten Up

What do we do when we are happy? We laugh. There is a theory that the more enlightened we become, the funnier things get. Laughter, if it's derived from a purely joyful, loving source, vibrates at very high frequencies.

In the 1980s, as an eighteen-year-old model, I traveled to China with a clothing company to do a photo shoot for their latest fashion catalogue. The Chinese client, photographer, stylists, and I drove for hours to a remote village planted along a river in the Guangzhou region. When we arrived I very quickly realized that few of the villagers had ever seen a white person before I showed up that day. There was a big buzz and tremendous tension.

I was immediately surrounded by about thirty or forty villagers who, shouting their excitement, reached out to touch my clothing and hair. There was a sea of rosy cheeks, beautiful little girls with their red-ribboned hair, and the contrast of the older folks with their weathered skin and dark clothes. I was unsure of my own safety in the advancing crowd and stood still as I was closely inspected and handled by the villagers. Just then, one person in particular became apparent to me. An old man, skinny as a stick, came close to my face and peered into my eyes. There was a breathless moment. Then he began to smile. His open, toothless grin was so full of humor that I couldn't help but relax and smile back. His head began to nod and his grin widened. Then a sound began to rise above the excited chatter. It was laughter. My new gentleman friend seemed to find the tension, and perhaps my odd appearance, all uncontrollably amusing. His cackle began to spread throughout, until each and every one of us was belly laughing— children, women, aged and youthful, the whole group—with me in the middle wearing the most ridiculous 1980s garb, massive shoulder pads and all, with tears streaming down my face. It was incredibly funny, relieving, and deeply connecting, the chasm of our different languages, cultures, and realities bridged, right then, by our mirth.

Laughter is a socially unifying trait. It brings people together and makes us feel part of something larger than ourselves. Even if one doesn't share the same views as others, a good laugh often eases tension, breaks down barriers, and restore balance to an otherwise challenging situation. We connect with our oneness.

It's estimated that as children we laugh approximately four hundred times a day. By the time we become adults we laugh, on average, a mere fifteen times a day. We play less, and take things more seriously. Actors tend to laugh more than the general population due to the kinds of playful activities that are part of the fiber of the craft of acting itself. However, even actors benefit from increasing the amount of laughter in their lives.

Laughter is connected to longevity and greater health. Studies have shown that cells in the body realign and heal faster when a person is laughing. Laughter activates the immune system, decreases stress hormones, is a muscle relaxer, reduces pain, exercises the heart, regulates blood pressure, and improves respiration and brain functioning. Laughing also benefits us on levels other than our physical well-being. It, of course, elevates mood and makes us feel good! It's a universal language and is communicated everywhere on the planet by every human being.

Laughing also occurs spontaneously. While we can consciously inhibit it, we have a tough time purposefully producing laughter. In other words, it's hard to fake. You will know that as an actor if you've ever needed to laugh on cue. It can be far more challenging than crying on cue! However, it's also contagious and even fake laughter can instigate real laughter in others. Laughter connects us to others and it makes us happy.

Laughter can provide powerful, uncensored insights into our unconscious. When we laugh, we are often communicating positive, playful intent. Yet laughter itself can be used negatively too. There is a difference between laughing *with* someone and laughing at someone else's expense. Of course a big part of being an actor, if you're going to do comedy or stand-up, is about making fun of others. I saw an interview with Martin Short where he admitted comedy can be cruel and suggested jokes should bend but not break the people at the receiving end of them. If you're conscious, you will know how far you're going and whether it's cruel or teasing. People who laugh at others in a cruel way are either casting them out of the group or are trying to force them to conform. They attempt to bond over the misfortunes or differences of others. Remember, the ego's way to feel taller is by "cutting off the heads of others".

Laughter's *real* gift to us is to bring us together, not to make us feel isolated and alone. There is always an opportunity to look at what you laugh at and to ask if you're being cruel, or empathetic and compassionate. It will always be the kinder choices in life that will bring long-term happiness to you, let alone to those around you.

We also laugh nervously to move energy. In some of the most inopportune times in my teens and twenties I would have intense laughing episodes, doubled over with tears streaming down my face and filled with absolute hilarity, often for no apparent reason. Everything was, out of the blue, very funny to me indeed. As I look back, I think it was probably a way for me to release the extraordinary tension I was under at the time. I was also connecting with how funny life at its hardest can really be!

To this day I have what I call my "laughing meditations," where in a very relaxed, trusting, and connected state during meditation practice I sometimes find, not only the human experience, but also the soul journey and the eternal nature of existence, to be so beautiful, ironic, perfect, and, well, funny, that I just laugh—deeply, fully, and ecstatically. If that sounds crazy, maybe it is, *and* it's a really fabulous and healthy "crazy" if there ever was one as far as I am concerned!

Even dogs need to laugh. Dog laughter (forced breathy exhalations through the mouth) is produced during play and friendly encounters with other dogs and people. Recorded playback in animal shelters of the sounds of dog laughter has been found to reduce barking, pacing, and other stress-related behaviors in the dogs kept there.

The intentions you make every day will create your reality. *It's a choice to be happy*, and aligning with the vibrational frequencies of happiness will create it. Meditate and focus on your happiness. Create it in your body by doing things that bring joy. Laugh, dance, be with people who inspire and uplift you. Pick up a funny book or movie, call a comedic friend, and play with your dog or child. And if you don't have any of those, borrow one. Create environments where you're at your best, where you feel good. We all need to laugh. When we laugh more, we have more fulfilling relationships, we are healthier and more fun to be around, and life is sweeter. After all, at the end of the day, if it's not fun, then why do it?

Begin Anew

As your consciousness is raised to a higher vibration, so is your level of sustainable happiness. Yes, life will continue to bring challenges, and it's how you travel through it that will determine the journey.

Let's look at some statistics for a moment. There is a small percentage of people pursuing acting who have become union members, and of the over one hundred and fifty thousand SAG-AFTRA members worldwide, only about fifty of those actors are reported to be high earners. The average income that the remaining union members earn from acting is low because employment is sporadic and most of them must supplement their incomes by holding jobs in other occupations. It's estimated that 95 percent of actors in Los Angeles work as waiters while they are hoping for their break in the business. Most acting jobs are short-term, lasting for a day to one week, and it's extremely rare for actors to have guaranteed employment that exceeds three to six months. For each single role that's put out by Breakdown Services, casting directors receive thousands of submissions online within minutes. The odds of getting auditions are low, the odds of booking work far lower than that. And even when work does come, how long does it last? In reality, even if you "make it" and get that big break, that big movie, or that television series, how long until the industry decides it's over for you? I share this with you, not to be negative or pessimistic. I bring it to the table to ask an important question: what's the purpose of all this? I suggest that perhaps it may be about something even more important than acting.

With the odds the way they lie, you must be passionate about acting. If you're on the fence about it, or if you think you would like to give it a try because it sounds interesting, you might consider a more stable career in which the odds of making a living are higher. If, however, this is your dream and you live, sleep, and eat acting, you have important choices to make that will determine the quality of your life.

I read a story once written by speaker and author Price Pritchett about a fly. This fly was buzzing against a window, attempting to get out. The window was closed, but the fly could apparently see through the glass to the outside world and that's where he wanted to go. The fly continued to throw his little body up against the glass, buzzing and thumping, banging and popping against the window. He continued on like this until eventually, his body beaten and exhausted from the futile attempt, he fell onto the sill and died. The thing is, if the fly had only turned around and gone in the other direction, he would have seen the open door not ten steps away that led, unrestricted, to the outside.

One of many things this story illustrates is how we can become so focused on a direction that we fail to see that the very thing we are dreaming about actually lies in another direction, and that it would take a fraction of the effort to get there.

Having explored your values, what's deeply important to you, you will see that the world outside the window may represent something deeper for you than acting. It may be something like a desire to connect with humanity or to serve good. Acting may very well turn out *not* to be the direction where you will find those values. This happened to me. Once I got the television series I had worked toward, I found myself asking, *What's the real purpose of all this? What is it that I want to do with this?* I quickly learned that my passion, though it could have been channeled through acting to some degree, would be far more directly delivered by being in the personal development profession. You, too, may find your calling lies somewhere else. The key is to focus on what you love, not how the outcome will look. That way you will be directed toward your calling, and what you love will be wherever you end up. There are many people each day finding their real passion as they turn in another direction.

On the other hand, for you the fly story could mean that the *ways* in which you've been going about making your dream happen haven't been working, and doing them *harder* is not the way to proceed. It may be that turning around and going the other way is more about shifting how you've been going about this whole acting thing. Some or all of the things in this book may be those new ways of doing things, and it may be that a whole new set of actions and habits needs to be changed. Relationships, attitudes, and approaches all get to be reviewed, and questions get to be asked. Has this really been working? What would work better? Have you been trying too hard? Is the lesson about trusting more? Have you been waiting and hoping and the lesson is about being more proactive? What if you went in the other direction with a number of things, and just noticed what happened? You can always switch back. Tenacity is important for an actor, especially considering the terrain. Optimism is invaluable. Giving up on your dream is not the answer. Your dream will always be a fundamental part of who you are. It's the fabric of your being, and it's the source for you. Yet the direction or the manifestation of it may change. Be open to possibilities in your journey. What other ways can you create, express, map out, dig for, and build your dream? Fill your life with experiences, relationships, travel, and study. Making life all about acting will limit you. Bring the world into you and let it fill you up. Make what lasts inside you the main thing, and gather life to you. Ask what the great lessons are in being an actor. What are you learning about yourself that will help you understand your true mission here on Earth? How will that then direct your path?

This is not a journey about whether you make it as an actor. This is a journey about who you are and who you want to become. If you place your identity on being solely an actor and acting ends for you, your identity ends. You are an eternal spirit having a human experience. The journey of being an actor is part of the journey of your soul. When anything brings out the best in you, you're where you're meant to be. You will know in your deepest heart, bones, guts, and essence when you take the path that's right for you. Nothing anyone else will say is the answer, even if it feels right. That "feeling right" is the answer coming from within you, even if it came out of someone else's mouth. The answer is ultimately yours and when you get still and quiet enough you will hear it. As you discover what it is that has driven you to be an actor, what it is that you love about it, and what inspires you, you're guided to your right path, whatever that is. You come to a place where vision shows you your purpose, and your actions take you on that path.

This is a journey. We are all unfolding into something we can only imagine. The mystery of our existence is something we all relate to, the unknown a given in life. We don't yet know what we don't yet know, and all we can do is keep growing and learning in the midst of impermanence and unknowing. As we turn toward what is good, we create good, and that, we can rest assured, will bring us into the happiness that is already who we are.

If you listen carefully, dear, creative spirit, you can hear yourself growing. You can hear your loved ones growing. You can hear strangers and those you are in conflict with growing. As the universe expands, so does everything in it; and the choices you make at every moment determine whether you are expanding toward light.

Give life all you have and claim your happiness.

About the Author

Justina Vail is a life coach, executive coach, speaker, award-winning author, and award-winning actor.

Justina was born in Malaysia to British parents. She lived there, in Hong Kong, and in England until immigrating to the US in 1989 for her acting career. She spent twenty-five years working as an actor in major motion pictures and on primetime network television series, winning a Saturn Award for Best Supporting Actress on Television in 1999. Two years later Justina chose to shift direction and move into the world of personal development and human potential. She has been in business as a life coach and consultant since 2002 and has helped hundreds of people—both in the film industry and in other professions—create happier, healthier lives.

Justina is a certified professional life coach, executive coach, Neuro-Linguistic Programming (NLP) Master Practitioner, hypnotherapist, and Grief Recovery Specialist®. She is a mentor for Women in Film, a member of the International Coach Federation (ICF), and co-developer and instructor at Envision Global Leadership's Executive Coach Training Program.

Justina has an overall history of more than thirty years in the entertainment industry. She is owner of Actors Life Coaching—a personal and professional life coaching service for entertainers. Her background and experience mean that Justina engages actors, at all levels of career success, with a deep understanding and experience.

Justina Vail lives in California with her husband, Jeff Evans, Ph.D., and their canines Ruby and Truman.

2290965R00108

Printed in Great Britain
by Amazon.co.uk, Ltd.,
Marston Gate.